GUIDEBOOK FOR

Day In and Day Out

by Mabel O'Donnell

Basic Primer

The Alice and Jerry Basic Reading Program

HARPER & ROW, PUBLISHERS

Evanston, Illinois   Elmsford, New York   Pleasanton, California

THE ALICE AND JERRY BASIC READING PROGRAM

Materials Comprising the Readiness Program

FIRST YEAR READINESS TEST—I
HERE WE GO, Diagnostic Readiness Book
OVER THE WALL, Developmental Readiness Book
PICTURE CARDS (63 pictures, 6½ x 9 inches, for use with HERE WE GO and OVER THE WALL)
TEXTFILMS (Filmstrips, 35 mm.)
        I Live in the City
        I Live in the Country
        Tell Another Story
        Away We Go
        Animals to Know
FIRST YEAR READINESS TEST—II
GUIDEBOOK FOR HERE WE GO and OVER THE WALL (no charge with basic orders)

Materials Comprising the Preprimer Program

SKIP ALONG, First Preprimer
UNDER THE SKY, Second Preprimer
OPEN THE DOOR, Third (Basic) Preprimer
HIGH ON A HILL, Fourth (Parallel) Preprimer
POCKET CARD HOLDER
BIG PICTURES FOR SKIP ALONG (24 pictures on 16- x 19-inch cards)
REBUS, WORD, PHRASE AND SENTENCE CARDS
PREPRIMER WORKBOOK (to accompany the first three preprimers)
A VOCABULARY PREPRIMER WORKBOOK (An additional workbook to be used in conjunction with the Preprimer Workbook; for use with immature groups only)
TEXTFILMS (to accompany each of the preprimers)
PREPRIMER ACHIEVEMENT TEST (in packages of 25)
GUIDEBOOK FOR TEACHERS FOR THE PREPRIMER PROGRAM (no charge with basic orders)
HAPPY DAYS, Supplementary Preprimer
RIDES AND SLIDES, Supplementary Preprimer
HERE AND THERE, Supplementary Preprimer
MY OWN BOOK, Preprimer Level (a series of books to give to pupils to take home upon completion of Preprimer Program; in packages of 16 books, 4 each of numbers 1, 2, 3, 4)

3

Materials Comprising the Primer Program

DAY IN AND DAY OUT, Basic Primer

THE WORKBOOK FOR DAY IN AND DAY OUT

A VOCABULARY PRIMER WORKBOOK (to be used in conjunction with the Workbook for Day In and Day Out; for use with immature groups only)

TEXTFILM (to accompany Day In and Day Out)

PRIMER ACHIEVEMENT TEST (in packages of 25)

GUIDEBOOK FOR TEACHERS FOR DAY IN AND DAY OUT (no charge with basic orders)

WISHING WELL, Parallel Primer

ONCE UPON A TIME, Wonder-Story Book (Primer)

MY OWN BOOK, Primer Level (a series of books to give to pupils to take home upon completion of Primer Program; in packages of 16 books, 4 each of numbers 5, 6, 7, 8)

WORDS I LIKE TO READ AND WRITE (a picture dictionary for primer and first grade levels)

Materials Comprising the First Reader Program

ROUND ABOUT, Basic First Reader

WORD CARDS FOR ROUND ABOUT

THE WORKBOOK FOR ROUND ABOUT

A VOCABULARY FIRST READER WORKBOOK (to be used with The Workbook for Round About; for use with immature groups only)

TEXTFILM (to accompany Round About)

FIRST READER ACHIEVEMENT TEST (in packages of 25)

GUIDEBOOK FOR TEACHERS FOR ROUND ABOUT (no charge with basic orders)

ANYTHING CAN HAPPEN, Parallel First Reader

I KNOW A STORY, Wonder-Story Book (First Reader)

MY OWN BOOK, First Reader Level (a series of books to give to pupils to take home upon completion of First Reader Program; in packages of 16 books, 4 each of numbers 9, 10, 11, 12)

WORDS I LIKE TO READ AND WRITE (a picture dictionary for primer and first grade levels)

CONTENTS

TIME CHART

This chart shows the relative rates at which the three ability groups can be expected to complete the primer.

Teaching plans covering the units as shown in the chart are developed in this Guidebook. A unit *may* provide more work than some classes can do in one reading period. In such cases, take as much time as necessary to complete the unit.

The program for the Immature Group can be most effectively carried out if all 79 units are taught. However, the 25 supplementary units can be omitted without interrupting the development of the basic reading skills.

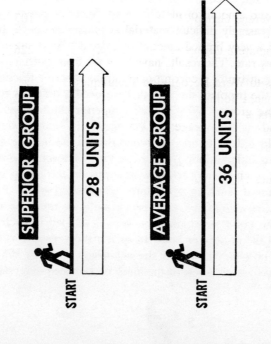

SUPERIOR GROUP

START

28 UNITS

AVERAGE GROUP

START

36 UNITS

IMMATURE GROUP

START

79 UNITS (54 regular units; 25 supplementary)

INTRODUCTION

The Three-Level Program

For many years research workers in the field of reading and child development have been pleading for greater attention to the problem of individual differences. Teachers entering the elementary field from schools of education the country over have not only been cognizant of the problem; they have realized that its solution was the province of the classroom teacher.

Teachers have attempted to meet the needs of superior, average, and immature pupils through small-group teaching. The differences in the programs for the three groups have been largely in time allotment, and in ease and amount of material read. Superior pupils read a maximum of increasingly difficult material at maximum speed. Immature pupils read a very limited amount of extremely easy material at an extremely slow rate. The results have been far from satisfactory.

Now there is a constantly recurring query from superior teachers. Is not the crux of the problem the fact that we need a different type of teaching for these groups? Why should a superior child be taught by the same methods as the average; the average by the same methods as the immature? In differentiating the programs, should not the first and most important differentiation be in the type of teaching used?

This Guidebook is an attempt to show how this differentiating can be done. The different teaching procedures emphasized in the Pre-primer Guidebook are maintained, and specific skills are reviewed and carried on from the point to which they were developed in each of the three groups at the preprimer level. In such a short résumé as the following, it is impossible to list all the significant teaching differences in the three programs; a few of the more pronounced differences are pointed out.

7

Program for superior groups. This program is a challenge to the thinking of superior pupils. Reading techniques are numerous and varied. The amount of directed teaching is less evident than in the other two programs. Pupils are constantly challenged to "try their wings" and to help themselves. The amount of vocabulary review is far less than that outlined for the average and immature groups, and silent reading is done in much longer units.

Adequate direction is given in the use of picture, context, and phonetic clues. Pupils have countless opportunities to use these techniques independently in the reading of the text and carefully planned bulletin board materials.

The additional reading outlined for each story has been carefully graded so that pupils may read widely in context material which is not too difficult. Other suggestions listed under Supplementary Activities are a constant encouragement to pupils to use initiative to increase their vocabularies beyond the limits of the primer word list. By the end of the program a careful foundation has been laid for spelling and writing activities.

Program for average groups. It is the aim of this program to make pupils take pride in being self-reliant. Superior pupils profit by having word recognition techniques suggested to them. Average pupils profit by having such techniques carefully taught. A large amount of time is taken in guiding pupils in the use of picture, context, and phonetic clues and a combination of the three, thus laying the groundwork out of which power in independent word attack can emerge. Word recognition techniques are always developed in meaningful situations. Reading for meaning is never subordinated to mechanics.

This program, as do the other two, accepts the challenge that reading development is not possible without an adequate vocabulary of carrier and service words (all words other than nouns) which can be recognized automatically. Consistent, interesting, and varied vocabulary reviews which develop visual acuity are a part of most units.

Special care has been taken in the activities under Vocabulary Enrichment and Extension to increase the child's speaking vocabulary far beyond the limits of the Primer word list. At the same time, words within the Primer vocabulary have their meanings enriched in various situations in which the meaning of the words must change to meet the changed situation.

8

Program for immature groups. In this group the rate at which the Primer text is presented is extremely slow. Techniques are few and are repeated many times. Immature pupils need to learn to do a few things and do them well. Only in this way can they attain a feeling of security and confidence. At the same time a special effort has been made to present numerous and varied approaches to each learning situation so that pupil interest may be kept at a high level.

Reading ability is fostered by increase in language ability. All too often pupils in immature groups lack the requisite ability to express their ideas and feelings to other people. Therefore, great emphasis is placed upon the oral language approach to reading.

All too often immature pupils fail to develop any adequate method of word recognition because they have not been given adequate ear-training experiences. Therefore, special emphasis on the development of auditory, as well as visual, perception is given in the program for immature groups.

THREE LEVEL WORD RECOGNITION CHART

	Initial Consonant Sounds	Word Structure (Verb endings and s for plurals)	Phonetic Parts	Final Sounds	Initial Blends	Long Vowel Sounds
	s h b j c l r d w m n g f p t k th wh sh ch v		ay ew ar ow oo ir ou oy er	t n p d y g l	bl br gr pl tr st sn	a e o
SUPERIOR GROUP	███	███	███	███	███	███
AVERAGE GROUP	███	███	███	███		
IMMATURE GROUP	███	███	███			

Note: The different teaching approaches emphasized in the Preprimer Guidebook are maintained, and specific skills are reviewed and carried on from the point to which they were developed in each of the three groups at the preprimer level.

10

GENERAL NOTES ON USING THIS GUIDEBOOK

1. Independent and additional reading. The Supplementary Activities for the superior and average groups contain references to stories in a number of preprimers. These stories, if used in the units indicated, can be read with no supervision from the teacher except for help with character names and some other new vocabulary. New vocabulary (aside from the character names) is noted the first time a new word appears in each book.

The same preprimer stories can be used by immature groups, but here the teacher should supervise the reading at all times. For the immature groups the reading references are placed in supplementary units. This additional reading provides such a good opportunity for the application of known vocabulary to new context that it is hoped the teacher will find time to use these supplementary units.

It is not expected that teachers will have all the books listed, but in all three programs the reading of any particular book must be done in entirety and in the sequence indicated. Otherwise, the correlation of vocabulary will not hold.

In order that the teacher may assemble the books she has available for this reading, the titles are listed below:

> *All in a Day* (American Book Co., 1953)
> *Bill and Susan* (Silver Burdett Co., 1945)
> *Here and There* (Harper & Row, Publishers, 1956)
> *Molly, Pete, and Ginger* (D. C. Heath and Co., 1955)
> *My Little Blue Story Book* (Ginn and Co., 1948)
> *My Little Green Story Book* (Ginn and Co., 1948)
> *My Little Red Story Book* (Ginn and Co., 1948)
> *Ned and Nancy* (D. C. Heath and Co., 1955)
> *Ride Away* (American Book Co., 1953)
> *Time to Play* (American Book Co., 1953)
> *Under the Tree* (Silver Burdett Co., 1945)
> *We Come and Go* (Scott, Foresman and Co., 1946)
> *We Look and See* (Scott, Foresman and Co., 1946)
> *We Work and Play* (Scott, Foresman and Co., 1946)

2. Textfilm. The Textfilm for *Day In and Day Out* is a definite part of the program. Where Textfilm is to be used, the teacher is

11

referred to the separate manual which accompanies the Textfilm. In it, full instruction is given for the use of each frame.

3. Supplementary units for immature groups. In the program for the immature group, 25 units (one after each Primer story) are supplementary. They contain references to the Textfilm and lists of books for additional reading. The program for the immature group can be most effectively carried out if these units are not omitted.

4. Sounds, letter names. Whenever an initial or a final consonant is presented in the unit plans, the sound which the consonant represents should be associated with the letter name. For example, you might say, *"Come* and *cap* begin with the same sound. They also begin with the same letter, the letter *c*."

5. Workbook correlation. The correlation of each workbook page with certain pages in the Primer is given at the bottom of the workbook pages under the caption USE. If the workbooks are so used, no new vocabulary will be encountered except the word *no*. However, this does not mean that the workbook pages must be always so used. Very often in the Supplementary Activities in the Guidebook, a different use of the workbook page may be suggested if such a page correlates better with the activity being stressed in a particular unit. With this use, also, no new vocabulary will be encountered.

6. Bulletin board. Some of the most important activities in the Guidebook concern independent reading from the bulletin board. It is to be hoped that these activities will never be omitted and that pupils will be constantly stimulated to read the bulletin board.

7. Grouping. In rural schools or in situations where the number of pupils is so small that division into groups is not feasible, teachers should use the program for average groups. To meet the reading needs of each pupil in such small groups, it is to be hoped that teachers will read thoroughly the programs for superior and immature groups and modify their teaching accordingly.

8. Manuscript writing. It is assumed that all writing done by the teacher on the board or bulletin board will be in manuscript form.

9. Choral reading. For teachers who wish to give their pupils a beginning opportunity to know and appreciate poetry, *Let's-Read-Together Poems: An Anthology of Verse for Choral Reading in Kindergarten and Primary Grades,* selected by Helen A. Brown and Harry J. Heltman (Harper & Row, 1961), will prove invaluable.

PROGRAM FOR SUPERIOR GROUP

Unit 1: Introduction

Have the following materials ready for use:

Word Cards: 465 out   488 day

Introducing book and title. In what way is this book more like the ones Father and Mother read? (Call attention to thicker book and stiff covers.)

Glance at the pictures on the cover. Where are Alice and Jerry standing? What do they see?

Alice and Jerry have fun every day, all day long. They say they have fun day in and day out. So the title of our book is—(move hand from left to right under title and read). Find the word *day* in two places. Which word says *out?* Who can read the whole title? Turn to the title page and read the title again.

Enriching
speaking
vocabulary

Contents pages. Turn to page 2. This word (indicate *Contents*) says *contents*. The contents of my cupboard are all the things that are in it. The contents of your pockets are all the things you have in them. And the contents of a book are the stories which are in it. The contents pages tell us the names of the stories and the number of the page on which each story begins.

Our book is divided into parts. These large words (indicate unit title headings) tell us the names of the parts. You read the name of the first part, and I will read the others.

There are several stories in each part. Count to see how many stories there are in the part called "Alice and Jerry." The title of the first story is the name of a little animal. (Pupils may remember *rabbit* from rebus card. If not, have them think how the word begins and remember that it is the name of an animal.) This number (indi-

Guidance in
methods of
word attack

cate 6) tells the page on which the story begins. Turn quickly to that page. Did the contents pages give us the right information? Turn again to the contents pages. Can you read any other title and find on what page that story begins?

Frontispiece and unit title page. The next page is called the frontispiece. Here are Alice and Jerry in their favorite place high on a hill. How many new things can you find out about that hill?

And now page 5 tells us again the name of the first part of the book. Was this picture taken on the same day or another?

Now glance quickly through the book to find out what Alice and Jerry do day in and day out. Look for things you would enjoy most.

WORD RECOGNITION TECHNIQUES

Phonics

Auditory-visual perception. *Initial sounds.* If anyone can come to the board and show me how *day* begins, I will finish the word. How does it begin when it starts with a capital letter? (Have pupils write *d* and *D* in manuscript writing; then immediately finish words. Let pupils try their wings. If they suggest that they can write the whole word, let them try.)

Phonetic parts. The word *out* (write *out* on board) is very interesting. These two letters (draw line under *ou*) say what you say when you are hurt. They say *ou*. If you remember that, you won't have trouble with the word—. (Use *day* and *out* as flash cards. Have book title reread.)

SUPPLEMENTARY ACTIVITIES

Vocabulary review in new context

1. Bulletin board. Have the following riddle on bulletin board.

Day In and Day Out

Day in and day out,
I like to play
With a little brown puppy
And Jerry and May.

2. Independent reading. Have pupils read individually or in groups *Here and There* (Harper & Row, Publishers), pages 2-6. (See page 11.)

Unit 2: Little Rabbit

NEW VOCABULARY: hole   hop   oh   rabbit

PREPARATION

Have the following materials ready for use:

Readiness Card 37   **Pocket Card Holder**
Word Cards: 54 come   161 went   452 Oh   454 hole
                  144 saw   451 rabbit 453 Hop   488 day

INITIAL PROCEDURE

Introducing new vocabulary. Alice and Jerry have a surprise word. When they are surprised, they round their lips like this (illustrate) and say *Oh.* (Hold up word card as you say *Oh.*) Show me the letter which looks like their lips. Round your own lips and say *Oh.* (Reverse card to show lower-case form.)

Contents pages. Turn quickly to the contents pages. What is the title of the first part of our book? of the first story? On what page will we find it?

SILENT READING

Page 6. I know who discovered the rabbit. How can I tell? Read silently to find out what Jerry said.

Page 7. Alice uses the surprise word. Can you find it? Read silently to find out what Alice saw and said. I am sure the rabbit sees the children. What will happen next? The rabbit can help herself because she can—(hold up word card *Hop* but do not read). Think how the word begins. Think what a rabbit can do.

Independent word attack— hop

Page 8. How many times do you see the word *hop?* How many times does it begin with a capital letter? with a small letter? Read the page silently. The rabbit didn't have an easy time getting away. How do I know?

Independent word attack— hole

Page 9. You have sharp eyes. So have I. But the rabbit saw something before we did. What is it? Think how *hole* begins; then see how many times you can find it on the page. Find the surprise word. Read the page silently. Be ready to show by your voice how surprised the children were.

What do you think will happen next? Who can tell us a good ending for the story?

ORAL READING

Establishing standards. Choose one good reader to reread the whole story.

VOCABULARY ENRICHMENT AND EXTENSION

Word associations. (Write on board *Jerry went home.*) Think of all the ways in which Jerry might have gone home. Maybe he walked (ran, rode, skated, skipped). If he were in an airplane, maybe he—. Anyway he *went* home. *Went* can mean many things.

WORD RECOGNITION TECHNIQUES

Auditory-visual perception. *Initial sounds.* If someone will show me how *hole* begins, I will finish the word. (Continue with *hop, rabbit, day, come, saw, went.*)

Phonics

Final sounds. (DO NOT OMIT THIS ACTIVITY.) Listen as I say *rabbit.* (Be sure to say the final *t* sound clearly.) Now listen again. *Rabbit, went, boat!* My ears tell me that these words end with the same sound. Listen again. *It, want, what!* What did your ears tell you? Let's prove that we are right. (Write on board all words used and direct attention to final *t.* Do not ask pupils to suggest words, since they may suggest words ending in silent *e.*)

SUPPLEMENTARY ACTIVITIES

1. *Workbook for Day In and Day Out,* pages 1, 2, 3, 4.
2. Bulletin board. Have the following rhyme on bulletin board. Readiness Card 37 may be used as illustration.

Vocabulary
review in
new context

Little Brown Rabbit

"Little brown rabbit,"
Said Alice one day.
"Pretty brown rabbit,
Come out here and play."

Hop went the rabbit,
And what did he see?
A little brown hole,
And down went he.

3. Independent reading. Have pupils read, in their seats **or in** groups, the following preprimer pages: (See page 11.)

Bill and Susan (Silver Burdett Co.), pages 2-7. (Give help with the word *stop* on page 4.)

Here and There (Harper & Row, Publishers), pages 7-17.

Molly, Pete, and Ginger (D. C. Heath and Co.), pages 1-6.

My Little Red Story Book (Ginn and Co.), pages 2-8.

Ride Away (American Book Co.), pages 2-9.

We Look and See (Scott, Foresman and Co.), pages 3-6.

4. Textfilm for *Day In and Day Out,* Frames 1-2. See Textfilm manual for directions.

Pp. 10-15 # Unit 3: Toys

NEW VOCABULARY: ball   happy   so
                  fly   just   toys

PREPARATION

Have the following materials ready for use:

Pocket Card Holder

Word Cards: 92 is   133 have   455 toy   459 so
                 105 may   159 this   456 ball   460 happy
                 123 You   162 Yes   457 Just

INITIAL PROCEDURE

Have the following sentences written on board:

You look happy.   See this ball.
You looked so happy.   This is my ball.
See my toys.   Yes, it is.
Just one boat!   You may have it.
Play ball.

Using initial consonant and context clues

Introducing new vocabulary. I like to see you smile because then —(indicate sentence 1; stimulate pupils to use initial consonant clue to unlock new word; as soon as sentence is read, have word card *happy* added to card holder). When you came in this morning—(sentence 2; use same procedure; suggest that new word rhymes with *go*).

At home Jerry has drums and guns, trains and airplanes. He knows what all these things together are called. So he says—(sentence 3). Of course, if all he had were one train, he would say—(erase *s* on *toys;* have sentence reread; add *toy* to holder).

Guidance in methods of word attack

(As rest of sentences are read, have underscored words added to card holder.) Jerry has many trains but—(sentence 4; be sure pupils think how new word begins and then jump over it to read rest of sentence). Jerry has a new bat. So he liked to—(sentence 5). One day he lost his ball in a field. When Jack and Jerry went to look for it, they found two balls. Jerry pointed to one ball and said—(sentences 6 and 7). Jack knew that Jerry was right. So he said—(sentence 8). Jerry picked up the other ball and said—(sentence 9). (Have all words in card holder read.)

Contents pages. One of these words will help you with the title of our new story. Turn quickly to the contents pages and find the title. Now find the page on which the story begins.

SILENT READING

Page 10. We don't have to be smart to know the name of this store. If you were Jerry, what would you buy? How many times can you find the word *toys? toy?* Read the page silently. The best silent reader may read aloud and tell us what Jerry wants.

Pages 11-13. (Have pages read in usual manner.)

Page 14. Jerry changes his mind again. What does he want now? Read three sentences to find out.

Independent word attack— fly

There is a new word somewhere on the rest of this page (*fly*). Think how it begins. Think what the rest of the sentence says. Then you can get it. Finish the page. Then put your finger on the new word and be ready to tell what it says.

Page 15. Jerry looks very much like you. Read the first sentence and find out why. On the rest of the page, Jerry uses a word which makes me know that that airplane belongs to him. Finish the page and be ready to show me that word.

ORAL READING

Organization. *Following events in sequence.* (This story divides itself readily into parts. Have it reread orally, having different pupils find and read the part of the story that tells about the ball, about the boat, etc.)

WORD RECOGNITION TECHNIQUES

Auditory-visual perception. *Initial sounds.* (Erase all words from board; remove all cards from card holder.) I will finish the word *happy* if someone can show me how it begins. (Continue with *so, ball, rabbit, hop, hole, want, went, toys, just, day.* Give pupils a chance to finish some of the easier words if they can.)

Final sounds. (DO NOT OMIT THIS ACTIVITY.) Listen carefully. *Rabbit, it, want!* What did we discover about these words yesterday? There is a word in the title of our book which ends like *rabbit.* Day In and Day *Out!* Which word is it? I will say three of the new words we had today. Which one ends like *rabbit?* (*happy, ball, just*) I will write *rabbit* on the board, all but the last sound or letter. I hope someone can finish the word.

Phonics (margin note)

SUPPLEMENTARY ACTIVITIES

1. *Workbook for Day In and Day Out,* pages 5, 6, 7, 8.
2. Bulletin board. Have this rhyme on the bulletin board. Pupils may draw an illustration to go with it.

Vocabulary review in new context (margin note)

My Store

I have a store.
A big toy store.
So come to my store and see
In the window a train,
And a big airplane,
And red boats, one, two, three.

3. Independent reading. Pupils may read, individually or in groups, the following preprimer pages:
Bill and Susan, pages 8-15.
Here and There, pages 18-25.
Molly, Pete, and Ginger, pages 7-10.
My Little Red Story Book, pages 9-12. (Give help with the word *fast* on page 11.)
Ride Away, pages 10-15.
We Look and See, pages 7-10. (Give help with the word *funny* on page 10.)

4. Textfilm for *Day In and Day Out,* Frames 3-4. See Textfilm manual for directions.

Unit 4: Jip

Pp. 16-21

NEW VOCABULARY: away   bow-wow   came   for
                 bird   but   duck   out

PREPARATION

Have the following materials ready for use:

Pocket Card Holder   **Word Card:** 464 came

INITIAL PROCEDURE

Introducing new vocabulary. You remember this word in the title of our book, *Day In and Day*—(write *out* on board). These two letters say—(underscore *ou* and have pupils give sound). This morning a puppy will say—(write *Bow-wow*). These two letters—(underscore *ow* in both places) also say *ow*. Think how the word begins. Remember the sound *ow*. Think what a puppy would say. The new word is—.

Guidance in methods of word attack

Contents pages. Turn to the contents pages, find the name of the new story, the page on which it begins, and then turn quickly to that page.

SILENT READING

Independent word attack— away

Page 16. Alice and Jerry like books. Jip doesn't. How can I tell? If they insist on sticking their heads into books, what will he do? Run *away*, of course. If you see the little word *a* on the beginning of *away*, you can find *away* on this page. How many times? Jip has a sad look at the top of the page. What kind of look does he have when he runs away? Can you find the three words, the phrase, which say *a happy look?*

Now read the page silently. Why didn't Alice and Jerry stop Jip? Why did Jip run away?

Page 17. The pictures on this page tell what happened, but they don't tell me why. Read silently. Why did the kitten run away?

Page 18. Of course, you know what the new word on this page will be. How many times can you find *bird?* A pretty red bird like this has another name. What is it? (*cardinal*) Read silently to find out why the bird flew away.

Page 19. Read four sentences silently. What happens the minute Jip barks?

There is a new word in the next sentence. Think how it begins. Jump over it and finish the sentence. Now who is ready with that sentence and the next?

I see the same new word in the next sentence. Who else came to the rabbit hole? Finish the page. Jip uses a word from the title of our book. I hope you know it.

Page 20. Of course, you know what the new word on this page will be. How many times can you find *duck?* Read the entire page. What does Jip do to scare the duck?

Page 21. Look where Jip is now! May scolds him a little. Read three sentences to find out what she says. I see a new word in the next two sentences. Think how it begins. Jump over it. Who is ready? Of course, the new word is *for.* Often when we look, we look *for* someone or something. Read two more sentences. What will May make Jip do? The next two sentences tell exactly what Jip did and how he felt about it.

There is a new word at the beginning of the last sentence. Think how it begins. Jump over it. The very best readers can get it by themselves. Jip didn't want to go, b—— he went home.

Independent word attack— bird, came, duck, for, but

ORAL READING

Rereading by page units. (Have each child choose the animal or person he likes best in the story and read aloud the page which tells about his favorite.)

Audience reading

VOCABULARY ENRICHMENT AND EXTENSION

Word concepts. Jip did not want to go home. *But* he went. As you go to your seats, tell me something you can do. Then tell me something you cannot do and use the word *but*. Let me have a turn first. I can teach boys and girls, *but* I cannot fly an airplane.

Adding meaning to carrier words

WORD RECOGNITION TECHNIQUES

Accurate word recognition. Read this sentence. (Write *Come home, Jip.*) What does this word say? (Underscore *Come.*) Now read— (write *Jip came home* and underscore *came*). Here is the letter you must watch. (Indicate *a*.) The name of this letter is $\bar{a}$. You can hear its name as you say *came*. Say the word and listen for the *a* sound. When a printer prints the letter *a*, it looks like this. (Show word card and indicate *a*.) Let's play "Magic." Watch these words change. (Erase board; then alternate writing *come, came, have, had, do, did,* until words are easily recognized.)

Drill on carrier words

Auditory-visual perception. *Final sounds.* Who will finish the word *rabbit?* (Write *rabbi____* and have some child add *t*.) Three words we used today were *away, not, came*. Which word ends like *rabbit?* Let's prove that it is *not*. (Write *not* under *rabbit*. Repeat procedure with *bird, but, for*.)

Phonics

SUPPLEMENTARY ACTIVITIES

1. *Workbook for Day In and Day Out,* pages 9, 10, 11, 12.

2. Bulletin board. Have this rhyme on the bulletin board. Have pupils unlock new word by thinking how it begins and by thinking of a word which rhymes with *house*.

Independent word attack

What Is in the Hole?

I see a hole
Down here in my <u>house</u>.
The hole is so little.
Look! Out comes a <u>mouse!</u>

3. Independent reading. Pupils may read, individually or in groups, the following preprimer pages:

Bill and Susan, pages 16-23. (Help with word *Baby,* page 17.)
Here and There, pages 26-33.
My Little Red Story Book, pages 13-18.
Ned and Nancy (D. C. Heath and Co.), pages 1-8.
Ride Away, pages 16-23.
We Look and See, pages 11-14. (Give help with the word *Baby,*
   page 11.)
   4. Textfilm for *Day In and Day Out,* Frames 5-6. See Textfilm
manual for directions.

Pp. 22-28

Unit 5: The New Coat

NEW VOCABULARY: box   laughed   please
                 coat   new   then

PREPARATION

Have the following materials ready for use:

Word Cards: 457 just   459 so   472 then

INITIAL PROCEDURE

Guidance in
methods of
word attack

Introducing new vocabulary. One night Father was late getting
home. Mother was so worried that she walked out to the gate. (Write
Just then she saw Father.) This new word (indicate *then*) begins like
this. Think how it begins. Then jump over it. Who is ready to read?
   Mother was worried no longer. (Write *So then Mother looked
happy* and have sentence read.) Father opened the gate and—(write
Then he went in). Who will read this phrase (draw a line under *Just
then*)? and this one (*So then*)? and this word (*Then*)? (Use *just, so,*
and *then* as flash cards.)

Contents pages. Turn quickly to the contents pages and find the next story. I could help you with the title; but after you read the story, you can help yourselves. On what page will the story begin? Who will be the first to find that page?

SILENT READING

Independent word attack—new, coat, please

Page 22. The minute I see this picture I know what Alice needs. If she were my little girl, I would buy her—(write *a new coat*). Think how each new word begins. Think what Alice needs. Who is ready? Now what does the title say? What did the title on the contents pages say? Look to see if we are right.

Read the page silently. Good readers will find two things that are wrong with that coat and also what Alice does.

Page 23. What does Mother say when she sees the coat? Read four lines to find out.

If you have good manners, you always use this word when you ask for things. (Write *Please*.) It begins like *play*. How many times can you find *please* on this page? Now finish the page. What kind of coat does Alice want? Will Mother let her have it?

What do you think will happen next?

Page 24. Off for the store! We were right, weren't we? I hope Mother mended the hole. When they get to the store, Mother forgets something, but Alice doesn't forget. Read to find out what Mother forgets and Alice remembers.

Page 25. Dear me! What color is the man bringing? Has Alice changed her mind? Read and see.

Page 26. Can you read the sign in the picture? I hope you know how the first sentence starts. (Indicate *Just then, So then,* and *Then* on board.) Alice is disappointed on this page. Read the whole page and find out why.

Page 27. A red coat at last! Think where the coat is. Think how *box* begins. How many times can you find the word *box?* Now read the page silently. There is a new word in the last sentence. If you think how it begins and then think of what you do when you are very happy, I am sure you can get it. Each of you be ready to whisper the word to me.

Independent word attack—box, laughed

There is a big surprise for Alice on the next page. Turn and see what it is.

Page 28. Alice asks two questions. How do I know? Read the page silently. Does Alice like her coat and cap? How do you know?

Guidance in
methods of
word attack

Page 29. My, what a rainy day! I see a word in the title which begins like *puppy,* but it doesn't say *puppy.* When Jerry looks out at the rain, he may see a rain pu——. *Puddle,* of course! What kind of puddle? Read the title and see. Won't this story be fun?

ORAL READING

Rereading by page units. The one who finds the page where Alice discovers the hole in her coat may read that page. The one who can find the word *please* may read the page on which you find it. (Continue in similar manner.)

WORD RECOGNITION TECHNIQUES

Auditory-visual perception. *Initial blends.* When I write the word *play,* I begin it this way. (Write *pl____*; then pause before completing word.) If someone will show me how to begin *please,* I will finish the word.

Phonics

I know a color which begins like this. (Write *gr____*; pause for suggestion *green;* then finish word. Repeat with *bl____* for *blue* and *br____* for *brown.* Then use *tr____* for *train.*)

Final sounds. Listen carefully. *Rabbit—coat!* What did your ears tell you? If I write *coat,* all but the last letter, who will finish it for me?

Listen again. *Man, green, brown!* What did your ears tell you? Let's see if we are right. Do all the words end with the same sound or letter? (Write words on board and direct attention to final *n* in each.)

SUPPLEMENTARY ACTIVITIES

1. *Workbook for Day In and Day Out,* pages 13, 14, 15, 16.

2. Bulletin board. Have this rhyme on bulletin board. How many pupils can unlock new words by thinking how they begin and associating them with other rhyming words?

Independent
word attack—

In This Box

In this box is something new.
Red and blue, and just for you!

Is it a boat? Is it a train?
Is it a ball? A red airplane?

Is it a bird? A big toy <u>duck</u>?
Come look in the box and see!
A <u>truck</u>!

3. Independent reading. Pupils may read individually or in groups the following preprimer pages:

Bill and Susan, pages 24-33. (Give help with the words *help*, page 25; and *thank*, page 33.)

Here and There, pages 34-38.

Ned and Nancy, pages 9-16. (Give help with *no*, page 12.)

Ride Away, pages 24-29. (Give help with *stop*, page 24.)

We Look and See, pages 15-22. (Give help with *run*, page 18.)

4. Textfilm for *Day In and Day Out*, Frames 7-8. See Textfilm manual for directions.

Unit 6: The Big, Big Puddle Pp. 29-34

NEW VOCABULARY: into   jumped   puddle   rain   splash

INITIAL PROCEDURE

Contents pages. You remember the kind of day it was in the last picture we saw in our books. What did Jerry see from the window? Now use your contents pages. Find the story title, the number of the page it begins on, and then turn to that page.

SILENT READING

Independent word attack— rain, splash

Page 29. The minute Jerry heard the rain, I know what he did. Read the first sentence to find out. If you think how *rain* begins, I am sure you can find the new word. How many times? Now read the page silently. What did Jerry say? What did Mother do?

Page 30. I am so glad Mother let Jerry go out. What is the water in that puddle doing? Think how *splash* begins. Can you find the new word? How many times? Now read the page. Be ready to tell me why you see the word *splash* two times in one place and three times in another.

Page 31. (Proceed in usual way.)

Page 32. Now we come to the puddle told about in the title. What does Alice think about it? Read and see.

Guidance in methods of word attack

Page 33. Sometimes we put two words together to make a new word. If we put this word (write *in*) and this word together (write *to*), the new word will be—. Can you find *into* on this page? How many times? Read silently. How many splashes does the big, big puddle make?

Word structure

I saw a word on this page that grew up for you and didn't trouble you at all. Jerry wanted to—(write *jump*). So he—(add *ed* to *jump* and have word read).

Page 34. Someone else is splashing. Jerry isn't so smart as he thinks he is. Read to find out why I think so. How does Alice look in this picture?

Page 35. What a change in Alice! Do you ever act like this? Maybe you had better look at Alice. Then you will know better than to get cross and look as ugly as that. If you remember where the man found the coat, I am sure you can read the title. It sounds as if Alice will get a present. Then why in the world does she look like that? Do you think she is going to cry?

ORAL READING

Rereading by page units. I want to forget that cross face. So let's read the puddle story by pages, make Alice happy, and the puddles splash.

WORD RECOGNITION TECHNIQUES

Drill on carrier words

Accurate word recognition. I am going to write some sentences. I will underline a word. Keep your eye on it. (Write *Come on! Oh, my! Look out! Just one toy!* Have sentences read. Erase sentences, write *on* quickly, and erase as quickly as written. Have pupils tell what was written. Repeat with *oh, out, one.*)

Auditory-visual perception. *Initial sounds.* Show me how *puddle* begins, and I will finish the word for you. (Continue with *rain, laughed, kitten.*)

Phonics

Final sounds. Listen carefully. *Green, man, brown!* What did we find out about them? We had another word today which ends like *green.* Which of these three words is it? *Puddle, splash, rain!* Let's prove that you are right. (Write *green, brown, rain, man* on board and direct attention to last letter.)

SUPPLEMENTARY ACTIVITIES

1. *Workbook for Day In and Day Out,* pages 17, 18, 19, 20.
2. Bulletin board. Have this rhyme written on board.

Vocabulary review in new context

The Rain Puddle

It rains and it rains.
So I play with my trains.
Then I look out the window
And see
A big puddle of brown.
I want to jump up and down
And see it splash up
On me, on me.
And see it splash up on me.

3. Independent reading. Pupils may read independently or in groups the following preprimer pages:

Bill and Susan, pages 34-37. (Give help with the word *sleep* on page 34.)

Here and There, pages 39-47.

Ned and Nancy, pages 17-20. (Give help with the word *make* on page 18.)

Ride Away, pages 30-38.
We Look and See, pages 23-30.
4. Textfilm for *Day In and Day Out,* Frames 9-10. See Textfilm manual for directions.

Pp. 35-42 # Unit 7: A Box for Alice

NEW VOCABULARY:	by	dolls	that	wanted
	city	eat	walk	

PREPARATION

Have the following materials ready for use:

Pocket Card Holder
Word Cards: 120 want   482 by   486 wanted
            480 city   485 that

INITIAL PROCEDURE

Introducing new vocabulary. Alice and Jerry lived in a small town. Sometimes Mother could not get what she wanted in the stores there. So she went to the big–. *City,* of course! Take a good look at the word *city.* (Add word card to card holder.)

One morning Mother asked Father when he was going to the– (indicate word card *city*). Father might have said, "After a while," but he didn't. He said–(write *by and by*). You know how the new word begins. It rhymes with–(write *my* under *by*). Who can get it? Who can read what Father said? What is another way to say "after a while"? (Have word card *by* added to card holder.)

Another word will grow for you today. I asked the boy next door what he wanted for Christmas. He said–(write *I want a train* and have sentence read). Then he said, "Last Christmas–(write *I wanted*

Guidance in
methods of
word attack

Little words
in big words

a boat)." What does this word say? (Indicate *wanted.*) Can you find the little word *want* inside the word *wanted?* Who will draw a line under it? What does this word say? (Add *want,* then *wanted* to card holder.)

(Point to your book and say, "This is my book." Point to book in a child's hand and say, "That is Jane's book." Repeat with *this chair, that chair.*) When I point to a child close to me (carry out directions), I say, "This is Ann." When I point to one far away (point to

Guidance in
methods of
word attack

child in back of room), I say—(write and read as you write, "That is Carl"). Let's look at the word *That.* It begins like the word *this.* (Draw line under *Th.*) The rest of the word is the little word—(draw line under *at* and have it read). When I see the word *at,* I know that the big word says—. What word do I use when I point to something near? far away? Let's play "Magic." Close your eyes. What word did I write? (Alternate *this* and *that* until recognition becomes accurate. Add word card *that* to card holder.)

Contents pages. I will watch to see if each of you can use your contents pages to find the new story, just as grown-up people do. (Be sure no one turns to story without using contents pages.)

SILENT READING

Page 35. Alice looks just as disagreeable as she did the last time I saw her. Read silently and find out what is the matter!

Can you think of two or three good reasons why Mother might want to take Alice with her, but thought she had better not?

Page 36. Alice looks worse than ever. What do you think Father and Mother are trying to do? I hope you remember this word (write *What*) because Father is going to use it. He asks a question, too. How can I tell? Read to find out what he says to cheer Alice up.

Page 37. Well, at last Alice looks better. I am sure she will say this to Father. (Write *My name is Alice.*) If she wants him to be very sure who she is, she will say this word louder than the rest. So I will write it in capital letters. (Erase *is* and rewrite in capitals. Have sentence reread.)

Now read silently. See if Alice says "Good-by" and lets Mother go without any more temper tantrums.

32 SUPERIOR GROUP

Independent word attack—dolls

Page 38. Alice and May are enjoying themselves. Is Jip? If you think what the girls are playing with, if you think how that word begins, you can find the word in two places on the page. What is the new word (*dolls*), and where is it? Good readers will know exactly how many dolls May has altogether by the time they are through the page. See if you are a good reader.

Page 39. Don't you wish you were Alice? I can find the phrase which means "after a while." Can you? What does it say?

Independent word attack—eat, walk

Alice is having something good to—*eat,* of course. Can you find the phrase *something to eat? something good to eat?* the word *eat?* Now read to find out what Alice does when she is through enjoying that ice-cream.

Page 40. Here come Mother and Jerry up the—(write *walk*). (If children say *sidewalk,* remind them that *walk* is the short way of saying *sidewalk.* It couldn't be *sidewalk* because the word begins like *window.*)

Maybe Mother knows how disappointed Alice was. Maybe she will bring her something. Read and see.

Page 41. Jerry has the box. So Mother will have to point far away and use this word—(indicate *that* in card holder). This page won't tell what is in the box, but it will give some clues. Then maybe we can guess.

Page 42. Which guess was right? What will Alice do with all these ribbons? Alice will use this longer word when she talks to Mother. I hope you know what it says. (Indicate *wanted* in card holder.) I wonder if Alice will say "Thank you" for the ribbons or will say something else just as nice. Read and see.

Independent word attack—dog

Page 43. Jip doesn't look very happy on this page. I wonder why. If you read the sentence which says, "I like Jip," and the two following sentences, maybe you can find out what the new word in the title is. Maybe you can find out why Jip is unhappy.

ORAL READING

Audience reading

Rereading by page units; Expressing feeling of story character. (Have story reread by pages. Have children try to show by their voices the change in Alice's mood.)

VOCABULARY ENRICHMENT AND EXTENSION

Synonymous meanings. If you can whisper and tell me another way to say "after a while," you may go to your seats.

WORD RECOGNITION TECHNIQUES

Accurate word recognition. One day Jerry and Jack were trading toys. Jerry said—(write *See this boat*). Then he pointed to Jack's airplane and said—(write *I want that airplane*). "Suppose we trade," said Jerry. (Write *Then you may have my boat.*) Now watch this word. (Indicate *this.*) Use your eyes as cameras. Take a good picture of this letter. (Draw a line under *i.* Repeat procedure, drawing a line under the *a* in *that,* the *e* in *then.* Play "Magic" with the three words. Be sure pupils refer to sentences if they need help.)

Drill on carrier words

Word structure. What does this word say? (Write *go.*) Who can make it say *going*? (Repeat with *splash, eat,* and *walk.*)

Verbs ending in ing

Auditory-visual perception. *Final sounds.* If I write the word *got,* all but the last letter, will you finish it? (Continue with *that, eat, coat, but, out.*)

Phonics

Look at the word *green.* Watch how it ends. (Erase word.) Now who can finish the word *brown* if I write all but the last letter? (Continue with *man, then, rain.*)

SUPPLEMENTARY ACTIVITIES

1. *Workbook for Day In and Day Out,* pages 21, 22, 23, 24.
2. Bulletin board. Have this rhyme on bulletin board to be used in usual way.

Independent word attack

The Blue Box

A green box, a brown box,
A blue box, too.
What is in the blue box?
Something for you.

What is in the blue box?
Something blue and red!
Something for my little doll.
A pretty doll bed!

3. Independent reading. Use in usual way.

Bill and Susan, pages 38-47. (Give help with word *Daddy* on page 38.)

My Little Red Story Book, pages 19-22.

Ride Away, pages 39-47.

We Look and See, pages 31-38.

4. Textfilm for *Day In and Day Out,* Frames 11-12. See Textfilm manual for directions.

Pp. 43-48

Unit 8: A Dog for Jerry

NEW VOCABULARY:	again	day	garden	stay	will
	boy	dog	Mac	was	

PREPARATION

Have the following materials ready for use:

Pocket Card Holder

Word Cards: 490 stay   493 again   495 garden
              492 will   494 was

INITIAL PROCEDURE

Introducing new vocabulary. Mother loved flowers. Behind the house—(write *She had a garden*). Think how the new word begins. Think where flowers grow. Who is ready to read?

Mother was going to a garden show. (Explain.) Alice and Jerry wanted to go, too. Mother said, "One may go, and—(write *One will have to stay at home*)." This new word (underscore *will*) begins like *window,* and this one (underscore *stay*) begins like *store.* Think how each new word begins. Then jump over it. One w—— have to st——

Guidance in methods of word attack

at home. Who is ready? Who will find word cards for the three new words and add them to the card holder?

Mother didn't want any disappointed children today. So she said, "The show will last two days. Tomorrow—(write *I will go again*)." Do you see the little word *a* at the beginning of the new word? (Draw a line under *a* in *again*.) Think what Mother would say, "I will go a——." (Have *again* added to card holder.)

Mother played a game. She took two pieces of paper, a long one and a short one, and held one in each hand behind her back. Alice and Jerry had to choose. The one who got the short piece was to go today. Do you know who the lucky one was? (Write *It was Jerry*.) Think how the new word begins. Then jump over it. (Have *was* added to card holder.)

(Indicate the word *garden* in card holder.) Match this word with the same word in a sentence. Read the sentence and then the word. (Repeat with *will, stay, again, was*, two or three times.)

Contents pages. (Be sure pupils use contents pages before turning to story.)

SILENT READING

Page 43. I hope you haven't forgotten the new word in the title. Poor Jip! Jerry wants some other dog to take Jip's place. Read until you find out exactly what kind of dog Jerry wants. Then stop.

Jip will cheer up when he hears what Father says. Finish the page and find out why. What will happen next? Turn and find out if you are right.

Page 44. I know from the picture that a man has come to see Father. But I don't know how long it was before he came. If you know the word in our book title (write *Day*) and if you know what it says now (add *s*), you can read the first sentence and find out.

Independent word attack— boy

Of course, you know that Jerry is a—. Think how *boy* begins. Now find it in two places on the page.

Jerry is still talking about that dog. Read the first four sentences and find out what he says. I am sure he said it over and over again.

Read three more sentences. What question does the man ask Jerry? Finish the page. How does Jerry answer?

Page 45. Remember that when Jerry went to the flower show, Alice had to stay at home. Someone has to stay somewhere in the story on this page. Who has to stay? Where will he stay? And how long? Read three sentences to find out.

Independent word attack—Mac

If I tell you that the name of the man's dog is *Mac,* can you find the word *Mac* in two places? Think how it begins. Now read four more sentences. The man is having some trouble. What is it?

Will Jerry help him out? Finish the page and see. Do you think everything is all settled now? Why not?

Page 46. Father is going to have something to say about this plan. Read three sentences. Will he let the dog come?

I hope you remember what Mother said about going to the flower show the next day. (Indicate sentence *I will go again* and have it read.) The man talks again. Read five sentences. What does he say?

Does Father change his mind? Finish the page and see.

Page 47. Jerry is surer of Mother than Father is. What does he say and do? Read two lines to find out.

Jerry is teasing in the next three sentences. What does he say? When you tease, you generally say something again and again. Does Jerry? Read one more sentence to find out.

What is Mother's answer? Hurry and find out. If the dog cannot stay in the house, what might Jerry have to do?

Page 48. Oh, what a dog! Did the man tell the truth about him? He is certainly big. But is he good? How can you tell? Do you remember who was lucky when Mother held the papers? (Have the sentence *It was Jerry* reread.) Now read five sentences. One is a two-line sentence. So watch out. Two people are happy. Who are they? Who will read the two-line sentence as if it were all on one line? Now finish the page. Jerry likes the dog's name. How do I know?

Two-line sentences

Page 49. Watch the look in the children's eyes. How do Alice and Jerry look? I think they look surprised, too. Maybe that is why the title of the next part of our book is "Surprise."

ORAL READING

Rereading by page units. (Since "A Dog for Jerry" is a boy's story, have the group choose six boys to reread the story.)

WORD RECOGNITION TECHNIQUES

Auditory-visual perception. *Initial sounds.* (DO NOT OMIT THESE ACTIVITIES.) If you will show me how *dog* begins, I will finish the word. (Continue with *day, boy, Mac, garden, will, was.*)

Initial blends. It takes two letters to begin the word *store.* (Write *st____*; pause; then complete *store* and erase.) Show me how to begin *stay,* and I will finish it. (Continue in same way with *play, please, green, blue, brown, train.*)

Phonics

Final sounds. You remember how *green* ends (write *green* and draw a line under *n*); and *rabbit* (repeat procedure). If I write *kitten,* all but the last letter, will you finish it? (Continue with *went, rain, train, got, just, garden, eat, again.*)

Phonetic parts. Do you remember what we found out about this word? (Write *out* and draw a line under *ou.*) What does this word say? (Write *house.*) Can you hear the sound *ou?* Can you find the part which says *ou?* Draw a line under it.

What does this word say? (Write *May.*) This part (draw line under *ay*) says *ā.* Can you hear the part in this word? (Write *play.*) Can you find it?

SUPPLEMENTARY ACTIVITIES

1. *Workbook for Day In and Day Out,* pages 25, 26, 27, 28.
2. Bulletin board. Have this rhyme on the bulletin board to be used in the usual way.

One Day

Independent
word attack

I was so happy,
So happy one day,
I just had to go walking
Away and away.

I saw ducks in the puddles,
A red bird in a <u>tree</u>.
By and by a little rabbit
Came out and looked at <u>me</u>.

3. Independent reading.

My Little Red Story Book, pages 23-26. (Give help with the word *Bunny* on page 25.)

Ned and Nancy, pages 21-28. (Give help with the word *has* on page 27.)

Time to Play (American Book Co.), pages 3-9.

We Come and Go (Scott, Foresman and Co.), pages 3-8.

(Give help with the word *Baby,* on page 5.)

We Look and See, pages 39-47.

4. Textfilm for *Day In and Day Out,* Frames 13-14. See Textfilm manual for directions.

5. Tests. Before beginning the next unit, give the two informal tests on pages 29 and 30 of the Workbook. In each test pupils are to be given a score of 1 for each item marked correctly. Pupils in superior groups should make a score of at least 22 on Test 1, page 29; and a score of at least 5 on Test 2, page 30.

Informal tests

Pp. 49-55 # Unit 9: Something for Mother

NEW VOCABULARY: get   surprise

INITIAL PROCEDURE

Vocabulary review. Do you remember how Alice and Jerry looked when we last saw them? They looked as if they had had a—(write *surprise* on board). Maybe they will have more than one. Then they will have—(write *surprises*).

Contents pages. Turn quickly to the contents pages. Of course, you know now what the name of the second part of our book is. What is the name of the first story in that part? On what page will it begin?

SILENT READING

Oral language

Page 50. (Take time for picture discussion.) The picture tells me that Alice is talking to Mother. But words are better than pictures. They tell me what Alice and Mother are saying. Read the page silently and be ready to tell what Alice wants and what Mother says about it.

Page 51. It looks as if Alice were filling up a hole. What has happened? Read four sentences to find out.

Guidance in methods of word attack

If Jip did that to my garden, I would tell him to—(write *Get out, get out!*). This new word (indicate *Get, get*) begins like *good*. Think how it begins. Think what Alice would say. "G—— out!"

Alice not only wants Jip to get out. She wants him to do something else, and she tells him why. Does Jip mind Alice? Finish the page and find out.

Page 52. Look at the garden now. I know why it has grown so well. Read three sentences and find out.

I know how many days it took after the rain before the garden turned green. Read the next sentence and find out.

If you finish the page, you will find out to whom Alice is talking. What does she say?

Page 53. Alice invited Mother. But does she want that rabbit? Read five sentences and find out.

The rabbit is tricky. Finish the page and see what he does.

Page 54. See what has happened now. Alice looks as surprised as we do. I don't know exactly how long it took for those flowers to bloom; but when I read the first sentence, I get an idea. Read that sentence and see if you do. What kind of sentence is the next one? How do you know? Show me that you know how to read it.

Now read six sentences. What does Alice say when she sees the flowers? What do you think the surprise is, and for whom? Finish the page and find out.

Working for fluency

Page 55. Alice talks in a rhyme. Read four sentences and find out what she says. Then we will see if you can swing your voice along and read aloud just as Alice talked.

Of course, Mother couldn't help liking that surprise. Finish the page to find out what she says.

ORAL READING

Rereading by page units. (Since this is Alice's story, have the group choose six girls to reread the story by pages.)

WORD RECOGNITION TECHNIQUES

Accurate word recognition. Today Alice said—(write *Get out, get out*). Here are the words to watch, and here are the letters to "spot" with your eye cameras. (Indicate *Get—get* and draw line under the *e* in each.) This is what happened. (Write *Jip got out;* repeat procedure with *o* in *got.* Then erase sentences and play "Watch Me Go" with *come, came, get, got.*)

Drill on carrier words

Auditory-visual perception. *Phonetic parts.* What does this word say? (Write *house.*) Can you draw a line under the part which says *ou?* (Repeat with *ay* in *play, ow* in *bow-wow.*)

Phonics

Final sounds. If I write *just,* all but the last letter, can you finish it? (Continue with *rain, coat, then.*)

Now listen carefully as I say, "Jip can jump." Did you hear two words which ended with the same sound? Let's see if you are right. (Write *Jip—jump* on board and direct attention to final *p.*) *Walk, hop, run!* Which word shall I write on the board because it ends like *Jip* and *jump?*

SUPPLEMENTARY ACTIVITIES

1. *Workbook for Day In and Day Out,* pages 31, 32, 33, 34.
2. Bulletin board. Have the following on the bulletin board. How many superior pupils can use the word recognition techniques to unlock new words independently?

My Garden

Independent word attack

I like gardens,
in the rain.
To<u>day</u> the rain comes down
in <u>show</u>ers
on the <u>flow</u>ers in my garden.

I stay by the window
and look
at the flowers in my garden.
The blue flowers,
the red flowers,
and the green, green leaves.
My garden looks
so pretty in the rain.

3. Independent reading.
   Ned and Nancy, pages 29-36. (Give help with the word *bigger* on page 33.)
   Time to Play, pages 10-17. (Give help with *we,* page 11; and *stop,* page 16.)
   We Come and Go, pages 9-12.
4. Textfilm for *Day In and Day Out,* Frames 15-16. See Textfilm manual for directions.

Unit 10: A Good Wish

Pp. 56-62

NEW VOCABULARY: Jack   pony   wish

PREPARATION

Have the following material ready for use:

Word Card: 498 wish

INITIAL PROCEDURE

Introducing new vocabulary. Do you remember what Alice did when she blew out the candles on her birthday cake? She made a— (hold up word card *wish*). *Wish* begins like—(wait for suggestions *will, want,* etc.). I think you know something about the end sound,

Guidance in
methods of
word attack

too. (Indicate *sh.*) I hear that sound at the end of *fish* and *splash.* What is the sound? Now we know two things about the word *wish* which will make it easier to remember.

Contents pages. Someone in our story is going to make a wish and get a big surprise. So find the name of the new story and the page it begins on.

SILENT READING

Page 56. I wonder if the good wish will have something to do with that big airplane. Read six sentences to find out.

I imagine Mother thinks a little boy with a big airplane would be very funny. Does she think Jerry will get his wish? Read four sentences to find out.

Here comes another wish. Finish the page. You will find a word that begins like *Jerry* and rhymes with *back* (*Jack*).

Independent word attack— lack

Page 57. Will Mother let Jerry change his name? Read the page and find out.

Page 58. Mother thinks she should have a turn. Read two sentences and find out what she wishes.

Mother is the lucky one. Read three sentences and find out why. I hope you know what the children said before they left the house. I hope you have your eyes on that last sentence. Now finish the page.

Independent word attack— .pony

Page 59. I know what Alice and Jerry will wish now. Do you? If you think how *pony* begins, you can find it on this page.

Is this Jack or some other boy? Read two sentences and see what you think. Now read four more sentences. Were we right about Jerry's wish?

Does Alice make the same wish? Does she think the wishes will come true? Finish the page and see.

Page 60. Mother must have sent them to the toy store. Read the first sentence and find out where the children are. What do you notice about the sentence?

Now finish the page. Did Alice and Jerry really go to a toy store, or is someone just wishing for all these toys?

Page 61. Maybe it was a pet store Mother sent them to. Read the whole page and see.

Page 62. I hope Alice and Jerry haven't been so busy wishing that they forgot to get what Mother wanted. Read two sentences to find out. Was either sentence a two-line sentence?

Two-line sentence

I do hope Alice and Jerry make one wish that will come true. Read four more sentences. Are they still wishing? Read two more sentences. Make that wish come true. Now finish the page and tell what Alice and Jerry say between bites of those good cookies. (Call attention to cooky jar and enjoy inscription "Thou shalt not steal" with children.)

Page 63. Mother has Alice's coat and cap, but I don't see Alice. Mother seems to be talking to Jerry. If you think how the new word in the title begins, you can find out what Mother wants Jerry to do. Can you f—— Alice? Who is ready?

independent word attack— find

WORD RECOGNITION TECHNIQUES

Accurate word recognition. (DO NOT OMIT THESE ACTIVI-TIES.) (Write *I wish I had a ball* and have sentence read.) Here (indicate *wish*) is the word to watch. Here (draw a line under the *sh*) is the part to "spot" with your cameras. (Write *I will get you a ball* and *Jerry got a ball.* Repeat procedures with the *ll* in *will,* the *e* in *get,* and the *o* in *got.* Erase board and play "Watch Me Go" with *came, come, will, wish, get, got.*)

Drill on carrier words

Auditory-visual perception. *Phonetic parts.* (Write *out* and have someone draw a line under *ou;* then pronounce the word and the part. Continue with *ay* in *away, ow* in *bow-wow.*) Of course, you know this word (write *boy*); and this one (write *toy*). But you didn't know that this part in each one says *oy.* (Give sound and underline *oy.*)

Phonics

Final sounds. If I write *train,* all but the last letter, will you finish it? (Continue with *rabbit, went, green.*)

What did we find out about *Jip, cap, jump, hop?* (Write *Jip* on board and direct attention to final *p.*) If I write *jump,* all but the last letter, will you finish it?

SUPPLEMENTARY ACTIVITIES

1. *Workbook for Day In and Day Out,* pages 35, 36, 37, 38.
2. Bulletin board. Have this rhyme on bulletin board. Check to

see how adept pupils in superior groups are becoming in getting new words through the use of rhyme and initial consonant clues.

Independent
word attack

My Wish for You

I wish, I wish
Oh, what do I wish?
Oh, what do I wish for you?
Three little <u>kittens</u>
With little red <u>mittens</u>.
And that is my wish for you.

3. Independent reading.

My Little Red Story Book, pages 27-34. (Give help with the word *apple* on page 31.)

Ned and Nancy, pages 37-40. (Give help with the word *cake* on page 37.)

Time to Play, pages 18-25.

We Come and Go, pages 13-16. (Give help with the word *funny* on page 15.)

4. Textfilm for *Day In and Day Out,* Frames 17-18. See Textfilm manual for directions.

Pp. 63-69

Unit 11: Can You Find Alice?

NEW VOCABULARY: find   her   now   say

INITIAL PROCEDURE

Contents pages. When we closed our books the last time, Mother was asking Jerry this question. (Write *Can you find Alice?*) Who can read the question and draw a line under the new word? I hope you can find (point to word *find* on board) the story on the contents pages and the number of the page it begins on.

SILENT READING

Page 63. Read the title and the first sentence. When Mother wanted to talk to Jerry, what did she do?

When we see that cap, we might say, "It is Alice's cap." Or we might say—(write *It is her cap* on board). You know how the new word begins. (Indicate *her.*) If I were to tell you that this part of the word (underscore *er*) said (give sound), of course you could get the word. Who is ready with the sentence? Now read the next five sentences in your book. The best silent reader may be the one I choose to read aloud.

Jerry is pretty sure of himself. Finish the page and find out why I know.

Page 64. Jerry certainly sees something! Is it Alice? Read four sentences and find out.

Do you remember what Jip said? (Write *bow-wow.*) Do you remember what this part said? (Underscore *ow.*) We have a new word on this page. (Write *now.*) Think how it begins. Think what this part says. (Underscore *ow.*) The word is—. *Now* finish the page. Does Jerry find Alice?

Page 65. I know why Jerry liked the name Jack. One of his playmates is named Jack, and we hear about him on this page. Read three sentences. What question does Jerry ask Jack? Now read three more sentences. What is Jack's answer?

Jerry decides that he needs help. Read two more sentences and find out why I know. I hope Jack won't leave that new boat when he runs away with Jerry. Finish the page and see if he does.

Page 66. Evidently the boys think a toy store is a good place to look for a runaway little girl. Do you agree with them? Why? Jerry is sure he has found Alice this time. Read three sentences and find out why. Read the next sentence. What do the boys do now?

What happens in the store? Finish the page and find out.

Page 67. It looks as if Jerry will have more help. Read four lines. What does he tell Jip to do?

Do you remember this word in the title of our book? (Write *day.*) Do you remember what this part says? (Underscore *ay.*) Then you can get this new word. (Write *say.*) Think how it begins. Think what

Guidance in
methods of
word attack

Independent
word attack—
now

the part says. The word is—. When Jip barks, he is trying to *say* something. Now finish reading the page. What do you think he is trying to say?

Page 68. Here is the lost girl. I wonder who really found her and where she was. Read four sentences and find out.

Jack thinks Jip is much smarter than Jerry thinks he is. Finish the page and find out why I know.

Page 69. Will Jerry forget to give Alice Mother's message? Read three sentences and see.

Alice has an idea what Mother wants. The next two questions tell. Can Jerry answer Alice's questions? Read three sentences and find out what happens.

How many more sentences will it take to finish the page? The one who can read each two-line sentence as if it were all on one line may choose the readers to reread the story.

WORD RECOGNITION TECHNIQUES

Accurate word recognition. (Write *Here is Alice. Here is her coat.* Have sentences read. Underscore *here* and *her*.) I hope you notice the difference in these words. (Erase board.) Get your cameras ready to click. What word did I write? (Write *here;* erase immediately. Alternate with *her.*)

Drill on carrier words

Auditory-visual perception. *Phonetic parts.* What does this word say? (Write *boy.*) Who can draw a line under the part which says *oy?* (Give sound. Continue with *ay* in *say, ou* in *out, er* in *her, ow* in *now.*)

Phonics

Initial sounds. If someone will show me how *find* begins, I will finish the word. (Continue with *pony, Jack, wish, garden.*)

Final sounds. If I write *ship,* all but the last letter, can you finish it? (Continue with *nest, barn, help, goat, hen, fan, hat.*)

SUPPLEMENTARY ACTIVITIES

1. *Workbook for Day In and Day Out,* pages 39, 40, 41, 42.

2. Bulletin board. Have this rhyme on the bulletin board to be used in usual way.

The Toy Store

Independent
word attack

Here is my toy store.
Oh, what do you see?
You may look in the window.
Then come in with me.

A duck and a kitten,
A rabbit that <u>hops</u>,
And here in this box
Are two pretty red <u>tops</u>!

3. Independent reading.
Molly, Pete, and Ginger, pages 11-16.
My Little Red Story Book, pages 35-44.
Time to Play, pages 26-33.
We Work and Play (Scott, Foresman and Co.), pages 3-10.
(Give help with the words *work,* page 3; and *Baby,* page 6.)
4. Textfilm for *Day In and Day Out,* Frames 19-20. See Textfilm
manual for directions.

Unit 12: A Walk with Mother | Pp. 70-76

NEW VOCABULARY: mew

INITIAL PROCEDURE

Contents pages. Today the children are going away with Mother,
but not in the car. Find the story title on the contents pages and find
out how I know they will not go in the car. What page does "A Walk
with Mother" begin on?

SILENT READING

Page 70. I wonder why Mother and the children are going for a
walk. Read the title and three sentences and find out.

I know how Alice and Jerry will answer Mother's question. Do you? Read four sentences and see if we are right. How does Mother answer Alice's question? The next sentence tells.

I don't know how far they walked, but I think it was a long way. Read two sentences and see if you agree. How many sentences will it take to finish the page? Read and see who gets tired walking first.

Page 71. Mother tells three things about the surprise on this page. Be sure you find all three. What will the surprise be?

Page 72. Could this kitten be the surprise? Why not? Do you remember Alice's new coat? (Write *new*.) If I tell you that this part (underscore *ew*) says *ū* (give sound), maybe you could tell me what this new word says. (Write *mew*.) Think how it begins. Think what the part says. The word is—. And the kitten is the one who said—. The kitten wanted to say something else. Read four sentences to find out.

Alice is just as smart as you are. She knew why the kitten couldn't be the surprise. Finish the page and prove that she knows.

Page 73. I hope this is a friendly dog. He must be. Alice looks afraid, but Jerry doesn't. Could the dog be the surprise? Does Jerry think he is? Read the whole page and see.

Page 74. One of the pictures gives the surprise away. But won't that pony ride be fun? I think I know where the walk ended. Read two sentences and see if you do. Read two more sentences. What did Mother say, and what happened next?

Evidently the man has heard about the children. Read four sentences and find out why I think so. Now finish the page. I am sure you could answer those two questions without saying what the man says. See if you couldn't.

Page 75. The minute Alice and Jerry see the pony, what do they say? Read six sentences to find out. Finish the page. The man says something which makes me know how the children got up on the pony. See how you think they got there.

Page 76. Jerry remembers something and tells Mother about it. Read the whole page. What does Jerry remember?

Page 77. What do we call cows and pigs and goats and rabbits when they are all together? Then what do you think will be the title of the next part of the book? Each of you choose one animal in the picture and tell me its name and the sound it makes.

Guidance in
methods of
word attack

SILENT READING

Rereading by page units. Suppose I surprise you. I will write a name and a page number on the board. The person whose name I write may read that page. (Continue until story is reread.)

WORD RECOGNITION TECHNIQUES

Auditory-visual perception. *Phonetic parts.* (Write *say, mew, now, her, stay, boy, day, new, away, toys, out* on the board.) I see a word in which I hear the part $\bar{a}$. Who can find and read the word and draw

Phonics

a line under the part? (Continue in same way with *ou, ow, oy, er, ew.*)

Initial blends. It takes two letters to start the word *play.* If someone will start it, I will finish it. (Continue with *please, green, blue, brown, stay, store.*)

SUPPLEMENTARY ACTIVITIES

1. *Workbook for Day In and Day Out,* pages 43, 44, 45, 46.
2. Bulletin board. Have this rhyme on the bulletin board to be used in the usual way.

My Pony

Independent
word attack

I wish I had a pony,
   A little pony <u>brown</u>.
I want to name my pony Jack
   And ride away to <u>town</u>.

Please get me a little brown pony,
   So I can ride <u>away</u>.
Please get me that little brown pony
   <u>Today</u>, <u>today</u>, <u>today</u>!

3. Independent reading.
   Molly, Pete, and Ginger, pages 17-24. (Give help on page 22 with the sound word *Wuff* and the word *No.*)
   My Little Red Story Book, pages 45-48.
   Time to Play, pages 34-41.
   We Work and Play, pages 15-18. (Give help with the word *funny* on page 18.)

4. Textfilm for *Day In and Day Out,* Frames 21-22. See Textfilm manual for directions.

5. Tests. This story marks the close of the absorption unit. Before beginning the next story, give the two informal tests in the *Workbook for Day In and Day Out* (pages 47, 48). Pupils in superior groups should make a score of at least 22 on the vocabulary test and a score of at least 5 on the sentence-meaning test. If scores fall lower than this, check your teaching with the unit plans. It is suggested at this point that each child be tested individually with the word cards for the vocabulary developed so far. (See pages 158-59 of the Primer.)

Individual check on sight vocabulary

Pp. 77-83 # Unit 13: Little Goat

| NEW VOCABULARY: | am | are | goat | started |
| | animals | ate | old | stopped |

PREPARATION

Have the following materials ready for use:

Pocket Card Holder
Word Cards: 508 stopped   512 am
                      511 started   513 are

INITIAL PROCEDURE

Introducing new vocabulary. Jerry was riding on the train. All at once the train—(hold up word card *stopped*). The first thing I know about this new word is that it begins like *store*. I think how it begins. I think what the train did. All at once the train st——. The new word is *stopped*. (Put word card into card holder.)

Guidance in methods of word attack

The train waited at the station a few minutes. Then it—(hold up word card *started*). Here is another word which begins like *store*. I will tell you something else about it. This part (indicate *ar*) says—

(give sound of *ar*). You know how the word begins. You know what this part says. All at once the train star——. *Started,* of course. Now if I begin a word like this (write *st*), and then you see the part which says *ar* (give sound and write *ar* after *st*), you will tell me to finish the word—(add *started* to card holder). I know something about our

Opposites
new words. They mean different things. *Started* and *stopped* are—.

(Point to yourself and say, "I am a woman." Then write the sentence on the board.) If you were to tell me what you are, Ann, what would you say? (As soon as Ann has replied, "I am a girl," change the word *woman* to *girl* and have sentence on board reread.) Show me the word *am*. Find the word card on this chair and add it to the card holder.

If I were to point to John, I would say, "You are a boy." (Write sentence on board.) Show me the word *are*. Do you remember what I told you this part said in *started*? (Underline *ar* in *are*.) Here is that part again; and if you remember what the part says, you know the whole word. What does it say? (Have word card *are* added to card holder.)

In the next part of our book we will read about some—(*animals*). We wondered what animal we would read about first. If you know this word (write *coat* and have it read), if you think how this word begins

Oral language
(write *goat*) and make it rhyme with *coat,* you can find out for yourself. The first animal will be a g——. (Allow a few minutes for children to recount experiences with goats.)

Contents pages. We start on a new contents page today. Be ready to read the name of the new part of our book, the name of the first story in that part, and the number of the page on which it begins.

SILENT READING

Page 78. (Allow time for enjoyment of picture.) The minute I look at the picture I am sure Little Goat has—(indicate word card *stopped* in card holder). He looks as if he were ready for mischief. Read the page to find out what he is going to do.

Guidance in methods of word attack
Page 79. I know what happened to that cap because I see this new word. (Write *ate*.) If I tell you that the name of this letter (indicate *a*) is *ā* and that you hear the sound of its name in the word, I

am sure you can get it for yourself. Little Goat a—— the cap. Read the whole page. What did he say before he ate that cap?

Page 80. Little Goat won't eat that doll, will he? If I tell you that the first letter in this new word (write *old*) is ō and that you hear the sound of its name in the word, you will know that this is a little o—— doll. Read the page and see if Little Goat ate the little *old* doll.

Page 81. I think a little goat I know will be sick before long. What will he eat this time? Read and see.

Page 82. Little Goat gets fooled on this page. Maybe you are smarter than he. Maybe you know what is behind the tree. Read and see what he thinks it is.

Page 83. What a surprise for Little Goat! I don't believe he will eat that kitten. I hope you know these words. (Indicate *am, are,* and *started* in card holder and have them read.) You will need all three when you read. Now read to find out whether Little Goat finishes his dinner by eating a kitten.

ORAL READING

Fluency-expression. (It is important that children feel the rhythm in the sentences and read accordingly. Suggest that you enjoyed the story so much that you would like to read a page or two yourself.

Setting oral reading standards

Set the pattern; then on the board write a child's name and the page number he is to read. Continue procedure until story has been re-read by pages.)

VOCABULARY ENRICHMENT AND EXTENSION

Extending speaking vocabulary. Goats often do funny, or amusing, things. *Amusing* is a more grown-up word to use than *funny*. Be ready to tell one *amusing* thing a goat might do. Be sure it is something a goat could really do. Be sure it is *amusing*.

WORD RECOGNITION TECHNIQUES

Auditory-visual perception. *Phonetic parts.* (Write the following words on the board: mew, now, out, say, boy, her, are, started, garden.) I see a word on the board in which I hear the sound ā.

Phonics

(Give sound.) Who will find the word and draw a line under the part? (Continue in same way with sounds of <u>ow, ou, ar, er, oy, ew.</u>)

Long vowel sounds. Sometimes letter names help us to get words. (Write <u>eat.</u>) The name of this letter is *e,* and the word is—. (Write <u>ate.</u>) The name of this letter is *a,* and the word is—. (Repeat procedure with <u>old</u> and <u>oh.</u>)

Initial blends. If you show me how <u>store</u> begins, I will finish it. Maybe you could finish it for yourself. (Repeat procedure with <u>stopped.</u>) If you will show me how <u>started</u> begins, I will finish it. Maybe you could add the part which says <u>ar.</u> (Give sound.) If you know how <u>stay</u> begins, if you know how to write the part which says *ay* (give sound), maybe you could write the whole word.

SUPPLEMENTARY ACTIVITIES

1. *Workbook for Day In and Day Out,* pages 49, 50, 51, 52.

2. Bulletin board. Have this rhyme on the bulletin board to be used in the usual way.

Two Names

Independent word attack

I have two names,
    And so have you.
A rabbit is a rabbit,
    But it is a <u>bunny,</u> too.

One day I saw a little goat,
    And he looked oh, so <u>funny.</u>
He started to eat a rabbit,
    But hop, hop went the <u>bunny.</u>

3. Independent reading.

Molly, Pete, and Ginger, pages 25-28. (Give help with the words *cakes,* page 25; and *has,* page 28.)

My Little Green Story Book (Ginn and Co.), pages 3-10. (Give help with the word *work* on page 7.)

Time to Play, pages 42-51.

We Work and Play, pages 23-26.

4. Textfilm for *Day In and Day Out,* Frames 23-24. See Textfilm manual for directions.

Pp. 84-89 # Unit 14: The Little Duck

NEW VOCABULARY:	cluck	could	quack	talk
	cock-a-doodle-doo	hen	rooster	tweet

INITIAL PROCEDURE

Guidance in
methods of
word attack

Introducing new vocabulary. Alice went for a—(write *walk*). **If** you think how this word begins (write *talk* under *walk*) and make it rhyme with *walk,* you can find out for yourselves the new word you will need in today's story. *Walk, t——.* Of course, the new word is *talk.*

Contents pages. A good workman is an *efficient* workman. I am going to watch carefully today to see how efficiently you can use your contents pages and turn to the new story. Are you efficient workmen?

SILENT READING

Page 84. (Allow time for spontaneous discussion of pictures.) The little duck does something very much like something Alice did. Read the title and two sentences. Why is he like Alice? What does he see? The kitten says "Hello" in her kitten way, and the duck does something. Read two sentences to find out what happens.

Independent
word attack—
could, hen,
cluck

What do you notice about the next sentence? How will you read it? You will find a new word in the next sentence; but if you think how it starts and jump over it, you can get it.

Could Little Duck say "Mew"? Finish the page and find out.

Page 85. Now whom does Little Duck meet? You know how *hen* begins. You know how it ends. How many times can you find it on this page? What sound does Mother Hen make? Can you find that word on this page? How many times? Now read the whole page. Be ready to tell what happens when Little Duck meets Mother Hen.

Page 86. I do hope Little Duck learns to talk on this page. This word (write *tweet*) says *tweet*. It is the sound the—makes. How many times can you find it on the page? Now read the whole page. What happens when Little Duck meets the bird?

Independent word attack— rooster, quack, cock-a-doodle-doo

Page 87. Now, whom does Little Duck meet? How many times can you find the word *rooster?* What does a rooster say? *Cock-a-doodle-doo* is a long, long word. Can you find it? (Write *Cock-a-doodle-doo* on board.) These little marks are hyphens. They divide the word into parts. (Read word and pause slightly between parts.) Now finish reading the page. Does the rooster teach Little Duck to talk?

Page 88. I am afraid Little Duck is feeling downhearted and discouraged. Maybe he is going home to have Mother Duck cheer him up. Read the page. What happens?

Page 89. I hope you know what a duck can say. I hope you can find that word. How many times do you see it? How many times does it begin with a capital letter? with a small letter? Now read the page. Does Little Duck finally learn to talk?

ORAL READING

Fluency-expression. (Write *mew, cluck, tweet, cock-a-doodle-doo, quack* on board.) The one who can read and erase the word which tells what the kitten says may read the page that tells what happens when Little Duck meets the kitten. (Continue in similar way with other words until story has been reread. Stress rhythmic reading. Set pattern by reading one page, if necessary.)

VOCABULARY ENRICHMENT AND EXTENSION

Opposites

Word concepts. I will write a word. Read it for me; then tell me a word which means something very different. Tell me the word which is opposite in meaning. (Use *stopped—started, old—new*.) If we say that something happens *now* (write *now*), we probably mean that it happens today. When we say, *"Then* something happened," we may mean that it happened a long time ago. So *now* and *then* (write *then* on board) are—.

WORD RECOGNITION TECHNIQUES

Phonics

Auditory-visual perception. (DO NOT OMIT THESE ACTIVI-TIES.) *Long sounds of vowels.* The name of this letter is—(write *o*), and the word is—(add *ld* to make *old;* repeat with *e* for *eat, a* for *ate, o for oh*).

Phonetic parts. When Mother saw Alice's cap, she said, "Here is her cap." (Write *her*.) We found a part in this word which said *er*. (Give sound.) Who can draw a line under it?

Now read these words. How sharp are your eyes? (Write *Father, Mother*.) (Have words read and a line drawn under the *er* in each.) Today we read about this farm animal. (Write *rooster* and repeat procedure.)

Final sounds. Listen carefully. *Bird, could, red!* Listen again for the last, or final, sound. (Repeat words.) What did your ears tell you? Let's see if you are right. (Write the three words on board and direct attention to final *d*.) I will say three words to you. Which one shall I add to the list on the board because it ends like *bird, could,* and *red*? (Use *animal, tweet, old; cluck, good, big*.)

SUPPLEMENTARY ACTIVITIES

1. *Workbook for Day In and Day Out,* pages 53, 54, 55, 56.
2. Bulletin board. Have this rhyme on the bulletin board to be used in usual way.

Independent
word attack

Little Duck

Little Duck went out
  For a walk one day.
"It looks like rain,
  I am happy to say,"
Said this little <u>duck</u>.
"And that is good <u>luck</u>."

Little Duck walked on
And came to a pond
And walked in
With a splash, splash, splash.

"Good luck,"
Said the duck.
"Quack, quack! Quack, quack!
Here I will stay,
And I will not go back.
Quack, quack! Quack, quack!
Quack, quack!"

3. Independent reading.

Molly, Pete, and Ginger, pages 29-34. (Give help with the words make, page 31; and bigger, page 33.)

My Little Green Story Book, pages 11-18. (Give help with the words apples, page 11; and dinner, page 18.)

Ned and Nancy, pages 41-45. (Give help with school, page 41.)

Time to Play, pages 52-63.

We Work and Play, pages 35-38.

4. Textfilm for Day In and Day Out, Frames 25-26. See Textfilm manual for directions.

Unit 15: Little Jack Rabbit

Pp. 90-93

NEW VOCABULARY: all   nest   run
             lived   played white

PREPARATION

Have the following materials ready for use:

Pocket Card Holder
Word Cards: 522 lived   524 run   525 all

INITIAL PROCEDURE

Introducing new vocabulary. Mac did not stay in the house with Jerry. (Write He lived in a dog house.) Think how the new word

(indicate *lived*) begins; then jump over it. Let the meaning of the
sentence help you get the word. Who is ready? If I write this (write
liv____), what word would you tell me to finish? (Add *ed.*) Who
will find the word card which says *lived,* put it into the card holder,
and then use the word *lived* in a sentence?

Everyone is here today. So—(write *You are all here*). This sentence
makes me know that every boy and girl is here. There is a word
in it which means every boy and girl. Who can read the sentence and
show me the word? Now who can find the word card *all,* put it into
the card holder, and then use the word *all* in a sentence?

Mother was sewing. Jip kept jumping up on her. So Mother said
this. (Write *Run away, Jip, run away.*) Think how the new word
(indicate *Run, run*) begins and ends. Jump over it and let the meaning of the sentence help you. Who is ready? Of course, the new word
is *run.* (Have word card *run* added to card holder.) If I write—
(write *ru____*), what word will you tell me to finish? If I write—
(write *ra____*), what word will you tell me to finish? Now who can
read the three new words in the card holder?

Contents pages. Our new story is about another animal, and you
may be surprised to find that he has a name. Are you efficient workmen? Prove it by the way you use your contents pages.

SILENT READING

Page 90. (Discuss the difference between tame rabbits who live in
rabbit hutches and wild rabbits who live in holes.) You remember
that Mac—(indicate word *lived* in card holder, letting children supply
word) in a doghouse. Mother Rabbit lived in a hole, but down in that
hole she made something. If you think how the new word in the first
sentence begins, I am sure you can find out what she made. Who
is ready?

What do you notice about the next sentence? Who can read it as if
it were all on one line?

One little rabbit feels as Jip did when Jerry wanted a new dog.
Read two more sentences. What is the matter, and why?

How many sentences must you read to finish the page? Read to
find out what Jack Rabbit wants to do and what Mother Rabbit says.

Page 91. It looks as if Jack Rabbit decided to—(indicate *run* in card holder and let pupils supply word) away. He may get into trouble. The clouds in the sky suggest something to me. What do you think may happen?

How did Jack Rabbit get away without Mother Rabbit's seeing him? Read the first sentence to find out.

What do you notice about the next sentence? Read to find out what Jack Rabbit says the minute Mother is out of sight. What do you notice about the next sentence? What *can* Jack Rabbit do, and what *will* he do? Read to find out. Why does he think he can do as he pleases? The next sentence tells.

Two-line sentences

How did he go, and where did he go? Finish the page and find out.

Page 92. Jack Rabbit is a wild rabbit. These rabbits are—. They are someone's pets. What is the right name for their house? Who do you think made that hutch? Why? Look at the clouds. Do you still think it may storm? Will Jack know enough to go home? Let's read and see. Before we start, find out how many two-line sentences there are on the page. Now read five sentences. What does Jack Rabbit decide to do when he sees the garden?

Independent word attack— white

Finish the page. There is a new word which tells the color of the rabbits. You won't need help with that.

Page 93. What kind of sentence is the first sentence? Read to find out what Jack did when he saw the rabbits.

Maybe he will not have anything to do with white rabbits. Read four sentences and find out.

Guidance in methods of word attack

You remember this word. (Write *look*.) And this one—(write *looked*). Then you know this word. (Write *play*.) You can make *play* grow just as *look* changed to *looked*. (Write *played* and have word read.) What do you notice about the last two sentences? Read them silently and find out what the rabbits did. I am afraid Jack Rabbit won't get home before the storm. We will have to wait until the next time we read to find out.

ORAL READING

Rereading by page units. The one who can read this word (write *nest*) may read the page which tells about it. The one who can read this (write *garden*) may read the next page. The one who knows this word (write *lived*) may read the page which tells to whom the house in the garden belonged. The one who can make the word *play* grow into this word (indicate *played*) may read the next page.

WORD RECOGNITION TECHNIQUES

Verbs ending in ed, ing

Word structure. (DO NOT OMIT THESE ACTIVITIES.) Watch these words grow. (Write *play;* have it read and used in a sentence. Follow with *played, playing; wish, wishing, wished; stay, stayed.*)

Auditory-visual perception. *Phonetic parts.* The rabbits played in the—(write *garden*). Who can read the word and draw a line under the part which helps you remember the word? Can you find the same part in this word? (Continue with *started, are.* In the same way review the phonetic part *ew* in *mew* and *new* and the vowel digraph *oy* in *boy.*)

Phonics

Initial sounds. The question word is—(write *what* and have it read). It takes two letters to start the word *what.* (Write *wh;* then erase.) We had a color word this morning which begins like *what.* Two rabbits were—. If someone will show me how *white* begins, I will finish the word. Two letters start the word *that.* Show me how it begins, and I will finish it for you.

SUPPLEMENTARY ACTIVITIES

1. *Workbook for Day In and Day Out,* pages 57, 58.
2. Bulletin board. Have this rhyme on the bulletin board to be used in the usual way.

Independent word attack

Something to See

I have something
That can fly,
Up and up in the blue, blue sky.

I have something
Pretty and white.
Look up and see my pretty new kite.

3. Independent reading.
All in a Day (American Book Co.), pages 3-11.
My Little Green Story Book, pages 19-24. (Give help with the
words *chair,* page 19; and *Bunny,* page 21.)
We Come and Go, pages 17-22.

Unit 16: Little Jack Rabbit

(*cont.*)

Pp. 94-97

NEW VOCABULARY: gate   his   night   open

INITIAL PROCEDURE

Guidance in
methods of
word attack

Introducing new vocabulary. When Mother found Alice's coat on
the chair, she said—(write *Here is her coat*). We remember the word
her because we see this part in it. (Underline *er*.) What does the
word say? the part?

If it were Jerry's coat, Mother would say—(write *Here is his coat*).
Think what Mother would say, and you won't have any trouble with
the new word. Shall I tell you how I remember the word *his?* I think
how it begins. Then I see a little word right inside the big word.
(Draw a line under *is*.)

SILENT READING

Independent
word attack—
gate, open

Page 94. There is something besides a storm after Jack Rabbit
now. What is there around the garden to keep people out? How do
you get through a fence? If you think how the word *gate* begins,
you can find it in the first sentence. This gate opens into a garden.
So we call it—. Read the first three words and find out. I hope you
remember the name of this letter. (Write *o*.) It will help you with
the other new word. Someone has been careless. Read all the first
sentence and find out why I say that. The next sentence is a two-line

sentence. I see both new words in it. Who can read it as if it were all on one line?

I hope the rabbits have sense enough to stop playing. Read two more sentences. See if they do.

The white rabbits know how to take care of themselves. Finish the page to find out what they do.

Page 95. Now Jack Rabbit is certainly in trouble. What is the trouble? Read four sentences to find out.

The storm starts also. Poor Jack Rabbit! Finish the page to see if he feels just as you would if you were lost and cold and frightened.

Independent word attack— night

Page 96. (Allow time for picture discussion.) I think I know what time it is. Then I think how the first word begins, and I know what it says. Now read three sentences. How does Jack Rabbit feel, alone in the dark?

There are three ways in which Jack Rabbit recognizes his mother. Finish the page and find out what they are. Jack is happy. The weather grows more pleasant, too. How can I tell?

Page 97. Mother Rabbit has a right to be cross with Jack Rabbit, hasn't she? But if your mother found you lost and cold and wet, I am sure she would take you home before she said very much. Is Mother Rabbit like that? Read five sentences and find out.

I wonder if Jack Rabbit has learned his lesson. Will he mind Mother Rabbit after this? Finish the page and see.

ORAL READING

Rereading by page units. The one who can read these two phrases (write *The garden gate, the open gate*) may read the page on which you find them. The one who knows this word (write *find*) may read the next page. The one who can read these two opposites (write *night–morning*) may read page 96. The one who can tell me how many two-line sentences there are on page 97 may read the page.

WORD RECOGNITION TECHNIQUES

Word structure. *Little words in big words.* (DO NOT OMIT THESE ACTIVITIES.) Inside the word—(write *his* and have some child read) we find the word—(draw a line under *is* and have it read). Inside the word—(write *ball*) I see the word—(draw a line under *all*). Inside—(write *that*) I see the word—(draw a line under *at*).

Auditory-visual perception. *Long vowel sounds.* If I know the name of the first letter, it helps me get this word. (Write *eat*. Continue with *open, old, ate, oh.*)

Initial sounds. Show me how the word *night* begins, and I will finish it. (Continue with *white, then, she.*) Who can show us how *his* begins? Maybe you can remember the little word inside and write the whole word.

Phonics

Final sounds. If I write *nest*, all but the last letter, who will finish it? (Continue with *bird, run, hop, could, night, hen, jump.*)

I will say two words. Listen to see what you discover about the way they begin. (Say *fun, fat.*) Listen again. What do you discover about the way they end? I will write the words on the board. Which one says *fun?* How do you know? Then what does the other word say? What other word do you know which ends like *fat?* (THESE WORDS ARE NOT PART OF THE PRIMER VOCABULARY. CHILDREN ARE NOT EXPECTED TO REMEMBER THEM. THE PURPOSE IS TO SHOW PUPILS THE USE OF END SOUNDS IN UNLOCKING NEW WORDS.)

SUPPLEMENTARY ACTIVITIES

1. *Workbook for Day In and Day Out,* pages 59, 60.
2. Bulletin board. Have this rhyme on bulletin board to be used in usual way.

Independent word attack

One Night

I ran down to the garden gate.
Night had come,
And it was late.
I looked up, and what did I see?
The moon and the stars,
Looking down at me.

3. Independent reading.
   All in a Day, pages 12-19. (Give help with *stop,* page 15.)

Molly, Pete, and Ginger, pages 61-66. (Give help with the word *we* on page 64.)

My Little Green Story Book, pages 25-28. (Give help with the words *fast,* page 27; and *we,* page 28.)

We Work and Play, pages 39-42. (Give help with the words *makes,* page 39; and *yellow,* page 41.)

4. Textfilm for *Day In and Day Out,* Frames 27-28. See Textfilm manual for directions.

Pp. 98-104 Unit 17: A Good Breakfast

NEW VOCABULARY: barnyard   cow   pig
breakfast   moo   wee

PREPARATION

Have the following materials ready for use:

Pocket Card Holder
Word Cards: 532 breakfast   537 barnyard

INITIAL PROCEDURE

Guidance in methods of word attack

Introducing new vocabulary. This morning I hopped out of bed and dressed. Then—(write *I ate my breakfast*). The new word begins like *brown.* Think how it begins. Then let the sentence help you get the word. Find the word card *breakfast* and put it into the card holder.

Not long ago I visited a farm. The farmer kept his cows in the barn, but his pigs and chickens lived in houses in the yard outside the barn. Since the yard was near the barn, he called it the—(add the word *barnyard* to card holder and have it read). This big word has two little words in it. The first one (indicate *barn*) says—. And the other one (indicate *yard*) says—.

Contents pages. You will need one of these new words to be able to read the title of the next story. Which one will it be? Find the title and see. What page will the story begin on?

<h3 style="text-align:center">SILENT READING</h3>

Page 98. Someone has been careless. Who do you think that was? Someone will get into trouble. Who will that be? Think how *pig* begins. How many times can you find the word *pig*?

Read the title and the first four sentences. How did the little pig happen to come to the garden? What did he do before he went in? Now what do you notice about the next two sentences? Finish the page and find out what happens.

Independent word attack—pig, wee

Page 99. I am sure the little pig said this when he saw the white hen. (Write *wee, wee.*) Think how the word begins. Think of the name of the next two letters. Little pigs say—. How many times can you find *wee?*

Now read the whole page silently. Will the little pig chase the white hen away, or will he ask her in? Find out.

Page 100. (Call attention to page number 100. Explain that reddish brown cows are called "red cows" by farmers. Have pupils find the word *cow* by thinking how it begins. Have them tell the sound a cow makes and find *moo* in the same way. Then have entire page read silently.)

Independent word attack—cow, moo

Page 101. (Call attention to page number. Have page read in usual way.)

Page 102. That man is certainly excited. He knows where those animals belong. Read the page and find out why I think so.

Page 103. I don't believe those animals will go all the way home to the barnyard after all. Read the page, watch for the two-line sentence, and find out why I think so. I am sure I know something that man will do. Do you? Turn and see if we are right.

Page 104. So this is what the animals did instead of going home! I am glad the farmer learned a lesson. What are the animals saying as they look over the fence? Do they ever get in again? Read and see.

Page 105. I am sure you know what the next part of our book will be about. Maybe you wish to know the doll's name. It is Betsy Lee. Do you like that name? I do. Who will read the title? I hope you notice the decoration on Betsy Lee's cap.

ORAL READING

Rereading by page units. The one who can read the name of this animal (write *pig*) may read the first page. The one who can tell me what a pig says (indicate *wee, wee* on board) may read the next page. (Continue in similar fashion until story has been reread.)

WORD RECOGNITION TECHNIQUES

Compound words

Word structure. *Little words in big words.* (DO NOT OMIT THESE ACTIVITIES.) We found out that there were two words in this big word. (Write *barnyard.*) Can someone draw a line under the part of the word which says *barn?* If you think how *barn* ends, you will know where to stop your line. What does the rest of the word say? (Repeat technique with *into.*)

Auditory-visual perception. *Phonetic parts.* If I didn't have a picture to help me, I could still get this word. (Write *cow.*) I know how it begins, and I see a part I know. Who can tell me what the part says and draw a line under it? What does the word say?

(Write *are.*) What part do you hear and see in this word? Draw a line under it. Now listen carefully. *Barnyard!* Did you hear the *ar?* (Give sound.) How many times? (Write *barnyard.*) Can you find the part which says *ar* two times?

Phonics

Initial blends. Two letters start the word *brown.* (Write word and draw a line under *br.*) Listen carefully. *Brown, breakfast!* What did your ears tell you? Then how will *breakfast* begin? Show me, and I will finish the word. (Continue with *please* and *started.*)

Final sounds. Listen as I say *pig, big, dog.* What did you discover? Let's see if we are right. (Write words on board and direct attention to final *g* in each.) Suppose I wanted to add another word that ended like *pig.* Would that word be *arm* or *leg* or *foot?* (Write *leg* to prove that this is the correct choice.)

Will you finish the word *night* by adding the last letter? (Continue in the usual way with *lived, run, jump.*)

Listen as I say *moon—mop.* Which word did I write? (Write *moon* and have pupils identify it by last sound.) Listen again. *Mat-mad!* Which word did I write this time? (Repeat procedure by writing the word *mad.*)

SUPPLEMENTARY ACTIVITIES

1. *Workbook for Day In and Day Out,* pages 61, 62, 63, 64. (On page 61, help pupils identify pictures of jack and jug.)

2. Bulletin board. Have this rhyme on the bulletin board to be used in the usual way.

That Rabbit

Independent
word attack

Little Rabbit
Had a habit.
She said, "Please, please, please,
I want this.
I want that."
She liked to tease, tease, tease.
What a habit
For a rabbit!
But she did say, "Please."

3. Independent reading.

   All in a Day, pages 20-29. (Give help with the word *we,* page 26.)

   Molly, Pete, and Ginger, pages 35-40. (Give help with the words *there,* page 39; and *car,* page 40.)

   My Little Green Story Book, pages 29-34. (Give help with the word *stop* on page 29.)

   Under the Tree (Silver Burdett Co.), pages 9-13. (Give help with the word *stop* on page 12.)

   We Work and Play, pages 47-50.

4. Textfilm for *Day In and Day Out,* Frames 29-30. See Textfilm manual for directions.

5. Tests. Before beginning the next unit, give the informal tests on pages 65 and 66 of the Workbook. Pupils should make a score of at least 22 on the vocabulary test and 5 on the sentence-meaning test. Each item correctly marked scores 1. If scores fall lower than this, check your teaching with the lesson plans. It will be well at this point to check each child individually with the word cards for all vocabulary introduced so far (see pages 158-60 of the Primer).

Individual check on sight vocabulary

Pp. 105-9

Unit 18: The New Doll

NEW VOCABULARY: Betsy Lee   very   word

PREPARATION

Have the following materials ready for use:

Pocket Card Holder
Word Cards: 540 very   541 word

INITIAL PROCEDURE

Introducing new vocabulary. Listen as I say *valentine*. Watch as I write it. Remember the sound with which it begins. Mother's blouse was more than just pretty. (Write *It was very pretty.*) Remember that the new word begins like *valentine*. Then let the sentence help you get the new word. It was v—— pretty. And you are *very* good readers. Who will find the word card *very* and put it into the card holder?

Guidance in methods of word attack

Contents pages. I hope you remember what the new part of our book will be about. I hope you remember the doll's name. Maybe you remember what she had on her cap. When you turn to the contents pages, be ready to read the name of the new part of our book and the name of the first story in that part. What page will the story begin on?

SILENT READING

Page 106. Read the title and the first two sentences. How did Alice happen to be at the gate when the mailman got there?

Two-line
sentences

I wonder if he will leave the big box. Read three more sentences. Watch out for the two-line one.

Who in the world is Alice White? Finish the page and find out. Aren't you glad you know Alice's last name?

Page 107. I am glad Alice didn't tear the box open at the gate. I am glad she did what she did in the first sentence. Read and see what she does. Be ready to tell why that was a good thing for Alice to do.

Read four more lines. What does she find, and what does she say when she opens the box? Now finish the page. How does the doll look? Check with the picture. Do the words and the picture tell the of the name?

Page 108. (Allow time for picture discussion.) The first thing Alice must do is give her doll a—. Read the page. How does she happen to call her Betsy Lee and not just Betsy? What does Mother think of the name?

Page 109. There is a new word on this page. Good readers who

Independent
word attack—
word

think how it begins and then let the sentence help them can get it for themselves. (*word*) There is just one thing wrong with Betsy Lee. Find out what it is.

Well, it looks as if Betsy Lee were not a talking doll. She did not say a—(add **word** card *word* to card holder). I wonder what Alice and Betsy Lee will do next. We will find out tomorrow.

ORAL READING

Rereading by page units. The one who can tell me Jerry's full name may read page 106. The one who can tell me Mother's real name, besides "Mother," may read page 107. The one who can tell me Father's real name may read page 108. The one who can read the two new words in the card holder may read page 109. Try to talk just as Alice did.

WORD RECOGNITION TECHNIQUES

Auditory-visual perception. (DO NOT OMIT THESE ACTIVITIES.) *Long sounds of vowels.* (Write *ate* on board.) If you know the name of this letter, it will help you get the word. (Underscore *a.*) What is the name of the letter? What is the word? (Continue with *e* in *eat; o* in *old, open, oh; e* in *wee, Lee, see.*)

Phonetic parts. Betsy Lee was a (write *new*) doll. You know how the word begins. Can you draw a line under the part which says *ū?* (Give sound.) Can you find the same part in this word? (Write *mew.*) Read the word first. Then draw a line under the part and tell what it says. (Continue same techniques with *er* in *her, Mother, Father.*)

Phonics

Initial sounds. If you show me how *very* begins, I will finish the word. (Repeat with *word.*) People's names always begin with capital letters. If someone shows me how *Betsy* begins, I will finish it. (Repeat with *Lee.*)

Final sounds. Think how the word *breakfast* ends. If I write it, all but the last letter, who will finish it for me? (Continue with the words *find, cap, then.*)

Big, doll, flag! Which two words end with the same sound? Watch how *big* ends. (Write *big,* direct attention to final *g;* then erase word.) If I write *flag,* all but the last letter, can you finish it? (Continue with *pig, wag, dig.*)

Town, tap! Listen carefully. Look carefully. Which word did I write? How do you know? (Write *town* and have pupils identify it by last sound. Repeat with *fat, fed.*)

SUPPLEMENTARY ACTIVITIES

1. *Workbook for Day In and Day Out,* pages 67, 68, 69, 70.
2. Bulletin board. Have this rhyme on the bulletin board to be used in the usual way.

In the Box

Independent word attack

I like surprises in boxes.
Do you?
Here is a box with surprises
One, two!

Open the box
And what do you see?
Two bird houses
For one big tree.

3. Independent reading.

All in a Day, pages 30-41. (Give help with the word *fun,* page 30.)

Molly, Pete, and Ginger, pages 41-46. (Give help with the words *honk,* page 44; and *our,* page 46.)

My Little Blue Story Book (Ginn and Co.), pages 3-12. (Give help with the words *we* and *fast* on page 7.)

Under the Tree, pages 20-25. (Give help with the word *Baby* on page 20.)

We Come and Go, pages 23-28. (Give help with the word *work* on page 25.)

Unit 19: In the Garden

Pp. 110-12

NEW VOCABULARY: gave

PREPARATION

Have the following materials ready for use:

Pocket Card Holder
Word Card: 542 gave

INITIAL PROCEDURE

Introducing new vocabulary. (Give a book to some child; then write on board *I gave Ann a book*.) This sentence tells you exactly what I did. Think how this word (indicate *gave*) begins. Think of the name of this letter. (Indicate *a*.) Then let the sentence help you get the word. I ga—— Ann a book. Of course, the new word is *gave*. Who will find the word card and put it into the card holder? What two things help you remember this word?

Contents pages. Be an efficient workman. Find out from the title of our new story where Alice and Betsy Lee will go today. What page will the new story begin on?

SILENT READING

Page 110. If I had as lovely a garden as this, I would want to show it to Betsy Lee, too. Read the title and the first two sentences. What does Alice decide to do?

Alice makes up a rhyme. Read six lines. What is the rhyme? Does Alice like to say it?

Now read the last two-line sentence. What does Alice do?

Page 111. The picture tells me that Alice is talking to Mother Rabbit. But what is she saying? Read five sentences to find out.

I wonder if Mother Rabbit likes Betsy Lee. Read three sentences and you will know.

I think Alice knows what that rabbit was thinking even though it couldn't talk. She doesn't want Betsy Lee to have her feelings hurt. What does she say?

Page 112. Maybe Brown Bird will like Betsy Lee. What does he say? Is his home in the garden? Read two sentences and find out.

I am sure Alice is talking to Brown Bird. Read four sentences. What does she say? Does Brown Bird like Betsy Lee? Read the next sentence and decide.

Mother Rabbit can hop. Brown Bird can fly and sing. I believe Alice wishes Betsy Lee could do something, too. Finish the page and see if I am right. Poor Betsy Lee! She can't do a single thing.

Page 113. If you look at the picture and read the title on the next page, you will know where Alice goes next.

ORAL READING

Working for fluency

Fluency-expression. The one who can say the rhyme Alice made up, and make it sound like a rhyme, may read page 110.

The one who can read the new word in the card holder may read page 111. The one who can tell what a bird says, and make it sound like a bird, may read page 112.

VOCABULARY ENRICHMENT AND EXTENSION

Descriptive phrases. The bird in our story was *Little Brown Bird*. The rabbit was *Mother Rabbit*. The gate was the *garden gate*. When we use two or three words to tell about something, we can get a better mind picture. I will say a word to each of you. You add one or two words to it to make a better word picture. (Use such words as *rooster, pig, hen, goat,* etc.)

WORD RECOGNITION TECHNIQUES

Noting word details

Accurate word recognition. (DO NOT OMIT THESE ACTIVITIES.) Remember how magicians change one thing into another. These words will change, too. What does this word say? (Write *gave*.) Close your eyes. (Change *gave* to *gate*.) What does the word say now? (Continue with *came, name; get, got; eat, ate; coat, goat; Wee, Lee*.)

gate

gave

Phonics

Auditory-visual perception. *Initial blends.* Do you remember how *breakfast* begins? It takes two letters to begin *breakfast*. Begin it for me, and I will finish it. (Continue with *brown, play, please, started, store, stopped, stay*.)

Final sounds. I will write *rabbit*, all but the last letter. Who will put that on for me? (Continue with *word, open, hop, dog, could, big, night, jump, run*.)

n
t
r
d
g

I will write two words that you do not know. I will tell you what they say. They will begin with the same sound. You can tell which is which if you look at the last letter and remember its sound. (Write *wag, wet*. Wait until words are written. Then say, "Which word says *wet*? How do you know? Which word says *wag*? How do you know?" Repeat procedure with *Nan, Ned; mop, mud*.)

SUPPLEMENTARY ACTIVITIES

1. *Workbook for Day In and Day Out,* pages 71, 72, 73, 74.

2. Bulletin board. Have this rhyme on the bulletin board to be used in the usual way.

Independent word attack

Morning

Cock-a-doodle-doo!
Cock-a-doodle-doo!

The rooster up on the barnyard <u>gate</u>
Is saying, "Get up!
It is <u>late</u>, late, late."

I run down to breakfast
And then out to play.
Good morning, Red Rooster.
H<u>ow</u> are you today?

3. Independent reading.
   All in a Day, pages 42-51.
   Molly, Pete, and Ginger, pages 67-69. (Give help with the word *school* on page 67.)
   My Little Blue Story Book, pages 13-16. (Give help with the words *pie,* page 13; and *funny* and *apple,* page 16.)
   Under the Tree, pages 26-31.
   We Come and Go, pages 29-32.

4. Textfilm for *Day In and Day Out,* Frames 31-32. See Textfilm manual for directions.

Pp. 113-19 # Unit 20: In the Barnyard

INITIAL PROCEDURE

Contents pages. Do you remember where Alice and Betsy Lee were going today? Find the title of the new story and the page it will begin on.

SILENT READING

Page 113. Alice is rhyming again. Read the title and two sentences. What does she say?

I wonder if that big rooster belongs in the barnyard. Read three sentences and be ready to prove whether he does or not.

Alice is disappointed in her doll. Finish the page and find out why.

Page 114. By the time I finished reading this page, I knew four things about Red Cow. See if you are as good a reader as I am.

Page 115. The hens seem to be eating grain. By the time I am through reading, I know where the grain came from. See if you do. Will Betsy Lee do anything this time?

Page 116. By the time I am through reading, I know whether these baby ducks have learned to talk like their mothers. Read to see if they have. Poor Betsy Lee! She can't do a thing.

Page 117. Alice knows all about pigs. Maybe they like her, but they like something else better. Read to find out what it is.

Page 118. See what has happened now. Read three sentences. How did that goat get in here?

I suppose every animal in the barnyard ran as fast as it could. Read and see if I am right.

Page 119. Alice looks frightened, but I think she is more afraid for Betsy Lee than for herself. What does she think that goat may do? Read to find out. I'm glad they got home safely, aren't you? But I do wish Betsy Lee could show off a little. Maybe she will tomorrow.

ORAL READING

Rereading by page units. The one who can read this word (write *cock-a-doodle-doo*) may read the page which tells about the animal that makes this sound. (Continue in same way for pages 114-17. Then let the one who can tell the sound a goat makes read the last two pages.)

VOCABULARY ENRICHMENT AND EXTENSION

Word concepts. I will say a word to each of you. You tell me a word which is opposite in meaning. (Use *young, black, shut, walk, some, work, his, day, stopped, lose, go, this*.)

Opposites

WORD RECOGNITION TECHNIQUES

Noting word details

Accurate word recognition. (DO NOT OMIT THESE ACTIVI-TIES.) Watch these words change like magic. (Write *new* and have it read. Have children close eyes. Change *new* to *mew*. Continue in same way with *boy—toy, talk—walk, all—ball, pig—big.*)

Auditory-visual perception. *Phonetic parts.* Listen as I say *moo.* (Write word.) You know the sound with which *moo* begins. (Indicate *m*.) This part of the word (draw a line under *oo*) says *ōō* (give sound). Listen as I say two more words. In which word do you hear the sound *ōō? Rooster—hen!* Let's see if you are right. (Write *rooster* and have some child draw a line under *oo*. Continue in same manner with *toy—too*.)

I will write a word. Tell me the word and draw a line under the part which helps you get the word. (Use *boy, away, cow, out, new, are, her.*)

Phonics

Final sounds. Will you finish the word *find* if I write all but the last letter? (Continue with *get, garden, jump, dog.*)

(Write *tin* and *tent* on board.) Here are two new words. One says *tent* and one says *tin*. Which one says *tin?* How do you know? What does the other word say? How do you know? (Continue with *leg—lap, help—held.*)

SUPPLEMENTARY ACTIVITIES

1. *Workbook for Day In and Day Out*, pages 75, 76, 77, 78.
2. Bulletin board. Have this rhyme on the bulletin board to be used in the usual way.

Independent word attack

Words I Like

Jack and quack
And pack and sack
Are words I like.
    Do you?

Jerry and merry
And berry and cherry!
I can say the words.
    Can you?

3. Independent reading.

All in a Day, pages 52-61. (Give help with the word *make* on page 58.)

My Little Blue Story Book, pages 17-22. (Give help with the words *Bunny,* page 18; *cakes* and *dinner,* page 20.)

Under the Tree, pages 44-47. (Give help with the word *Daddy* on page 44.)

We Come and Go, pages 47-52. (Give help with the words *cars,* on page 47; and *yellow,* page 48.)

Unit 21: Betsy Lee Talks

Pp. 120-22

NEW VOCABULARY: hug   Ma-ma

PREPARATION

Have the following materials ready for use:

Pocket Card Holder
Word Cards

145 she	471 please	511 started	526 white	532 breakfast
453 hop	493 again	515 could	531 night	543 hug

INITIAL PROCEDURE

Contents pages. Alice has been disappointed in Betsy Lee. The title of the new story makes me know that she will be disappointed no longer. Find and read the title on the contents pages and tell me why I think so. What do dolls say when they talk?

SILENT READING

Page 120. Do you think these animals are in the room with Alice? I think she just remembers the animals and sees them in her mind as she talks to Betsy Lee. Is Betsy Lee talking to Alice? Read the whole page to find out.

Page 121. Now Alice talks about the animals she sees in her mind's eye. Read the page and check to see if Alice remembers every animal. Alice is sure Betsy Lee can't talk. Find the sentence which makes me know that she is sure. What do you think Alice will get on the next page? Turn and see if she does get a surprise.

Independent word attack— Ma-ma, hug

Page 122. (Allow time for enjoyment of picture.) You told me that talking dolls say "Ma-ma!" Since you know how *Ma-ma* begins, you can find it how many times?

If Betsy Lee can talk, I wonder why she hasn't been doing it. The first sentence is a long two-line sentence. Read that and the second sentence. You will find a new word. (*hug*) You will know how it begins and ends. Think of these things. Then let the picture and the sentence help you. Find out why Betsy Lee talks now when she couldn't talk before.

Now finish the page. How many hugs does Betsy Lee get?

Independent word attack— Carl

Page 123. You know one of these people. Jack, of course! The man's name is Mr.—(write *Mr.* on board; pause a moment; then write *Carl,* but do not pronounce word). You can get the rest of his name. You know how it begins. You know this part. (Draw a line under *ar.*) You know how it ends. Who is a competent reader who can get the new word for himself? (Diagnose ability of group in applying word recognition techniques which have been taught.) Now look at Mr. Carl. Do you think you will like him? Why? Do you think Jack does? Now who will read the title of the next part of the book?

ORAL READING

Dramatization

Audience reading. (Have pupils dress a doll to represent Betsy Lee. Have pupils try out for parts; then choose four readers to read the four Betsy Lee stories for a reading group in some other room.)

VOCABULARY ENRICHMENT AND EXTENSION

Synonymous meanings. When Betsy Lee could not talk, Alice was disappointed. How did she feel when she was disappointed? When

Betsy Lee finally did talk, Alice was delighted. How did she feel then? Each boy may tell me something which delighted him. Each girl may tell something which disappointed her.

WORD RECOGNITION TECHNIQUES

Plurals in s

Word structure. (DO NOT OMIT THESE ACTIVITIES.) *Plurals.* What does this word say? (Write *rabbit.*) Now what does it say? (Add *s.* Continue procedure, alternating singular and plural forms of *toy, ball, cow,* etc.)

Auditory-visual perception. *Phonetic parts.* Who will read this word and then draw a line under the part which helps you get the word? (Write *moo;* follow with *rooster, too.*) Listen as I say three words. In which one do you hear the sound $\overline{oo}$? (Give sound.) *Moon, stars, sky!* Let's prove that you are right. (Write *moon* and have pupils underline part. Follow with *early, late, soon.*)

Phonics

Initial sounds and blends. (Put the following words in card holder: *she, please, started, breakfast, white.*) Who will read and bring me the word which begins like *whistle?* (Continue in similar manner until all words are removed.)

Final sounds. (Put the following words in card holder: *again, night, could, hug, hop.*) Who will bring me a word which ends like *man?* (Continue in similar way until all cards are removed.)

I will write two words on the board. One will say *soap.* One will say *soon.* Which word says *soon?* How do you know? (Continue with *bag—bed; seat—seed.*)

SUPPLEMENTARY ACTIVITIES

1. *Workbook for Day In and Day Out,* pages 79, 80, 81, 82.

2. Bulletin board. Have this rhyme on the bulletin board to be used in usual way.

Vocabulary
review in
new context

What Will He Say?

Oh, I have a pretty doll,
    And her name is Betsy Lee.
She can say, "Ma-ma! Ma-ma!"
    So come to my house and see.

> Now I want a boy doll
> To go with Betsy Lee.
> Will he say, "Pa-pa, Pa-pa"?
> Oh, what will he say to me?

3. Independent reading.
   All in a Day, pages 62-71.
   My Little Blue Story Book, pages 23-32.
   Under the Tree, pages 32-37. (Give help with the word *we* on
   page 36.)
   We Come and Go, pages 33-42. (Give help with the words *help,*
   page 33; *we,* page 37.)
4. Textfilm for *Day In and Day Out,* Frames 33-34. See Textfilm
manual for directions.
5. Tests. Before beginning the next story, give the two informal
tests in the Workbook (pages 83 and 84). Pupils in superior groups
should make a score of at least 22 on the vocabulary test and a
score of at least 5 on the sentence-meaning test. If scores fall lower
than this, check your teaching with the unit plans. It is suggested at
this point that each child be tested individually with the word cards
Individual for the vocabulary developed so far. (See pages 158-60 of the
check on sight Primer.)
vocabulary

Pp. 124-29 ## Unit 22: My Little Girl

NEW VOCABULARY: Carl   girl   hello   liked   Mr.

PREPARATION

Have the following materials ready for use:
   Pocket Card Holder
   Word Cards: 546 Carl   547 girl

INITIAL PROCEDURE

Guidance in methods of word attack

Introducing new vocabulary. If you think how this new word begins (put word card *girl* in card holder) and if you think what Alice is, you can get this new word. Listen carefully: *Carl—girl*. What did your ears tell you? Let's prove that you are right. (Compare word cards *Carl* and *girl,* directing attention to final *l*.)

Contents pages. Turn quickly to the contents pages. Be ready to read the title of the new part of the book and the title of the first story. Do you suppose Mr. Carl has a little girl of his own?

SILENT READING

Page 124. Mr. Carl certainly does have a pretty garden, doesn't he? When I look at the roof, I see something else that likes the garden. What do you notice about both sentences on this page? Read the page and find out one thing about Mr. Carl.

Verbs ending in ed

Page 125. It looks to me as if Mr. Carl were in a bird store. Do you think he is? I am sure you know this word (write *look*); and this one (write *looked*). Then you can read these words. (Write *like* and *liked*.) Read three sentences. Find out two more things about Mr. Carl.

Has he a little girl of his own? The next two-line sentence tells.

What did Mr. Carl like besides Alice? Is he in a bird store? Read two sentences and find the answers. Now read the three short sentences. What kind of birds did he have? Now finish the page. What did "my little girl" like to do?

Page 126. (Allow time for enjoyment of picture.) Read the first two sentences. What happened this morning?

Independent word attack— hello

Whom did Alice see? What did she say? Read two sentences to find out. You will come across a new word. Think how it begins. Think what you would say if you met someone. Get the word for yourselves. Finish the page. To whom is Alice talking? What does she say?

Page 127. Will Betsy Lee talk this morning? Will Alice and Mr. Carl stay in the garden? Read the entire page to find out.

Page 128. (Allow time for enjoyment of pictures.) I really believe the birds know that Betsy Lee is a *little* doll and that Alice is a *big* girl. Read six sentences. See if you can find out why I think so.

Alice makes a discovery. She finds out something. What is it? Finish the page and see.

Page 129. If birds are hungry, there is just one thing to do. Alice seems to be doing it. I wonder if she feeds all the birds. I wonder if they say, "Thank you," in their bird way. Read the page and see.

ORAL READING

Two-line sentences

Fluency. (The story is full of rhythmical two-line sentences. Have pupils discover how many two-line sentences there are on a page. Have the child who can read each two-line sentence as if it were all on one line read the entire page.)

VOCABULARY ENRICHMENT AND EXTENSION

Word associations. When Alice met Mr. Carl, she said "Hello!" What else might she have said? if it were morning? afternoon? evening? Christmas? Mr. Carl's birthday? (Etc.)

WORD RECOGNITION TECHNIQUES

Verbs ending in ed

Word structure. (DO NOT OMIT THESE ACTIVITIES.) I like to—(write *talk* on board and have word read) on the telephone to my mother. Yesterday I—(write *talked* and have word read) for a long time. Who can read and erase the two words I have written? (Continue with *like—liked, look—looked, walk—walked, jump—jumped.*)

Phonics

Auditory-visual perception. *Phonetic parts.* Mr. Carl liked birds. (Write *birds* on board.) There is a part in this word which says *ir.* (Give sound.) It helps me remember the word. (Draw line under *ir.*) Can you find the same part in this word? (Write *girl.*) Read the word and draw a line under the part. What part helps you to remember each of these words? (Use *boy, say, Carl, out, now, new, moo.*)

Initial sounds. Who can show me how *she* begins? If you can show me, I will finish it, or maybe you can finish it for yourself. (Continue with *white, then.*) Mother Hen had some chickens. (Write *chickens.*) Two letters make the first sound in *chickens.* (Draw a line under *ch.*) Alice was a girl, but she was also a child. If someone can show me how *child* begins, I will finish it.

wh
th —
ch —

Phonics

Final sounds. What did we find out about the words *Carl* and *girl?* (Write words on board and underline final letter in each.) I will say three words. Which one shall I write because it ends like *Carl?* (*Bob, Dick, Earl; cart, corn, curl*)

Here are two new words. (Write *fun—fat.*) Which one says *fun?* How do you know? Which one says *fat?* (Continue with *dig—dead, step—steal.*)

SUPPLEMENTARY ACTIVITIES

1. *Workbook for Day in and Day Out,* pages 85, 86, 87, 88.

2. Bulletin board. Have this rhyme on the bulletin board to be used in usual way.

Independent
word attack

My Garden

I have a pretty garden
With a bird house in a tree.
A brown bird saw the bird house.
"Tweet, tweet!" he said.
"I see
A home,
For me."
Today I saw a bluebird
Fly in at the garden gate.
He can not stay in my bird house.
He came
Too late,
Too late.

3. Independent reading.

My Little Blue Story Book, pages 33-40. (Give help with the words *chair,* page 34; and *work,* page 35.)

Under the Tree, pages 48-51. (Give help with the words *make* and *Thank* on page 50.)

We Come and Go, pages 43-46. (Give help with the words *cookies,* page 44; and *Where,* page 45.)

We Work and Play, pages 27-30.

Pp. 130-33 # Unit 23: The Big Green Bird

NEW VOCABULARY: help

INITIAL PROCEDURE

Contents pages. Today we will not read about red birds, blue birds, brown birds. We will read about a different kind of bird. Find out from the title of the new story what kind it will be.

SILENT READING

Page 130. Can you find the big green bird? He is not in these cages. Alice is very sure about something, and she tells you why she is sure. Read the title and two sentences to find out.

Mr. Carl doesn't agree with Alice. Read three sentences to find out why *all* the birds are not happy.

Does Alice find the bird? Finish the page and see.

Page 131. (Allow time for picture discussion.)

Independent word attack— help

When you just *can't* do something, you sometimes have to ask for—. You will find a new word on this page. (*help*) You know how the word begins and ends. Jump over it and let the sentence do what the word says. Read the whole page and be ready to tell what Alice says to Mr. Carl.

Page 132. (Allow time for pupils to identify bird as *parrot* and to recall that parrots can talk.)

I wonder if this parrot can talk? Will he say, "Polly wants a cracker"? Read five lines and find out.

I am sure Alice heard the bird before she saw him because she asks a question two times. Read the next line. What is the question?

Finish the page. What did Alice do when she saw the bird and heard him talk once again? (Bring out idea that Mr. Carl has had the bird for days and as a surprise has taught him to say, "Hello, Alice!")

Page 133. I wonder what Betsy Lee will say? Can she say anything except "Ma-ma"? Read six sentences and find out.

Will Alice feed the green bird? Finish the page and find out.

ORAL READING

Working for fluency

Fluency-expression. There are parts of this story I like especially well. I would like to read them for you. (Read most rhythmical portions of each page.) Would you like to choose your favorite page and read it? Can you make your reading swing along as mine did?

VOCABULARY ENRICHMENT AND EXTENSION

Word associations. I have a bird cage for a little yellow bird. What shall I put into my bird cage? (*Seed cup, water cup, cuttlebone, swing, perch,* etc.)

WORD RECOGNITION TECHNIQUES

Auditory-visual perception. (DO NOT OMIT THESE ACTIVITIES.) *Long vowel sounds.* The name of the first letter makes me remember this word. (Write *ate*.) What does it say? What is the name of the letter? (Continue with *eat, old, open, oh*.)

Phonics

Phonetic parts. Tell me this word (write *bird*) and draw a line under the part which helps you remember it. (Repeat with *her*.) What did you notice about this part (indicate *ir*) and this part (indicate *er*)? (Repeat with *ou* in *out* and *ow* in *now*.)

Final sounds. I will write the word *animal,* all but the last letter. Who will finish it? (Continue with *help, hug, word, night, open.*)

Here are two new words. (Write *wig—win*.) Your doll has a wig. Which word says *wig*? How do you know? (Continue with *chirp—child, shawl—shoot.*)

SUPPLEMENTARY ACTIVITIES

1. *Workbook for Day in and Day Out,* pages 89, 90, 91, 92.

2. Bulletin board. Have this rhyme on the bulletin board to be used in the usual way.

Vocabulary
review in
new context

Hello

Do you like to say, "Good morning"?
Do you like to say, "Good night"?
I like to say, "Hello, hello!"
   Hello, hello,
   And away I go,
   Hello, hello, hello!

I was playing ball this morning.
   I saw Jack going by.
I did not say, "Hello, hello!"
   But I did say, "HI, JACK, hi!"

  3. Independent reading.
    My Little Green Story Book, pages 35-42 .
    Under the Tree, pages 2-7.
    We Work and Play, pages 31-34.
  4. Textfilm for *Day In and Day Out,* Frames 35-36. See Textfilm
manual for directions.

Pp. 134-39 # Unit 24: The Best Store

NEW VOCABULARY: best   Snap

PREPARATION

Have the following materials ready for use:

    Pocket Card Holder
    Word Cards: 551 best   552 Snap

INITIAL PROCEDURE

Introducing new vocabulary. Birds live in a—(write *nest*). Today
we have a new word which rhymes with *nest*. Alice thinks that Jip is

the—(put word card *best* in card holder but do not read the word)
dog in the world. Think how the word begins. Make it rhyme with
nest. It says—.

You wear this on your head on cold days. (Write *cap.*) We have
another new word, which rhymes with *cap*. (Put word card *Snap* in
card holder but do not read.) It tells what a puppy sometimes does
when he is not very friendly. It begins like *snow*. Think how it begins.
Make it rhyme with *cap*. A puppy will sometimes sn——. *Snap,* of
course! Who will read both new words?

Contents pages. I wonder if our story today will be about a puppy.
Turn to the contents pages and see. What kind of store do you think
might be the best store?

SILENT READING

Page 134. (Allow time for discussion of picture. Emphasize idea
that kittens, puppies, and rabbits collectively are called animals. So
the store may be called either a pet store or an animal store.)

I wonder if this is the store Jack liked best. Read the whole page
and find out.

Page 135. The third sentence ends with a question mark. Can you
find the question mark? Now read that far. Find out what time of day
it is, and be ready to answer the question.

Read two sentences. What were the first animals Jack saw? Read
two more sentences. What animals did he see next? Finish the page.
What else did he see, and which animal did he like best?

Page 136. When Jack got around to the puppy side of the window,
what happened? Read two sentences to find out. Now read until you
find out everything Jack said. Finish the page. Does the puppy like
Jack? Be ready to prove it.

Page 137. Maybe Jack will change his mind when he sees what is
in the cage. Do you think the man is telling Jack to get away from
there? How can you tell that he isn't? Why do you think Jack's hand
is in his pocket? Read until you find out the man's name. What do
you think may happen next? (If children suggest that the man may
give Jack the dog, emphasize the idea that dogs in pet stores are too
expensive to give away.)

Page 138. Can you find the first question mark? Read until you come to it. Be ready to read and answer the question.

Can you find the second question mark? Read until you come to it. Be ready to tell how Jack answers Mr. Green's question.

Mr. Green doesn't agree with Jack that the little dog is the best pet in the store. Find out why by reading five sentences. You might even discover the dog's name.

Does Jack change his mind? Finish the page and see.

Page 139. I hope Jack doesn't get bitten. Read three sentences. What does Mr. Green do, and what happens? Does the puppy snap? Read three sentences to find out.

Mr. Green gives a good reason why the puppy didn't snap. Finish the page and see what it is.

ORAL READING

Two-line sentences

Fluency-expression. The one who can tell me how many two-line sentences there are on page 134 may read the page for us. (Continue in same manner for each of the other pages. Read a sentence now and then yourself to set the pattern for expressive, rhythmical reading.)

VOCABULARY ENRICHMENT AND EXTENSION

Word associations. I will say the name of a store for each of you. You tell me what would be sold in that store. (*hardware store, department store, millinery store, drugstore,* etc.)

WORD RECOGNITION TECHNIQUES

Verbs ending in ed, ing

Word structure. (DO NOT OMIT THESE ACTIVITIES.) Do you know this word? Can you use it in a sentence? (Write *like*. Continue with *liked; play, played; look, looked; go, going.*)

Auditory-visual perception. *Rhyming words.* I will write six words on the board. (Write *toy, say, walk, boy, talk, day.*) Who can read and erase two words which rhyme?

Initial sounds. Who will show me how *nest* begins? Then I will finish it. Now think. *Best* rhymes with *nest.* How does *best* begin?

Who will show us? The rest of the word is just like *nest.* Could you
finish the word *best?* I will write the word *snap* for you. These two
letters (write *sn*) begin the word. It ends like this. (Add *ap.*) Now *cap*
rhymes with *snap.* You know how *cap* begins. Who could write the
whole word?

*Phonics—
initiating
spelling
ability*

Final sounds. Sometimes I drink from a mug. If I write *mug,* all
but the last sound, will you finish it? (Continue with *pet, kitten, animal, help, bird.*)

I will write two new words. One will say *hard.* One will say *hit.*
Which one says *hit?* How do you know? (Continue with *tail—tag,
chin—cheap,* in same manner.)

SUPPLEMENTARY ACTIVITIES

1. *Workbook for Day In and Day Out,* pages 93, 94.
2. Bulletin board. Have this rhyme on the bulletin board to be
used in the usual way.

One Day

*Independent
word attack*

What did I have in my house?
What did I see today?
Something little, something gray!
A little gray mouse
In my house.

What did I see in my house?
What did I see today?
Snap, went the trap,
But the little gray mouse
Ran away and away and away.

3. Independent reading.
My Little Green Story Book, pages 43-54.
We Work and Play, pages 11-14.

Pp. 140-43 # Unit 25: The Best Store (*cont.*)

SILENT READING

Page 140. We left Jack playing with Snap. Read **two** sentences. What does Mr. Green finally say, and what happens? I wonder if Jack can make that puppy mind. The next three sentences will tell you.

Remember what Mr. Green wanted. Read as far as the question mark to find out what question he asks Jack. Do you know what Jack's answer will be? Finish the page to see if you are right.

Oral language

Page 141. (Have children identify types of dogs they know. Have them decide what Jack will do with each tool shown.) I think I know what Jack's work is going to be. Do you? I wonder if he will play favorites. Will he treat Snap a little better than he does the rest of the dogs? Read the page and see.

Page 142. I wonder if Jack has been a good workman. Will Mr. Green want him to come again? Read three sentences to find out. Finish the page. Whom did Jack see on the way home, and where?

Page 143. It looks as if Jack and Alice are having a quarrel. What a face on Alice! I don't like it a bit, do you? Read the whole page and find out what the quarrel is about.

Of course, Jack had to talk to Mother. What do you think she may say about the job Jack has found?

ORAL READING

Dramatization

Reading to prove a statement. One page in our story today proves that Mr. Green had too much work to do. Which page is it, and who will read it? Another page proves that Jack plays favorites. Who will find and read that page? Who will find and read the page which proves that Jack was a good workman? Who will read what Jerry says on page 143 and talk like Jerry? like Jack? like Alice?

WORD RECOGNITION TECHNIQUES

Noting word
details

Accurate word recognition. (DO NOT OMIT THESE ACTIVI-
TIES.) What does this word say? (Write *nest*.) Close your eyes. The
camera clicked, the picture changed. What does the word say now?
(Change *nest* to *best*. Continue with *cap—snap, cow—now, pig—big,
help—hello, gave—gate, wee—Lee*.)

Auditory-visual perception. *Phonetic parts.* Read this word and
underline the part which helps you remember it. What does the part
say? (Use *now, out, too, are, boy, mew, play*.)

Phonics

Initial blends. If I wanted to write *snow*, I would begin it like this.
(Write *sn;* pause; then finish the word.) Who can show me how *Snap*
begins? Maybe you can finish it. If not, I will. (Continue with *please,
green, started, blue, brown, train*.)

Final sounds. (Have pupils add final letter in the usual way: *hug,
help, Carl, word, night, man*.)

(Write *land* and *lap* on board.) The name of the *land* I live in is
America. Which word says *land*? How do you know? (Continue in
the same way with *rug—right, pencil—pen*.)

SUPPLEMENTARY ACTIVITIES

1. *Workbook for Day In and Day Out,* pages 95, 96.
2. Bulletin board. Have this rhyme on the bulletin board to be
used in the usual way.

The Dog for Me

Independent
word attack

Mac was a pretty good dog.
Jip was a good dog, too.
But the best dog in town
Had a coat white and brown.
So he was the dog for me
You see.
Snap was the dog for me.

3. Independent reading.
My Little Green Story Book, pages 55-63. (Give help with the
word *cake* on page 59.)
Under the Tree, pages 58-63.

We Come and Go, pages 53-60. (Give help with the word *make* on page 54.)

Pp. 144-46 # Unit 26: A Dog for Jack

INITIAL PROCEDURE

Phrase meaning. (Have the following sentences written on the board.)

> You will have to go
> day in and day out.
> You can not go now and then.

Phrase meaning

When Mother heard Jack's story, she tried to explain to Jack what it meant to take a job, a real job. He would have to be on hand every day. He could not stay home some morning when he wanted to play ball. She said—(sentences 1, 2). Jack was sure he wanted that job. Who will read the phrase which means "every day"? the one which means "once in a while"?

Contents pages. The title of our new story gives away a secret to me. See if it does for you. What do you expect will happen in this story?

SILENT READING

Page 144. Here is Jack hard at work. Read three sentences. Did he do what he promised Mother he would do? Why did he play with Snap only now and then?

Do you see the two questions at the end of the page? Finish reading and be ready to tell me how Jack answered those questions.

Page 145. Jack can't believe that Mr. Green means what he says. He thinks Mr. Green is joking. Read four sentences. Find out what Jack says and what Mr. Green's answer is.

I suppose Jack says, "Oh, thank you." Finish the page and see if he does. Do you think Jack said, "Thank you," with his eyes? How could he do that?

Page 146. The minute the window was open, what happened? Read four sentences and find out. I don't believe we can call this dog "Snap" any more. Finish the page and find out why. If you were choosing a name, what name would you choose?

Page 147. Well, aren't you glad that Miss Alice has cheered up again. What are the children saying as they go upstairs?

ORAL READING

Rereading by page units. Would someone like to read the page which has the title of our book on it? the page where Jack's eyes say, "Thank you"? the page which tells me to stop calling that dog "Snap"? (In this or another period, reread the group of stories "Mr. Carl and Jack" in a similar way.)

VOCABULARY ENRICHMENT AND EXTENSION

Synonymous meanings

Descriptive phrases. Jack went to Mr. Green's store every day. What is another way of saying "every day"? Once in a while he played with Snap. What is another way to say "once in a while"?

WORD RECOGNITION TECHNIQUES

Recognizing word details

Accurate word recognition. (DO NOT OMIT THESE ACTIVITIES.) I am watching for my best reader. He will be the one who will not fall off as he climbs up and down these word ladders. (Write the following words in a column: a, and, at, away, am, are, again, ate, all. If any child has trouble with ate, are, or away, be sure to make him help himself by using techniques which have been taught. Repeat procedure with big, boat, ball, bow-wow, bird, but, box, by, boy, Betsy, best.)

Auditory-visual perception. *Phonetic parts.* Read this word. (Write Carl.) Draw a line under the part which helps you; then tell me what the part says. Maybe you can get this word for yourselves. (Write car. Continue with day—gay, toy—joy.)

Phonics

Initial sounds. I will write the word sheep for you if you will show me how it begins. (Continue with whistle, chimney, and thumb.)

sh—
wh—
ch—
th—

Final sounds. (Have pupils add the final letter in the usual way: *help, pig, again, coat, Carl, find.*)

(Write *cut–curl* on board.) I tried to *curl* my hair. Which word says *curl?* How do you know? (Continue with *fan–fog, ship–shed.*)

SUPPLEMENTARY ACTIVITIES

1. *Workbook for Day In and Day Out,* pages 97, 98, 99, 100.
2. Bulletin board. Have this rhyme on the bulletin board.

Independent word attack

Girls and Boys

Girls like to play
   With kittens and <u>cats</u>.
Boys like dogs
   And balls and <u>bats</u>.

But, now and then,

A boy likes a kitten,
   A boy likes a cat,
And a girl wants to play
   With a ball and a bat.

3. Independent reading.
   Molly, Pete, and Ginger, pages 47-52. (Give help with the words *cat,* page 51; and *kitty,* page 52.)
   My Little Blue Story Book, pages 41-48. (Give help with the word *make* on page 43.)
   Under the Tree, pages 14-19.
   We Work and Play, pages 19-22.

4. Textfilm for *Day In and Day Out,* Frames 37-38. See Textfilm manual for directions.

5. Tests. Give the informal tests on pages 101 and 102 of the Workbook. Pupils should make a score of at least 22 on the vocabulary test and a score of at least 5 on the sentence-meaning test. If Individual check on sight vocabulary scores fall lower than this, test your teaching with the unit plans. It is suggested at this point that each child be tested individually with the word cards for the entire Primer vocabulary. (See pages 158-60 of *Day In and Day Out.*)

Unit 27: A Happy Day

Pp. 147-49

INITIAL PROCEDURE

Contents pages. I am sure Alice and Jerry had many happy days. Maybe our story this morning will tell about one. Find the title on the contents pages and see if it will.

SILENT READING

Page 147. Do the children look as if they had had a happy day? Who is ready to read the title of the last part in our book? Turn quickly to find out what happened.

Page 148. I know what Jerry did on his happy day. Do you? Read the title and the first two sentences. How did the day start?

Two-line sentences

I see two long two-line sentences. Only very good readers can read as if each sentence was on one line. Find out what Jerry decides to do to have a good time.

Finish the page. Did Jerry do what he set out to do? Does the puppy get a name? If he doesn't, try to decide why he doesn't. The picture may help you.

Page 149. How does Alice's happy day start? Read two sentences to find out. What does she decide to do? What happens then? The next three sentences will tell you.

After a morning's fun, what else happens to make this a happy day? Finish the page and find out. Would you call this a happy day? Why?

ORAL READING

Two-line sentences

Fluency. One sign that tells me that boys and girls are good readers is the way they can find and read long two-line sentences. How many can you find on page 148? Read each one silently. I will ask someone to read the page. The rest of us will judge whether he reads as smoothly as if he were talking, not reading.

I have discovered something interesting about page 149. How many two-line sentences are there? How smoothly can a good reader read the page?

VOCABULARY ENRICHMENT AND EXTENSION

Word associations. When people are happy, there are always signs to show that they are *happy*. What are the signs of a happy boy? a happy dog? a happy kitten? a happy bird?

WORD RECOGNITION TECHNIQUES

Noting word details

Accurate word recognition. (DO NOT OMIT THESE ACTIVITIES.) (Write the following words on the board. Have a child choose some word he knows, use it in a sentence, and then erase it. How fast can board be cleared? *Come, came, can, cap, coat, city, could, cluck, cock-a-doodle-doo, cow, Carl.*)

Auditory-visual perception. *Initial sounds.* (Have pupils show, by writing on board, how *what,* *she,* and *this* begin. Finish each word for them as soon as word-beginning is written.) Jerry and Alice are *children.* (Write word on board as you say it.) Two letters start the word *children.* (Draw line under *ch;* then erase word.) If you can show

Phonics

me how the word *chair* would begin, I will finish it for you.

Final sounds. Listen as I say *Jerry, pretty, puppy.* What did your ears tell you about the way these words end? Let's prove that they end alike. (Write words on board and call attention to the final *y.*) I want to add another word to our list which ends like *Jerry.* Which word shall it be? (*What, happy, open.* Write *happy* on board to prove that the choice is the correct one. Continue with the words *Carl, Jack, Betsy.*)

(Write *rug—rap* on board.) I have a *rug* on my floor at home. Sometimes someone will *rap* on my door. I know which of these new words says *rap.* Do you? How do you know? (Continue in same manner with *feel, feed; barn, basket.*)

SUPPLEMENTARY ACTIVITIES

1. *Workbook for Day In and Day Out,* pages 103, 104, 105, 106.
2. Bulletin board. Have this rhyme on the bulletin board to be used in the usual way.

A Happy Day

Independent
word attack

I wish I could have a boat ride.
I wish I could ride on a train.
I wish I could <u>fly</u>
Up into the <u>sky</u>
In a big, big airplane.

I wish you could come to my house
To play with my new red ball.
Then I could say,
"I had the best day,
The very best day of all."

3. Independent reading.
   Molly, Pete, and Ginger, pages 53-56. (Give help with the sound word *Meow* on page 53.)
   My Little Blue Story Book, pages 49-52. (Give help with the word *stop* on page 52.)
   Under the Tree, pages 38-43. (Give help with the word *cake* on page 38.)
   We Come and Go, pages 61-64.
   We Work and Play, pages 43-46. (Give help with the word *cars* on page 43.)

Unit 28: Good Night   Pp. 150-57

INITIAL PROCEDURE

Contents pages. Today we say, "Good night," to Alice and Jerry. When you are tucked into bed, do you always go right to sleep? If your brother or sister sleeps with you, what do you sometimes do? I wonder if Alice and Jerry are that kind of children. Use your contents pages to find the page on which the story begins.

SILENT READING

Page 150. Is this the bed in which we saw Alice when she first took Betsy Lee to bed with her? Whose room do you think this is? Yes, I think Jerry has a new two-bunk bed, and Alice wants to try it out. Even Jip is trying it out. Will Mother let him stay there all night? Would your mother? In which bunk would you like to sleep? I think Jerry has the fun of climbing upstairs because it is his new bed.

Read the whole page. What does Mother do? What do the children say to her?

Page 151. It looks to me as if two children I know are going to spoil a happy day by getting into mischief. What do you think? Even Jip is doing something he has no business doing. Read three sentences. Alice wants to play a game. Find the name of the game. Will Jerry behave and go to sleep? Or will he play, too? Read two more lines and find out.

Now the game begins. Finish the page and see how it goes. Have you ever played a game like this? (Recall "I Packed My Grandmother's Suitcase" or some similar game.)

Page 152. Read five lines. What will Alice add to the barnyard? Now finish the page. What does Jerry add?

Pages 153-55. (Have pupils read by page units in usual way.)

Page 156. The fun is over. How do I know? Read the first sentence to find out. Is Mother very, very cross? Read everything she says and find out.

Will Alice and Jerry and Jip behave themselves now? Finish the page and see.

Oral language

Page 157. Read the page quickly. Did Alice keep her promise? Now look at the picture. (Allow time to discuss picture details—lamp, book ends, etc. Explain the banner with initials for Friendly Village, the place where the children live.) Is this a good way to end a book—saying, "Good night," to Alice and Jerry? I hope they wake up in another book, don't you?

ORAL READING

Dramatization; Fluency. (Choose one child to read pages 150-51 through line 6. Then have pupils choose an Alice and a Jerry to read the portion of the story in which each child talks. One other **pupil** may read pages 156-57. Watch for rhythmical reading.)

VOCABULARY ENRICHMENT AND EXTENSION

Word associations. Suppose we play Alice's game in another **way.** I went to the zoo, and I saw a camel with a big brown hump. (Have each pupil repeat each animal named and add a new one with some descriptive phrase.)

WORD RECOGNITION TECHNIQUES

Noting word details

Accurate word recognition. (DO NOT OMIT THESE ACTIVI-TIES.) (Have the following words written on board. Have each pupil read a word, use it in a sentence, and then erase it: *did, do, down, duck, dog, doll, day.*)

Auditory-visual perception. *Phonetic parts.* (Write the following words on the board. Have pupils read each word and then draw a line under the parts which help them remember the words: *new, toy, moo, stay.*)

Phonics

Initial blends. (Have pupils show on board how the following words begin. Finish each word for them as soon as initial blend is written: *please, brown, store, train, snap, blue, green.*)

Final sounds. If I write *Jerry,* all but the last letter, can you finish it? (Continue with *pretty, happy, puppy, Betsy.*)

(Write *mend—moon* on board.) I know which of these new words says *moon.* Do you? How do you know? (Continue with *pail—pet, mug—mop.*)

SUPPLEMENTARY ACTIVITIES

1. *Workbook for Day In and Day Out,* pages 107, 108, 109, 110.
2. Bulletin board. Have this rhyme on the bulletin board to be used in the usual way.

Good Night

Independent
word attack

Good night, rabbit,
In your little dark hole.
Good night, little bird,
On your nest.

Out in the barn
Is the one I like best.
Good night, Brown Pony.
Good night.

3. Independent reading.

Molly, Pete, and Ginger, pages 57-60.
My Little Blue Story Book, pages 53-63.
Under the Tree, pages 52-57. (Give help with the words *bed,*
page 52; and *sleep,* page 57.)
We Come and Go, pages 65-71.
We Work and Play, pages 51-62.

4. Textfilm for *Day In and Day Out,* Frames 39-40. See Textfilm
manual for directions.

5. Informal tests, pages 111-12, Workbook. Scores on vocabulary
test should be at least 22; on sentence-meaning test at least 5. If scores
fall lower than this, check your teaching with the unit plans. It is
suggested at this point that each child be tested with the word cards
for the Preprimer and Primer vocabulary. See pages 158-60 of *Day
In and Day Out.*

Individual
check on sight
vocabulary

My Own Book

WHAT IT IS

My Own Book is the title of a series of books. Each book is 4 x 5½
inches in size and is delightfully illustrated.

PURPOSE AND USE

My Own Book, Nos. 5, 6, 7, and 8, are books written in the vocabulary of *Day In and Day Out,* the Primer of The Alice and Jerry Basic Reading Program.

When a child has finished reading *Day In and Day Out,* he can be given, or can purchase, copies of these four books. He will be thrilled by ownership of new books which he can read independently. It is also desirable that he take the books home to read to his mother and father so that his parents will, in turn, become conscious of his reading progress.

PACKAGING

Four copies of *My Own Book,* No. 5; four copies of *My Own Book,* No. 6; four copies of *My Own Book,* No. 7; and four copies of *My Own Book,* No. 8 constitute one package (16 books to a package), labeled *My Own Book for the Primer Level.* This scheme of packaging has made it possible to sell these books inexpensively.

HOW TO ORDER

Order one package of *My Own Book for the Primer Level* for every *four* pupils in your primer class. You will then have on hand appropriate books to give to each child as he finishes the primer. Order from Harper & Row, Publishers, Evanston, Illinois; Elmsford, New York; or Pleasanton, California.

STANDARDIZED ACHIEVEMENT TEST

A Reading Achievement Test for use at the end of the Primer can be bought from Harper & Row, Publishers. This test should be given before beginning the Basic First Reader, *Round About.*

PARALLEL PRIMER

The Parallel Primer, *Wishing Well,* can be read with a minimum of vocabulary difficulty upon the completion of *Day In and Day Out.*

Diagnosis of Pupil Growth

(Upon completion of *Day In and Day Out*)

1. Are pupils having a thoroughly enjoyable time learning to read? Can they enter into the spirit of a story so that characters and occurrences seem real to them as they read?

2. Can they read silently with little or no evidence of head or lip movement? Has the habit of reading silently before reading orally become well established? Do they understand the purpose and use of the period and the question mark?

3. Is oral reading fluent, rhythmic, and expressive?

4. Have pupils mastered the 180 words of the basic vocabulary so well that they can apply these words with ease and confidence to the reading of new context?

5. Has pupils' ability in auditory and visual perception developed to the degree that they can:

   a) hear as well as see that certain words begin with the same sound?

   b) hear as well as see that certain words end with same sound?

   c) combine picture clues with initial consonant clues to unlock new words?

   d) combine context clues and initial consonant clues to unlock new words?

6. Are they applying reading ability in the activities of the school day: reading signs, bulletin boards, etc.?

7. Are you, the teacher, diagnosing the needs of individuals in this group and doing something to meet these needs, instead of rushing on to new text material?

8. Have you a sense of satisfactory accomplishment? Are you enjoying with your group the experience of learning to read?

PROGRAM FOR AVERAGE GROUP

Unit 1: Introduction

(See Program for Superior Group, Unit 1, page 13.)

Unit 2: Little Rabbit

Pp. 5-9

NEW VOCABULARY: hole   hop   oh   Rabbit

PREPARATION

Have the following materials ready for use:

Pocket Card Holder
Word Cards:

74 see	144 saw	451 Rabbit
103 Little	145 she	452 Oh
143 said	161 went	453 hop

INITIAL PROCEDURE

Introducing new vocabulary. (Have the following sentences written on board: *Alice went, too. Hop went Jerry. Hop, hop hop!*)

Alice and Jerry have a surprise word. When something surprises them, they round their lips (illustrate) and say, "Oh!" (Put word card *Oh* in card holder.) Show me the letter which looks like their lips. When they are not quite so surprised, their lips are not quite

Guidance in
methods of
word attack

103

so big and round (reverse card), but they still say—. We have other words which begin like *oh*. So take a good eye picture of this letter. (Indicate and trace *h*.) When I write—(write *Oh*), you will know that the word is—.

Every summer morning Jerry went to the hill, and—(indicate first sentence on board). Let's think about this word. (Indicate *went*.) It begins like *want*. Think how it begins. Then jump over it. Alice w——, too. (Form *w* with lips, but do not give sound.) Of course, the word is *went,* and this is the letter to watch carefully. (Indicate *e*.) If I write—(write *we_____*), what word will you tell me to finish? (Have word card *went* read and added to card holder.)

Guidance in methods of word attack

One day a big rock fell on Jerry's foot. Jerry could not walk. He had to—(hold up word card *hop*). Think how the new word begins. Think what Jerry did. The new word is—. (Add card to card holder.) Now read what Jerry did. (Sentences 2, 3.)

I hope you have not forgotten the little animal about which we are to read today. (Build *Little Rabbit* in card holder.) I am sure that when Jerry saw the rabbit, he said—(indicate *Oh*). I am sure the rabbit—(indicate *went;* then *hop*).

Contents pages. How many remember the number of the page on which the story "Little Rabbit" begins? (Wait for a few guesses.) We are wasting time guessing, aren't we? We have contents pages so that we won't waste time. Turn to the contents pages. How quickly can you find the number of the page on which "Little Rabbit" begins?

Purpose of contents pages

SILENT READING

Oral language

Page 6. (Allow time for picture discussion.) Jerry has made a discovery, but I don't believe he really knows what he has found. Read the whole page silently. Find out why I think he does not know what he has found.

Page 7. Some rabbits are tame. Some are wild. Which kind is Little Rabbit? Alice is certainly surprised. Read to find out what she sees and what she says.

Page 8. One look at the rabbit's eyes and I know how the rabbit feels. What does it do? What do Alice and Jerry do? Read and see.

Page 9. Another discovery for Alice and Jerry! What is it? Is it a discovery for the rabbit, or did the rabbit know the hole was there? You know how the word *hole* will begin. How many times can you find the word *hole*? Now read the page. One sentence tells exactly what Little Rabbit is doing in the picture. Who can find it?

(margin: Independent word attack— hole)

Predicting outcomes. (Discuss with pupils the possibility that Alice and Jerry will watch that hole for a time. But finally they will grow tired of waiting and will run off to play.)

ORAL READING

Expressing feelings of story characters. (Discuss the loud, excited voice with which Jerry probably talks on page 6, Alice's soft voice on page 7, the speed suggested on page 8, etc. Have story reread to see if children can express spirit of story through voices.)

VOCABULARY ENRICHMENT AND EXTENSION

Classification. Suppose you discovered a tame rabbit on your front steps. What color would he be? What would you call the house you might build for him? Suppose it were a wild rabbit. What color would it be? What would that rabbit make in your garden? Which rabbit could you have for a pet?

WORD RECOGNITION TECHNIQUES

(margin: Phonics)

Auditory-visual perception. *Initial sounds.* You know this word. (Write *here—Here.*) Watch how *here* begins. (Trace *h* and then *H* with colored chalk. Then erase words.) We had another word this morning which began like *here.* It was—. If someone will show me how to begin *hop,* I will finish it. (Have some pupil write *h;* then finish the word for him. Repeat with *H.* Use same procedure for *hole.* Write *ran* on board and repeat entire procedure for *ran, rabbit.*)

(margin: Drill on carrier words)

Accurate word recognition. (Put word cards *see, saw, said, she* in a column in card holder. Have some child hop down the rabbit hole by reading the column from top to bottom. Repeat with *hop, Oh, went.*)

SUPPLEMENTARY ACTIVITIES

1. *Workbook for Day In and Day Out,* pages **1, 2, 3, 4.** Take time to discuss directions. Have text read if necessary. If adequate help is given in first portion of Workbook, pupils will grow in ability to work independently.

2. Bulletin board. *Developing ability to use context clues and initial consonant clues to unlock new words:* REMEMBER THAT NEW WORDS INTRODUCED ON BULLETIN BOARD ARE NOT PART OF PRIMER VOCABULARY. Pupils are not expected to remember them as sight words. Have the following caption on the bulletin board and read it for children: *I can get new words. Can you?* Underneath write:

Independent word attack

Little Rabbit

Look at little rabbit.
She lives in a hole.
I live in a house.

3. Independent reading. Pupils may read in groups, at their seats, or at the library table the following preprimer pages. (See page 11.)
Bill and Susan (Silver Burdett Co.), pages 2-7. (Give help with the word *stop* on page 4.)
Here and There (Harper & Row, Publishers), pages 7-17.
Molly, Pete, and Ginger (D. C. Heath and Co.), pages 1-6.
My Little Red Story Book (Ginn and Co.), pages 2-8.
Ride Away (American Book Co.), pages 2-9.
We Look and See (Scott, Foresman and Co.), pages 3-6.

4. Textfilm for *Day In and Day Out,* Frames 1-2. See Textfilm manual for directions.

Unit 3: Toys

NEW VOCABULARY: ball   happy   so
                  fly   just   toys

PREPARATION

Have the following materials ready for use:

Pocket Card Holder
Word Cards

159 this	451 rabbit	454 hole	457 just	460 happy
161 went	452 oh	455 toy	458 fly	
162 Yes	453 hop	456 ball	459 so	

INITIAL PROCEDURE

Introducing new vocabulary. (Have the following sentences on board. Underscore new words.)

Jerry looked <u>happy</u>.
You look <u>so</u> happy.
<u>Yes</u>!
You may have <u>just</u> one.
I want <u>this</u> one.
He did not want a <u>toy</u>.
I want to play <u>ball</u>.

Guidance in
methods of
word attack

Jerry ran into the house with a big smile on his face. (Indicate sentence 1.) Think how this new word begins. (Indicate *happy*.) Then let the meaning of the sentence help you. Jerry looked h——.

Happy, of course. Who will find the word card *happy,* read it, and put it into the card holder? (Use similar technique for other new words. Add word card for each underscored word to card holder.)

Using initial consonant and context clues

Jerry's smile was so big that Mother said—(sentence 2). Jerry saw some cookies on the table and said, "May I have one?" Mother answered—(sentence 3). It was almost lunch time. So Mother said—(sentence 4). Jerry looked for the biggest cookie, pointed at it, and said—(sentence 5). Don't forget the pointing word. It says—.

When the cooky was gone, Jerry looked at the box where he kept drums and boats, trains and airplanes. He knew the name for all these things put together. He called them his—(write *toys*). But—(sentence 6). He saw his new bat standing in the corner, and he said—(sentence 7).

(Have pupils hop down the rabbit hole by reading word cards in card holder.)

Contents pages. The title of our new story is one of our new words. Find the title of the new story and the number of the page on which it begins. We have just begun our book. Will the story be toward the front or back of *Day In and Day Out?* We have already read one

Guidance in locating page numbers

story. So I will not turn page by page until I come to page 10. I will take a very few pages (illustrate) and turn them all at once. I turned to page 9. How many more pages must I turn before I come to page 10? I must turn forward, or ahead, until I come to page 10. How quickly can you find page 10?

SILENT READING

Page 10. One look at this page, and I know why the story title is a good one. Do you? (Allow time for identification of toys.) Watch Jerry's pointing finger. What toy does he want? Now read the page. Did we discover the right toy?

Page 11. I suppose Jerry will buy the boat and go home. Read to see if he does.

Page 12. How many new toys can you see? Does Jerry change his mind again? Read to see.

Page 13. Will Father spend money for three toys? Count six lines, six sentences. Read just that far. What does Father say?

Jerry must make up his mind. Finish the page. Has he decided what toy to buy?

Page 14. Maybe Jerry changes his mind and makes up his mind at the same time. Read three lines, three sentences, and see if he does.

Father doesn't want to waste his money. He wants Jerry to get a—(write *good* on board and have some child read) toy. I wonder if Father thinks this is a good airplane. If it is, it must be able to do something. I discover a new word in the last sentence. (*fly*) I know how it begins. I can get it. So can you. Finish the page. Will Father waste his money? Why not? What new word did you discover? Show it to me.

Page 15. The minute Father pays for the airplane, Jerry stops calling it *the* airplane or *this* airplane. What does he call it? Read and see.

Predicting outcomes; Extending speaking vocabulary. Let's add a good ending to this story. What happens when Jerry gets home? If he is *careful,* what will he do? If he is *careless?*

Independent word attack— fly

ORAL READING

Organization. *Following events in sequence.* Suppose we follow Jerry into the toy store. First he wanted a—(write: [1] *Jerry wants a boat*). Who will read the page in the story which tells about that? Next he wanted a—(write: [2] *He wants a ball;* continue in similar manner to add outline of events to board and have rereading follow outline).

WORD RECOGNITION TECHNIQUES

Auditory-visual perception. *Initial sounds.* Of course, you know this word. (Write *see—See.*) Watch how it begins. (Trace *s, S* with colored chalk; then erase words.) If someone will show me how *said* begins, I will finish the word. (Continue with *saw, so, something.* Have some pupil play "See Me Go" to read and erase words.)

If someone will show me how *happy* begins, I will finish it. (Continue with *hop, hole.* Repeat procedure with *ran, rabbit.*)

Phonics

Accurate word recognition. The best toys are always on the top shelves in toy stores. If you can climb to the top shelf on this word ladder, you may tell me what toy you want, and I will write its name for you. (Arrange all word cards listed under Preparation into two word ladders.)

Building sight vocabulary

SUPPLEMENTARY ACTIVITIES

1. *Workbook for Day In and Day Out,* pages 5, 6. On page 6 be sure directions are understood and text read, if necessary.

2. Bulletin board. For purpose, caution, and caption, see Unit 2.

Independent word attack

My Ball

Oh, look, Father.
See my ball.
It is a football.
Come and play football with me.

3. Independent reading. Pupils may read in groups, at their seats, or at the library table the following preprimer pages:

Bill and Susan, pages 8-15.
Here and There, pages 18-25.
Molly, Pete, and Ginger, pages 7-10.
My Little Red Story Book, pages 9-12. (Give help with the word *fast* on page 11.)
Ride Away, pages 10-15.
We Look and See, pages 7-10. (Give help with the word *funny* on page 10.)

4. Textfilm for *Day In and Day Out,* Frames 3-4. See Textfilm manual for directions.

Unit 4: Preparatory Unit for "Jip"

NEW VOCABULARY: away   but   for
                  bow-wow   came   out

PREPARATION

Have the following materials ready for use:

Pocket Card Holder
Word Cards

51 and	135 house	458 fly	465 Out
54 come	155 had	461 away	467 for
84 big	156 home	462 Bow-wow	468 But
133 have	452 oh	464 came	

INITIAL PROCEDURE

Introducing new vocabulary. Have the following sentences on the board:

He _had_ a happy look.
Out came Jerry.
So here I come.
Look out _for_ me.
Jip ran _away_.
Bow-wow, bow-wow!
_Up_ and away went Alice.
Not with a puppy like Jip!
But Jerry did not go.
He had to play at _home_.

I have a book. (Hold up book and write sentence on board.) Who will show me the word *have?* Take a good eye picture. Then when I write—(write *hav*_____), you will tell me to finish—.

(Give the book to some child. Then say, "I had a book, but I do not have one now." Write *I had a book* as you say the words.) Who will show me the word *had?* Take a good eye picture of this letter. (Indicate *d.*) Then when I write—(write *had*), you will know it says—. (Have child who holds the book read the sentence that applies to him. Have him give the book to someone else and read the sentence which then applies. Repeat procedure until meaning has been added to *had* and *have.* Use the word cards *had* and *have* as flash cards.)

Jerry was like other boys I know. When he was cross, he had a cross look. When he was sorry, he had a sad look. But most of the time—(sentence 1).

Alice was having a tea party for her dolls under the apple tree. Jip was there, too. All at once the back door opened and—(indicate sentence 2). This word was in the title of our book, *Day In and Day Out.* I remember that this part (draw a line under *Ou*) says—(give sound), and the word is—. You know how the next word begins; jump over it and let the sentence help you. (Have sentence read.) Take a good eye picture of this letter. (Indicate *a.*) Then if I write—(write *cam*_____), you will tell me to finish—.

Jerry jumped into his wagon and called, "Here comes the fast train. It is going to wreck your house. I can't stop it." (Sentence 3.) Just as he got to the tree he called—(sentence 4; use usual techniques for new word *for*). If I were to write—(write *fo*_____), what word would you tell me to finish?

Jip was scared. I hope you remember this word. (Write *a.*) You see it on the beginning of this new word. (Indicate *away* in sentence 5.) Now read and tell what Jip did. As he ran, he barked and said—(sentence 6). What a long word *bow-wow* is! I remember it because of this little line (indicate hyphen) which separates *bow* and *wow.*

Alice picked up her dolls, and—(sentence 7; have sentence reread until the children sense the rhythm of the phrase *Up and away*).

By and by, Jip came back. But Jerry had more exciting things on hand. He did not want to play. (Sentence 8. If capitalized *N* causes trouble, help children to remember how word begins; then have them jump over it to read the rest of sentence. Have sentence reread until children sense rhythm.)

Mother soon came out and put a stop to Jerry's mischief. Later that morning Alice went to see May—(sentences 9-10; use usual techniques for *But* and *home*).

(Have the sentences reread and have underscored words added to card holder. Have pupils "hop down the rabbit hole" and read the words.)

VOCABULARY ENRICHMENT AND EXTENSION

Extending speaking vocabulary. Will you help me finish my sentences? A brown rabbit that lives in the woods is—(*wild*). A pet rabbit is—(*tame*). A pet rabbit lives in a—(*hutch*). When I turn ahead in my book, I turn—(*forward*). Jerry was careful with his airplane, but when he ran into Alice's tea party, he was—(*careless*).

I like this word. (Write *but*.) I will use it to tell you one thing I can do and one thing I cannot do. I can drive a car, but (indicate *but*) I cannot drive an engine. Use the word *but* and tell me something you can do and something you cannot do.

WORD RECOGNITION TECHNIQUES

Accurate word recognition. I will give each word in the card holder a partner. (Arrange as follows: *come—came, big—but, and— away, fly—for, had—have, house—home, oh—out*.) Who will read and bring me one word and its partner? (Continue until all cards are removed.)

Building sight vocabulary

Auditory-visual perception. *Initial sounds.* Of course, you know this word. (Write *father—Father*.) Watch how it begins. (Trace *f* and *F*; then erase words.) If someone will show me how *for* begins, I will finish it.

Phonics

If someone will show me how *hop* begins, I will finish the word. (Continue with *hole, home, rabbit, so*. Have pupils play "One, Two, Three! How Many for Me?" to read and erase the words from the board.)

SUPPLEMENTARY ACTIVITIES

1. *Workbook for Day In and Day Out,* pages 7, 8. Be sure to discuss picture sequence on page 7 with pupils.

2. Bulletin board. Use usual caption. Have pupils make an illustration for story.

Away with Father

Independent word attack

Jerry went away with Father.
He did not go on the train.
Father had a big red car.
So Jerry and Father went in the car.

3. Independent reading. Conduct in usual way.
   Bill and Susan, pages 16-23. (Give help with *Baby,* page **17.**)
   Here and There, pages 26-33.
   My Little Red Story Book, pages 13-18.
   Ride Away, pages 16-23.

Pp. 16-21   Unit 5: Jip

NEW VOCABULARY: bird   duck

INITIAL PROCEDURE

Contents pages. Use the contents pages to find the name of the new story and the number of the page on which it begins. Be sure you turn

Guidance in locating page numbers

more than one page the first time. Then turn page by page until you come to page 16. Don turned to page 13 with his first turn. In which direction did he have to turn to find page 16?

SILENT READING

Page 16. What kind of look does Jip have in the picture at the top of the page? Do you know why? Has his look changed in the picture at the bottom? Why? Do Alice and Jerry discover that he is running away? Read to see if they do.

Page 17. Does the kitten have a happy look? I don't believe Jip means to frighten her. Read four lines. See if you agree.

That kitten does something which reminds me of Alice when Jerry broke up her tea party. Finish the page and see what she does.

Page 18. You know what Jip discovers now. You know how *bird* begins. How many times can you discover the word *bird* on this page? This bird is certainly—(write *pretty* on board and have the word read). Now read the page. Will the bird play with Jip?

Independent word attack— bird, duck

Page 19. Read two sentences. What does Jip say to the rabbit?

The rabbit doesn't give Jip time to ask her to play. Read four sentences. What does she do?

Will Jip go down the rabbit hole after her? Finish the page and find out.

Page 20. My, what a big—! You know how *duck* begins. How many times can you discover the word on this page? Everyone is running away from Jip. He is growing braver and braver. Read four sentences. Find out why I think so.

That duck knows the safest place for her. Where is that place? Finish the page and see.

Page 21. Now who does not have a happy look? Why not? Read the first sentence. What happens when the duck flies home?

If I found a runaway puppy, I think I would scold him pretty hard. Read six sentences. Does May scold Jip?

I wonder if Jip gets out of that basket and away from May. Finish the page and see.

Predicting outcomes. What may happen when Jip gets home? If Alice is worried because Jip is lost, what might she do? It isn't all Jip's fault that he ran away, is it?

ORAL READING

Following events in sequence

Organization. The first thing that happened in our story was this. (Write: [1] *Jip ran away.*) Who will read the page which tells about that? The next thing was—(write: [2] *Jip saw a kitten;* continue with outline and rereading in similar fashion).

VOCABULARY ENRICHMENT AND EXTENSION

Extending speaking vocabulary. (Have children turn back to page 18.) I know another name for this bird. Do you? (Add some interesting facts about cardinals.)

When Jip came home, I am sure Alice was delighted to see him. How did she feel if she was delighted? I am sure May took care to see that Jip did not fall from her basket. I am sure she was very— (*careful*).

WORD RECOGNITION TECHNIQUES

Drill on
carrier words

Accurate word recognition. Get your cameras ready to play "Magic." (Write *come*. Have some child read the word and use it in a sentence.) Close your eyes. (Change *come* to *came*.) Open your eyes. What does the word say now? Use it in a sentence. (Continue with *had—have, the—this, went—want, yes—you, just—jump, big—but*.)

Phonics

Auditory-visual perception. *Initial sounds.* Of course, you know this word. (Write *big—Big*.) Watch how *big* begins. (Trace *b—B;* then erase words.) Now if you will show me how *bird* begins, I will finish it. (Continue with *but, ball, bow-wow, hop, hole, happy, rabbit, so, for*.)

SUPPLEMENTARY ACTIVITIES

1. *Workbook for Day In and Day Out,* pages 9, 10, 11, 12.
2. Bulletin board. Use the usual caption.

Independent
word attack

The Play House

Alice had a pretty play house.
It had three big windows.
It had two <u>doors</u>.
It had a pretty red <u>roof</u>.

3. Independent reading. Conduct in usual way.
   My Little Red Story Book, pages 19-22.
   Ned and Nancy (D. C. Heath and Co.), pages 1-8.
   Ride Away, pages 24-29. (Give help with the word *stop,* page 24.)

We Look and See, pages 11-14. (Give help with word *Baby,*
page 11.)
    4. Textfilm for *Day In and Day Out,* Frames 5-6. See Textfilm
manual for directions.

Unit 6: The New Coat   Pp. 22-25

NEW VOCABULARY: coat   new   please

PREPARATION

Have the following materials ready for use:

Pocket Card Holder
Word Cards: 162 Yes   459 So   468 But   471 Please
Phrase Cards

224 Good morning	294 It is	388 She went
244 Here is	298 I want	399 This is
276 I have	381 She had	446 You may have

INITIAL PROCEDURE

Vocabulary review. (In the card holder have all the word and
phrase cards listed above, except the word card *Please.*)

*Drill on
sentence
beginnings*

Something exciting is going to happen to Alice today. Before we
can find out what it is, we must be sure we can get our sentences
started correctly. How quickly can we each take a card from the
card holder, read it, and then use it to begin a sentence? The card
I take says *It is.* It is a cold day. (As soon as all cards are removed,
have pupils exchange cards, reread, and return to card holder to form
two word ladders. How quickly can they climb the word ladders
without "falling off"?)

Introducing new vocabulary. (*Please; My, oh, my!*) Sometimes when Alice is surprised, she uses the surprise word. (Write *Oh!*) But sometimes she says—(write *My, oh, my!*). Can you read what she says and be as surprised as she is?

Guidance in
methods of
word attack

Whenever she asks for something, Alice does not forget to use a word (write *Please*) which begins like *play*. She says pl——. *Please,* of course! It takes two letters to begin *Please.* (Trace *Pl.*) Then keep your eye on this letter. (Indicate *e.*) If I write—(write *Ple_____*), you will tell me to finish—. Please find the word card *Please* and add it to the card holder.

Contents pages. Turn quickly to the contents pages and find the new story. You have made a discovery, haven't you? You can't read the title. When we turn to the story, you can help yourselves. What page shall we turn to?

SILENT READING

Page 22. The minute I look at the picture, I know what Alice needs. If she were my little girl, I would buy her—(write *a new coat*). Think how each new word begins. Think what Alice needs. Now who can read the title? Was that title on the contents page? Turn back and see.

Independent
word attack—
new, coat

What do you find wrong with this coat in the picture? Read five sentences. Does Alice agree with you?

There is only one person who can do something about this shabby coat. Does Alice know who that is? Finish the page and see.

Page 23. There is some good news for Alice in the first four sentences. Find out what it is.

When I buy something new, I like to change colors. Does Alice? Read until you find out.

Maybe Mother says, "No, I think we had better get another brown coat." See if she does. What do you expect may happen on the next page?

Page 24. Off for the store! We were good guessers, weren't we? I know from the pictures that the clerk is going to be a—. You know how *man* begins. How many times can you find the word *man* on page 24?

Using initial
consonant clues

Read the first two sentences. Get Mother and Alice started on their way. Then Mother introduces Alice to the man, but she forgets something. Read four sentences. What does she forget? Alice doesn't forget. Finish the page and find out why I know.

Page 25. I hope the man doesn't think they want that coat. What color is it? It takes two letters (write *gr*_____) to start the word *green*. How many times can you find the word *green* on this page? What does the man say as he shows the green coat? Read three sentences and see. Does Mother change her mind? Read until you find out. Does Alice? Finish the page and see.

What do you think will happen the next time we read?

ORAL READING

Following
events in
sequence

Organization. What was the first thing which happened in the story? (*Alice finds her old coat.*) Who will read the page which tells the first thing that happened? What was the next thing that happened? (*Mother promises Alice a new coat.*) Who will read the page which tells about that? (Continue in similar fashion.)

VOCABULARY ENRICHMENT AND EXTENSION

Extending speaking vocabulary. Alice was very happy when she heard about that new coat. I can think of a grown-up word which means happy. Can you? (*delighted*) When Mother told the clerk Alice's name and what Alice wanted, she— Alice to the man. Suppose I have never met Carl before. How would you introduce him to me?

WORD RECOGNITION TECHNIQUES

Building sight
vocabulary

Accurate word recognition. Alice is going to change the color of her coat. These words are going to change for you. (Write *play;* change to *please.* Continue with *oh—on, hop—hole, too—toy, fly—for, so—go, out—one.*)

Phonics

Auditory-visual perception. *Initial sounds.* Of course, you know this word. (Write *mother—Mother.*) Watch how *mother* begins. (Trace *m* and then *M;* erase words.) If someone will show me how *man* begins, I will finish the word. (Continue with *may, morning, ball, had, rabbit, for, so.*)

SUPPLEMENTARY ACTIVITIES

1. *Workbook for Day In and Day Out,* page 14.
2. Bulletin board. Change caption to *Are you as smart as Jerry? He can read this. Can you?* Read caption for pupils.

Something New for Jerry

> Look, Alice.
> See my new coat.
> See my <u>pants</u>.
> I have a new <u>suit</u>.

Independent word attack

3. Independent reading.
   Here and There, pages 34-38.
   My Little Red Story Book, pages 23-26. (Give help with the word *Bunny* on page 25.)
   Ride Away, pages 30-38.

Pp. 26-28 # Unit 7: The New Coat (*cont.*)

NEW VOCABULARY: box   laughed   then

PREPARATION

Have the following materials ready for use:

Pocket Card Holder
Word Cards: 457 Just   468 But   472 then   474 laughed
Phrase Cards: 244 Here is   273 I do not   298 I want
                  272 I do   276 I have

INITIAL PROCEDURE

Vocabulary review. (In the card holder have all the word and phrase cards listed above, except *laughed* and *then.*)

Drill on sentence beginnings

I hope there is a lovely red coat for Alice somewhere, don't you? Let's be sure we know how to start our sentences so that, when we begin to read, we can find out in a hurry. (Use techniques suggested in Unit 6.)

Introducing new vocabulary. When Mother saw Alice in that old coat, she thought Alice looked funny. Mother—(write *laughed*). Think how the new word begins. Think what you do when you see something funny. What did Mother do? *Laughed,* of course! Take a good eye picture of this letter. (Indicate *a.*) Then when I write—(write *la_____*), you will tell me to finish—. (Have word card *laughed* added to card holder.)

Guidance in methods of word attack

The man held up the green coat, and—(write *Just then Alice said, "I want a red coat"*). The new word (indicate *then*) begins like *this.* Think how it begins. Jump over it to let the sentence help you. Just th— Alice said—. *Then,* of course! Watch how it begins. (Trace *th.*) Watch these two letters. (Indicate *e* and *n.*) Then when I write—(write *then*), you will know it says—. (Have word card *then* matched to word in sentence and added to card holder.)

This is what happened next. (Write *So then the man looked.*) I hope this is what happened after that. (Write *Then he saw a red coat.*) Don't forget—(indicate word card *then*). You will need it in your very first sentence this morning. If the man did find a red coat, I am sure Alice—(indicate word card *laughed*).

Guidance in locating page numbers

Now make one turn and see how near you come to page—(write *26*). Jack turned to page 30. Did he turn far enough or too far? (Count to 26, then to 30, if necessary.) In which direction must Jack turn now? (Emphasize term *backward.*)

SILENT READING

Page 26. Can you read the sign? I hope you remember the first word in the first sentence. (Indicate word card *then.*) The man is certainly busy looking for coats. What does he say as he looks? Read four sentences and see.

Maybe Alice will take one of these coats. Finish the page and see.

Page 27. I am almost as pleased as Alice when I look at this page. If you think where the coat is, if you think how that word begins, you can discover the new word and tell me what it says. How many times did you find the word *box?* I hope you remember how this sentence started. (Indicate *Just then* on board.)

The man is as excited as Alice. Read four sentences and find out why I think so. Did Alice do this? (Indicate *laughed.*) Finish the page and see. I suppose you think the surprises are over. Well, they aren't. Turn the page and see why I say that.

Page 28. Where did that cap come from? Read until you find out. Alice looks beautiful, doesn't she. I wonder how she likes her new clothes. Finish the page and see.

Page 29. I am sure Alice will not wear that new coat on this kind of day. Why not? *Rain* begins like *ran.* Maybe you can discover the word *rain* on this page. How many times can you find it? When it rains hard, I see something on the walks and pavements which begins like the word *puppy.* I see pu——. Now maybe someone can read the title. What do you suppose will happen in that big, big puddle?

Independent word attack— box

Independent word attack— rain, puddle

ORAL READING

Organization. *Following events in sequence.* (Bring out through suggestion that the three things which happened in the story today were: [1] *The man looks for a red coat.* [2] *The man finds the coat.* [3] *The man finds the cap.* Have story reread according to this outline. In this or another period have the entire story reread.)

WORD RECOGNITION TECHNIQUES

Word structure. What does this word say? (Write *look.*) Watch it grow. (Write *looks;* then *looked.* Repeat with *jump* and *play.*)

Auditory-visual perception. *Initial sounds.* Of course, you know what this word says. (Write *come—Come.*) And you know how it begins. (Trace *c—C;* then erase words.) If you will show me how *coat* begins, I will finish the word. (Continue with *came, cap, box, for, happy, man, rain, so.*)

Verbs ending in s, ed

Phonics

SUPPLEMENTARY ACTIVITIES

1. *Workbook for Day In and Day Out,* pages 13, 15, 16.
2. Bulletin board. Use caption from Unit 6.

Independent
word attack

What Father Said

Father said, "I like this red coat.
I like this red cap, Alice.
Do you want a new dress, too?"
  "Yes," said Alice.
"And I want new shoes and new socks."

3. Independent reading.
   Bill and Susan, pages 24-33. (Give help with the words *help,* page 25; and *thank,* page 33.)
   Ned and Nancy, pages 9-16. (Give help with *no,* page 12.)
   Ride Away, pages 39-47.
   We Look and See, pages 15-22. (Give help with *run,* page 18.)
4. Textfilm for *Day In and Day Out,* Frames 7-8. See Textfilm manual for directions.

Unit 8: The Big, Big Puddle   Pp. 29-34

NEW VOCABULARY: into   jumped   puddle   rain   splash

PREPARATION

Have the following materials ready for use:

Pocket Card Holder
Word Cards:

65 jump	147 walked	464 came	474 laughed
94 it	159 This	465 out	478 jumped
131 did	161 went	468 But	
132 Do	457 Just	471 Please	
139 not	459 So	472 then	

INITIAL PROCEDURE

Vocabulary review. (Have the following sentences on board. Add to card holder word cards for underscored words as soon as each sentence is read.)

Please, may I go?
Alice walked down to see May.
Just then May came out.
This is my new coat.
Do you like it?
So she jumped.
But Alice did not jump.
She went home.
Mother laughed.

The minute Alice got home she put on her new coat and cap. She wanted to go down to May's house. So she said—(sentence 1). Mother said, "Yes." So—(sentence 2). Alice was going to ring the bell, but—(sentence 3). Alice said—(sentences 4, 5). May did like the coat and cap very much. May had a new jumping rope, and she had been waiting to try it all afternoon. (Sentences 6, 7, 8.) When Alice told Mother that she did not jump for fear her new cap might fly off and get dirty—(sentence 9). Mother was glad that Alice was so careful.

May can jump. See if you can read and make these words jump right out of the card holder.

Compound words

Introducing new vocabulary. Sometimes we put two words together to make one. If I were to put this word (write *in*) and this word (write *to*) together, the new word would be—(write *into*). Alice went into the house. We call *into* a compound word. That means it is two words put together.

Guidance in methods of word attack

May wanted to—(write *jump*). So she—(write *jumped*). I don't suppose you can read this. (Write *jumping*.) I hear this word when I say, "May had a *jumping* rope." Now do you know what it says? When I put this ending on a word (draw a line under *ing*), the ending says *ing*.

Alice said, "I will—(write *go*) home." I saw her—(write *going*) home. Do you see the ending *ing*? (Draw a line under the *ing*.) It makes *go* say—.

Contents pages. Do you remember what kind of day it will be in our story today? Do you remember the title? Find the title on the contents pages. Read the title and tell the number of the page on which the story begins. Each day our first turn must include a few more pages. Make your turn. Now think. Will you have to turn forward or backward to find page 29?

Guidance in locating page numbers

SILENT READING

Page 29. The minute Jerry sees the rain, what does he do? What does he say? Read until you find out. Did Mother come? Finish the page and see.

What will happen next? If you were Jerry, what would you want to do?

Independent word attack—splash

Page 30. What did the water do when Jerry walked in the puddle? Can you find the word *splash?* How many times? Read three sentences. Find out what Jerry said to Mother.

Jerry finds two kinds of puddles. Read to find out what each kind is and how many splashes it makes.

Page 31. (Follow usual procedure.)

Page 32. I think the title of our story belongs with this page. Why? The minute Jerry sees that big puddle, what does he say? Read three sentences and see. Alice looks as if she might not like the puddle. Finish the page and see.

Page 33. There goes Jerry. What does he say as he jumps? Read four sentences and see.

Reading a two-line sentence

You remember we put a period (make one) at the end of a sentence. Sometimes a sentence won't fit on one line. We have to use two lines. Then the period comes at the end of the second line. How sharp are your eyes? What do you discover about the next sentence? I also see the compound word. (Indicate *into.*) Who can read the sentence as if it were all on one line? Read with your eyes first. (Let several children read.) Now finish the page. How many splashes does the big puddle make?

Page 34. What a surprise for Mr. Jerry! I hope you remember what this word says when we put the ending *ing* on it. (Indicate *going.*) Is Jerry as smart as he thinks he is? Read three sentences and see.

The joke is on Jerry. Read four sentences and find out why. If I look at the picture, I can certainly read the last sentence. Can you?

Page 35. How Alice has changed! You had better take a good look at her. Then I am sure you will never again be cross or pouty. If you remember where the man found Alice's coat, maybe you can read the title. *A Box for Alice* sounds as if she were going to get a present. A present for that cross girl! Aren't you eager to find out what is the matter?

ORAL READING

Organization. *Following events in sequence.* (Have pupils suggest a simple outline of events, as in previous units. Have them read to tell what happened first, second, etc.)

VOCABULARY ENRICHMENT AND EXTENSION

Extending speaking vocabulary. When Jip played the joke on Jerry, Alice looked happy. In the next picture she looked very, very unhappy. What do you think "unhappy" means?

WORD RECOGNITION TECHNIQUES

Verbs ending in ing

Word structure. (Write *go* on board; then change to *going*. Continue with *look, looking; splash, splashing; play, playing.*)

Compound words

If I write this word (write *blue*) and this word (write *bird*) and put them together, the compound word is—. (Continue with *greenhouse, onto, today.*)

Phonics

Auditory-visual perception. *Initial sounds.* Jip is a—(write *puppy*). Watch how *puppy* begins. (Trace *p.*) Show me how *puddle* begins, and I will finish the word. (Continue with *rain, man, coat, but, for, home, so.*)

SUPPLEMENTARY ACTIVITIES

1. *Workbook for Day In and Day Out,* pages 17, 18, 19, 20.
2. Bulletin board. Have this rhyme on bulletin board. After children have worked it out for themselves, read it for them to set the pattern of the rhythm.

Today

Vocabulary
review in
new context

I ran to the window
   And then out to play.
Oh, what did I do
   Today, today?

I walked in a puddle.
   I jumped in one, too.
I like rain puddles.
   Do you? Do you?

3. Independent reading.
   Bill and Susan, pages 34-37. (Give help with *sleep* on page 34.)
   Here and There, pages 39-47.
   Ned and Nancy, pages 17-20. (Give help with *make* on page 18.)
   We Look and See, pages 23-30.
4. Textfilm for *Day In and Day Out,* Frames 9-10. See Textfilm manual for directions.

Unit 9: A Box for Alice

Pp. 35-39

NEW VOCABULARY: by   city   dolls   eat

PREPARATION

Have the following materials ready for use:

Pocket Card Holder
Word Cards

92 Is	155 had	162 Yes	472 Then	483 eat
94 it	156 home	461 away	474 laughed	
131 did	158 name	467 for	479 into	
150 going	159 this	468 But	480 city	
151 good-by	161 went	471 Please	482 by	

INITIAL PROCEDURE

Vocabulary review. (Have the following sentences on the board. Add word cards for the underscored words to card holder as soon as each sentence is read.)

> Mother is <u>going away</u>.
> <u>Please</u> come <u>home</u>.
> Mother <u>had</u> something <u>for</u> Alice and Jerry.
> <u>Is it</u> something good?
> <u>Then</u> Mother <u>laughed</u>.
> <u>Yes, this</u> is something you like.
> Alice and Jerry <u>went into</u> the house.
> <u>But</u> Jip <u>did</u> not go.

While the children played in the puddle, Mother went to the store. Jerry saw her and said—(sentence 1). By and by Mother came back. She met the children far down the street and said—(sentence 2). This is the reason she wanted them to come home. (Sentence 3.) Alice asked a question. How do I know the next sentence is a question? Now read Alice's question and what Mother did and said. (Sentences 4, 5, 6.) What happened next? (Sentences 7, 8.) Jip was too wet and muddy. The children had milk and fresh cookies. (Erase sentences. Have children play, "One, Two, Three! How Many for Me?" with words in card holder.)

Drill on carrier words

Introducing new vocabulary. Alice and Jerry were hungry. They wanted—(write *something to eat*). Watch how *eat* begins. (Trace *e*.) I'll tell you something interesting. The name of this letter (indicate *e*) is *e*. You hear it as you say the word. Say *eat* and listen for the letter name. If I write—(write *e*_____), you will tell me to finish the word—. (Have word card for *eat* and for each of the other new words added to card holder as introduction progresses.)

When Jerry introduces himself, he says—(write *My name is Jerry*; use usual techniques for *name*).

Guidance in methods of word attack

Alice and Jerry wanted to go out again. Mother might have said, "After a while!" But she didn't. She said—(write *by and by*). The new word begins like *but*. It rhymes with—(write *my* above *by*). *My*, *b*——(form *b* with lips, but do not make sound). Can you make the words rhyme? Now read the phrase and tell me how Mother said "after a while." If I write—(write *by*), the word says—. But this word—(write *my*) says—. By and by when the children go out again, they will say this to Mother. (Write *good-by*.)

Alice and Jerry live in a small town, or village. Sometimes Mother cannot get what she wants in the stores there. Then she goes to the big—(write *city* and read if suggestion does not come from children). Take a good eye picture. (Trace *ci*.) Then when I write—(write *ci*____), you will tell me to finish—. What do you think of when I say *city*? (Have each child tell one thing he associates with a big city.)

This is the day when we find out the reason for Alice's cross face. Aren't you eager to find out?

Contents pages. (Use in usual way.)

SILENT READING

Page 35. By the time I have read the title and the first two sentences, I know the reason for that cross face. See if you do. Will Alice tease? Read the next three sentences and find out. Will Mother change her mind? Finish the page and see.

Page 36. Still as cross as ever! (Have children decide what Father is doing, and why.) Does Alice give up teasing? Read three sentences and see. Father doesn't know who this pouting, cross little girl is. Finish the page and find out why I think so. Did you notice the question mark? What question did Father ask?

Page 37. Smiling at last! I think Alice knew that Father was joking. Read two sentences. What did she do?

I am sure if she wants Father to know that her name *is* Alice, she will say *is* in a loud voice. Then it will look like this. (Write *IS*.) Read three more sentences and see what she says.

Two-line sentences

People with sharp eyes will notice something about the next two sentences. As soon as you know, stand. (Let each child who discovers the two-line sentences try to read each one as if it were all on one line.)

Independent word attack—dolls

Page 38. How many big dolls can you find? How many little ones? Now think how *dolls* begins. Can you discover the word? How many times?

As soon as Mother went away, what happened? Read two sentences and see. Now read four more sentences. Did you find the right number of dolls? Someone might be smart enough to know how many dolls May had altogether.

Now I know why Jip is yawning and what he does about it. Finish the page and see.

Phrase
meaning

Page 39. Don't you wish that you were Alice? Do you remember how Mother said *after a while?* (Indicate *by and by.*) By and by what happened? Read two sentences and see.

Alice asks a question. How do I know? What is her question and how does Father answer it? Read until you find out. When that ice-cream is gone, what happens? Finish the page and see.

Predicting outcomes. When I think of the title of the story, I think I know what will happen when Mother comes home. Do you? What might be in the box? We will find out tomorrow.

ORAL READING

Expressing feelings of story characters. (Have pupils decide that there are two pages in the story where Alice is cross and three where she is happy. Have the story reread by pages to show by the reader's voice the change in mood.)

Audience
reading

VOCABULARY ENRICHMENT AND EXTENSION

Extending speaking vocabulary. When Jerry heard that he was going to the city, he was happy. Can you think of a grown-up word for "happy"? (*delighted*) When we have a good time, we *enjoy* ourselves. Can you tell me something Jerry enjoyed today? two things Alice enjoyed? Whisper and tell me how Mother said *after a while.*

WORD RECOGNITION TECHNIQUES

Drill on
carrier words

Accurate word recognition. This word says—(write *my*). The camera will click. The word will change. What does it say now? (Change *my* to *by*. Continue with *this—then—the; laughed—looked; did—do; new—not.*)

Auditory-visual perception. *Initial sounds.* This word says—(write *not—Not*). Watch how it begins. (Trace *n;* then *N;* erase words.) Show me how *name* begins so that I may finish the word. (Continue with *new, but, came, for, happy, man, puddle, rain, so.*)

SUPPLEMENTARY ACTIVITIES

1. *Workbook for Day In and Day Out,* page 22.
2. Bulletin board. Use caption from Unit 6.

Independent word attack

To The City

Father went to the city.
He did not go on the train.
He had a car at home.
But he did not go
in the car.
He went on the bus.

3. Independent reading. Conduct in usual way.
   My Little Green Story Book (Ginn and Co.), pages 3-10. (Give help with the word *work* on page 7.)
   Time to Play (American Book Co.), pages 3-9.
   We Look and See, pages 31-38.

Unit 10: A Box for Alice (*cont.*)   Pp. 40-42

New Vocabulary: that   walk   wanted

PREPARATION

Have the following materials ready for use:

Pocket Card Holder

Word Cards:	120 want	152 got	484 walk	486 wanted
	147 walked	159 this	485 that	

INITIAL PROCEDURE

Introducing new vocabulary. (Have the following sentences on board.)

> What do you want?
> She saw what she <u>wanted</u>.
> She <u>got</u> the big, big doll.

This chair is close to me. (Point to chair near at hand.) *That* chair (point to one at back of room) is far away. *This girl* (point to child in reading group) is—. *That* girl (point to one far away) is—. When we point to something near at hand, we say—. (Put word card *this* in card holder.) When we point to something far away, we say—. (Hold up word card *that*.) My eyes tell me two things about this word. It begins like *this*. (Trace *th*.) Inside I see the little word. (Write *at*.) So when I write—(write *th*) and then add the little word *at* (write *at*), the word says—. What word do I use when I point to something near at hand? far away? (Use *this* and *that* as flash cards.)

You know this word. (Write *look*.) Now it says—(add *ed*). But I see *look* (draw a line under *look*) in *looked*. When Alice went down to see May, she—(write *walked*). There is a little word inside *walked*. (Draw a line under *walk*.) Alice went down the—(write *walk;* use *walk* and *walked* as flash cards).

When Alice got to May's house, May told Alice she could have anything she wanted to play with. Then May said—(sentence 1). Alice looked at all the toys, and—(sentence 2). What does this word say? (Indicate *want;* then *wanted*. Use *want* and *wanted* as flash cards.)

Then Alice said, "I will get the doll I want." So—. (Sentence 3. Use usual techniques for word *got*. Arrange word cards for *this—that, want—wanted, walk—walked* by pairs in card holder. Add *got*. Have one pupil see how quickly he can read and remove words; another how quickly he can reread and return them.)

It is time for Alice to get that box. What will be in it? Remember, our first turn gets a little bigger each day, but not too big. How near did you come to page 40? In what direction did you have to go for your next turn?

SILENT READING

Page 40. I hope you remember the phrase which means "after a while." I don't believe Alice saw Mother the minute she got out on the walk. Read three sentences and see why I think so.

What did she say and what did she do when she saw Mother? Read until you find out. What did Mother say? Finish the page and see.

Page 41. Who is carrying the box? I am sure if Mother points to it, she will use this word. (Indicate word card *that*.) Alice asks a question. How do I know? What is her question? Read to see. Jerry answers the question first. Read two sentences. What does he say? Now Mother answers. Finish the page to see what she says. What can be in that box that is red and blue and green and brown? Can you guess?

Oral language

Page 42. (Allow time for picture discussion.) I am sure Alice hasn't seen those pretty ribbons yet when she talks at the top of the page because she asks three questions. Can you find three question marks? Now read three lines and find out what Alice asks. How does Mother answer her questions, and what does Alice do? Read until you find out. Has Alice been wanting new ribbons? Finish the page and see what you think.

Predicting outcomes. As I look at the rest of the pictures in this book, I know what I will be watching for. Will you be watching for something? What will it be? Which ribbons will Alice wear?

Page 43. What can be the matter with Jip? Maybe if you find the sentence which says *I like Jip,* and then read the next two sentences,

Independent
word attack—
dog

you will find out. You will find a new word, but you know how it begins; and the sentence will help you. (*dog*) What does Jerry say to Father? Now maybe someone can read the title. Do you suppose Jerry wants to give Jip away? Will Alice let him do that?

ORAL READING

Organization. *Following events in sequence.* (Have pages 40-42 reread to follow a simple outline: [1] *Alice waits for Mother.* [2] *Mother tells Alice about the box.* [3] *Alice opens the box.* In this or another period have the entire story reread.)

VOCABULARY ENRICHMENT AND EXTENSION

Extending speaking vocabulary. Alice was delighted to see Mother. Was she happy or unhappy? She was disappointed when she could not go to the city. Does disappointed mean "happy" or "unhappy"? She enjoyed her ice-cream. That means that she—. Mother came home by and by. What is another way of saying "by and by"?

WORD RECOGNITION TECHNIQUES

Drill on
carrier words

Accurate word recognition. This morning we had fun with some partner words. I will write two partner words for each of you. Can you read them and use each one in a sentence? (Use *this—that, the— then, want—wanted, walk—walked, went—want, had—have, come— came, did—do.*)

Phonics

Auditory-visual perception. *Initial sounds.* (Write *want* on board and have word read; then trace the *w* and erase word. Have pupils show how *with* begins and finish word. Continue with *window, name, by, my, coat, for, hop, puppy, rain, saw.*)

SUPPLEMENTARY ACTIVITIES

1. *Workbook for Day In and Day Out,* pages 21, 23, **24.**
2. Bulletin board. Use caption suggested in Unit **6.**

Independent
word attack

<u>Candy</u> for Jerry

Mother went to the city.
Alice went, too.
Alice looked in a window.
"Jerry wants something good to **eat,**"
said Alice.
"He wants <u>candy</u> in a box.
See this good candy, Mother."

3. Independent reading.
Bill and Susan, pages 38-47. (Give help with word *Daddy* on page 38.)

My Little Green Story Book, pages 11-18. (Give help with the
words *apples*, page 11; and *dinner*, page 18.)

Time to Play, pages 10-17. (Give help with the words *we*, page
11; and *stop*, page 16.)

4. Textfilm for *Day In and Day Out*, Frames 11-12. See Textfilm
manual for directions.

Unit 11: A Dog for Jerry   Pp. 43-45

NEW VOCABULARY: boy   day   dog   Mac   stay

PREPARATION

Have the following materials ready for use:

Pocket Card Holder
Word Cards

54 come	123 you	155 had	457 just	485 that
65 jump	131 Did	159 this	458 fly	486 wanted
84 big	132 Do	161 went	464 came	488 day
108 on	133 have	162 yes	467 for	489 boy
120 want	147 walked	452 oh	468 but	490 stay

INITIAL PROCEDURE

Vocabulary review. (Have the following words arranged in pairs
in card holder: *but—big, came—come, Do—Did, for—fly, have—had,
just—jump, oh—on, this—that, walked—wanted, went—want, yes—you.*
Have each child read and remove one pair. When all cards are removed, have cards exchanged, reread, and returned to card holder.
Watch for words which cause trouble.)

Introducing new vocabulary. (Have the following sentences on
board. Have underscored words added to card holder as soon as
sentences are read.)

One <u>day</u> Mother went to the city.
Jerry had to <u>stay</u> at home.
Jerry is a <u>boy</u>.
Days and days went by.

You know the title of our book. (Indicate title.) You know this word. (Indicate *DAY*.) When *day* is written in small letters, it looks as it does in this sentence. (Indicate *day* on board.) Read the sentence and tell what Mother did. This time it was Alice, not Jerry, who went with Mother. So—(sentence 2). The new word—(indicate *stay* and trace *st*) begins like *store*. Jerry had to st—— at home. But Jerry does not care. He did not like to go shopping anyway. I guess that was because—(sentence 3; use usual techniques for *boy*). After that Mother did not go to the city for a long, long time. The next sentence makes me know that. (Sentence 4.) Can you find a phrase, three words, in that sentence which means *a long time?* Now who will show me the two new words which rhyme? Who will read the other new word?

Guidance in methods of word attack

Contents pages. (Use in usual way.)

SILENT READING

Oral language

Page 43. (Have pupils discover the golf bag and decide what Father may be doing.) Read until Jerry is through talking. Find out what kind of dog he wants. Finish the page. Will Father go right out and buy that dog for Jerry?

Page 44. Father doesn't change his mind. Read the first two sentences and find out why I know. Jerry doesn't let Father forget about that dog. I know that when I read the next two sentences. Now finish the page. I wonder what this man has to do with our story. Find out.

Page 45. When I read three sentences, I find out three things. I find out something this man has, where he is going, and how long he is going to stay. Are you as good a reader as I am? See if you are.

If I were to tell you that the dog's name was Mac, could you find his name? How many times? Now read two more sentences. Why can't Mac go to the city, too? (Discuss differences between city dogs and small-town dogs.)

That man wants something very much. Read two more sentences to find out what it is. Can Jerry help him? Finish the page and see. Do you suppose Father and Mother will agree? We will find out tomorrow.

ORAL READING

Following
events in
sequence

Organization. (Have children suggest a simple outline, such as: [1] *Jerry tells Father what he wants.* [2] *A man comes to see Father.* [3] *Jerry and the man make a plan.* Have the whole story reread by pages.)

VOCABULARY ENRICHMENT AND EXTENSION

Extending speaking vocabulary. Do you know how to say *after a while* in another way? Can you use the title of your book and tell me how to say that I do something *over and over and over again?* I know you liked the story this morning. How could I say *liked* in another way? (*enjoyed*)

WORD RECOGNITION TECHNIQUES

Phonics

Auditory-visual perception. *Phonetic parts.* You remember this word from the title of our book. (Write *day.*) I will tell you something interesting about this word. This part (underline *ay*) says *ā*. Say the word. Now tell me what this part says. (Indicate *ay.*) How sharp are your eyes? (Write *May.*) Can you read the word? Can you draw a line under the same part and tell me what the part says? (Follow with *play, away, stay.*)

SUPPLEMENTARY ACTIVITIES

1. *Workbook for Day In and Day Out,* pages 25, 26. Discuss picture sequence on page 26 and be sure directions are understood. Have text read if necessary.
2. Bulletin board. Have this jingle on bulletin board. Help children to see how initial sound plus the sound of the part *ay* will help

them get *say* and *Ray*. After they have worked out jingle, read it for them to set rhythmic pattern.

Independent word attack

What I Can Say

Day and play
And stay and away.
Do you like to say that?
I do!

Ray and May
May come out to play.
I can say that.
Can you?

3. Independent reading.
   Time to Play, pages 18-25.
   We Come and Go (Scott, Foresman and Co.), pages 3-8. (Give help with the word *Baby,* page 5.)
   We Look and See, pages 39-47.

Pp. 46-48

Unit 12: A Dog for Jerry (*cont.*)

NEW VOCABULARY: again   garden   was   will

PREPARATION

Have the following materials ready for use:

Pocket Card Holder
Word Cards

155 had	460 happy	471 please	490 stay	495 garden
159 this	464 came	472 then	492 will	
161 went	467 for	482 by	493 again	
162 yes	468 but	485 that	494 was	

INITIAL PROCEDURE

Drill on carrier words

Vocabulary review. (Have all word cards listed above, except *again, garden, was,* and *will,* in card holder.) Read and bring me the word I use when I point to something near at hand; far away; a word which rhymes with *day;* with *my;* a word which begins like *play;* like *the;* a word which begins like *bird;* two which begin like *hat;* one that begins like *window;* like *foot;* a word that begins like *cap;* a word which means the opposite of *no.* (Have pupils exchange and reread cards and return them to card holder.)

Introducing new vocabulary. (Have the following sentences on board. Add underscored words to card holder as soon as each sentence is read.)

I will go.
I will go again.
I will go to the garden.
It was Father.

Guidance in methods of word attack

Mother was expecting company, and she was very busy. "I should go to the store," said Mother. "But I haven't time." Jerry heard her and said—(sentence 1; use usual techniques for *will*). Be sure to notice how *will* begins and these two letters. (Indicate *ll*.)

When Jerry came back, Mother said, "I forgot to tell you to bring eggs." If you know this word (write *a*), and can see it at the beginning of the new word in the next sentence, I am sure you can read the sentence and tell what Jerry said. (Sentence 2.) Take a good eye picture of this letter. (Indicate *g*.) Then when I write—(write *ag*——), you will tell me to finish—.

Then Mother said, "I want sweet corn for dinner. So—(sentence 3; use usual techniques for *garden*)."

Just then the doorbell rang. "My company already!" thought Mother. But it wasn't the company. (Sentence 4. Use usual techniques for *was*.) Who can read all the new words in the card holder? Be sure to use the sentences if you need help.

SILENT READING

Page 46. Someone besides Father will object to that dog. Read three sentences. Who will object?

Before we read further, let's see what the man's plan is. When the man goes to the city, where will Mac be? When the man comes home again, what will happen? Read five sentences. Is that the way he explains things to Father?

I believe Father will give in. Will Mother? Finish the page and see if they do.

Oral language

Page 47. (Allow a few minutes for identifying electric sewing machine, dress form, etc.) Jerry has faith in Mother. Read five sentences. What does he say and do? I believe Jerry is teasing. When we tease, we say things (indicate *again* in card holder and wait for the word to be read) again and again. Does Jerry? Read the next sentence and see. Does Mother give in? Finish the page and find out.

If that dog can't stay in the house, where will he stay? Will he fit in Jip's doghouse? Then what do you expect to see in the next picture? Turn and see if you are right.

Page 48. What a dog! He certainly is big, but is he good? How can you tell? Is this a new doghouse? How do you know? Who do you think made it? Why is Jip staying close to Mother?

Jerry and Father couldn't waste any time making that doghouse. Read two sentences. Why do I say that? Read two more sentences. Where did they put the house? The first one to notice something about the next sentence may read it. What is Jerry saying to Mother as he sits astride Mac? Can you read aloud what he says and sound like Jerry?

Two-line
sentence

Page 49. How do Alice and Jerry look on this next page? Don't you wish you knew what they see to surprise them? Maybe Jerry is saying—(write *Oh!*). Maybe Alice is saying—(write *My, oh, my!*). Anyway, I think I know why the new part of our book is called "Surprise." (Run your hand under title and have children read.)

Predicting outcomes. Jerry is very happy today. I imagine he will be happy with Mac for days and days to come. But what may happen then? Is it really a good thing to borrow a dog? Why not?

ORAL READING

Audience reading. (Since this is a boy story, have each of six boy readers choose a page and reread the story for the group.)

VOCABULARY ENRICHMENT AND EXTENSION

Synonymous
meanings

Extending speaking vocabulary. When Mac came, Jerry was happy. What other words do you know which mean "happy"? (*delighted, glad, merry, joyful,* etc.) When Mac goes home, I am sure Jerry will be—(*unhappy, sad, disappointed, miserable,* etc.).

WORD RECOGNITION TECHNIQUES

Auditory-visual perception. *Phonetic parts.* Can you read this word? (Write *stay.*) Can you draw a line under the part which helps you to remember the word and tell what the part says? (Continue with *play, day, May, away.*)

Phonics

Do you remember what this part said in *out?* (Write *out* and draw a line under *ou.*) Now say *house.* I hear the part *ou* in house. Do you? Now watch while I write *house.* Who can find the part *ou* and draw a line under it?

Initial sounds. Of course, you know this word. (Write *go—Go.*) Watch how *go* begins. (Trace *g;* then *G;* erase words.) Show me how *garden* begins, and I will finish the word. (Continue with *boy, coat, day, for, happy, man, name, puppy, ran, said, will, was.*)

SUPPLEMENTARY ACTIVITIES

1. *Workbook for Day In and Day Out,* pages 27, 28.
2. Bulletin board.

One Day

Independent
word attack

I was so happy,
  So happy one day,
I just had to go walking
  Away and away.

I saw ducks in the puddles,
  A red bird in a <u>tree</u>.
By and by a little rabbit
  Came out and looked at me.

3. Independent reading.
Ned and Nancy, pages 21-28. (Give help with *has,* page 27.)
Time to Play, pages 26-33.
4. Textfilm for *Day In and Day Out,* Frames 13-14. See Textfilm manual for directions.
5. Tests. Before beginning the next unit, give the two informal tests on pages 29 and 30 of the Workbook. In each test pupils are to be given a score of 1 for each item marked correctly. Pupils in average groups should make a score of at least 20 on the vocabulary test, 4 on the sentence-meaning test. If scores are lower than this, CHECK YOUR TEACHING WITH THE UNIT PLANS. It is important at this point that each child be tested individually with the word cards for the new vocabulary that has been introduced so far in the Primer. (See page 159 of *Day In and Day Out.*)

Individual check on sight vocabulary

Pp. 49-53 # Unit 13: Something for Mother

NEW VOCABULARY: get   surprise

PREPARATION

Have the following materials ready for use:

Pocket Card Holder
Word Cards:

133 have	465 out	482 By	493 again
161 went	467 for	485 That	494 was
457 Just	472 then	490 stay	497 get
464 came	479 into	492 will	

INITIAL PROCEDURE

Vocabulary review. (Have the following sentences on the board. Add word cards for underscored words to card holder as soon as each sentence is read.)

One day the rain came down.
You can not go out in the puddles.
You will have to stay in the house.
Just then two boys came into the house.
That was a surprise for Jerry.
By and by the boys went home.
Come again! Come again!

Drill on carrier words

Jerry liked sunny days. But—(sentence 1). Jerry had a cold that day. So Mother said—(sentences 2, 3). Jerry felt sorry for himself. But—(sentence 4). "Oh!" said Jerry when he saw them. If you know what we call the word *oh* (surprise word), you will know this long word in the next sentence. (Indicate *surprise* and have sentence 5 read.) What a good time the boys had that morning! But—(sentence 6). As they went away, Jerry called—(sentence 7; have each word in card holder matched to same word on board; have sentences reread).

Guidance in methods of word attack

Introducing new vocabulary. Mother cleaned the kitchen floor. She opened the back screen door to get something, and in popped Jip, wet and muddy. Mother said—. (Write *Get out, Jip, get out!* Use usual techniques for word *get.*) Can you carry out three directions in just the right order? Find the word card *get,* read it, and match it with the word *get* in the sentence. Can you carry out three more? Read the sentence, read the word card, and then put the card into the card holder.

Contents pages. If you remember the look in the eyes of Alice and Jerry the last time we saw them, you remember the title of the new part of our book. (Indicate the word *surprise* on board.) Find that title on the contents pages. Then read the title of the first story in that part and the number of the page on which it begins. If the new story begins on page 50, how many pages have we read? (Count to 49, if necessary.) Then our first turn will have to be quite a big one. See how close you can come to page 50. Which way did you have to turn the second time?

Guidance in locating page numbers

SILENT READING

Page 50. (Allow time for picture discussion.) Have you any idea what the something for Mother might be? I have noticed something about little girls. Whenever Mother has something, they want the same thing. Is Alice like that? Read the title and four sentences and find out. Generally if mothers can give little girls what they want, they do so. I wonder if Alice's mother is like that. Finish the page and see.

Page 51. It looks to me as if Jip has been into mischief. Did you discover something which should not be in that new garden? Read four sentences and see if you discovered the right thing. I think Alice has reason to be cross. Finish the page and see if she is.

Two-line sentence

Page 52. The garden is brown no longer. What has happened? How sharp are your eyes? Who can find a two-line sentence? I think I know why the garden turned green. Read three sentences and see if they give the reason. How many days after the rain did the garden turn green? Read until you find out. Alice is so surprised. She wants to share her surprise with someone. Read the page and see who it is.

Page 53. Alice has one visitor she wants. Who is that? She also has an unexpected visitor. Who is that? Is a rabbit a good visitor for a garden? Why not? I wonder if Alice will tell him to get out. Read five sentences and see. How many visitors leave the garden? Read the next two sentences and see. What do you notice about the last sentence? Someone plays a trick on Alice. See who it is.

Predicting outcomes. If that rabbit keeps coming back, what may happen to Alice's garden? I hope he isn't so hungry that he will eat it all up. We will find out tomorrow.

ORAL READING

Following events in sequence

Organization. (Suggest that two things happen on each page of the story. For example, Page 50: [1] *Mother makes a garden.* [2] *Alice has a garden.* Page 51: [1] *Jip makes a hole.* [2] *Alice chases Jip.* Etc. Have two pupils read each page to follow the simple outline.)

VOCABULARY ENRICHMENT AND EXTENSION

Descriptive words. If you say the word *boat,* I get a mind picture of any kind of boat. But if you say a blue boat with a white sail, I have a much better picture. Can you add two other words to the word *rabbit* so that I will see the rabbit that hopped into Alice's garden? two words to the word *garden* so that I will know how Alice's garden looked after the rain? two words to the word *dog* so that I will know what kind of dog Mac was?

WORD RECOGNITION TECHNIQUES

Auditory-visual perception. *Phonetic parts.* (Write the following words on the board. Have pupils read each word and draw a line under the part which they hear and see in each word: *stay, day, away, out, house.*)

Phonics

You know this word. (Write *boy*.) This part in the word *boy* says —(give sound of vowel digraph *oy,* and draw a line under it). Say *boy*. Can you hear the sound *oy?* (Give sound.) How sharp are your ears? Listen as I say *toy*. Did you hear the sound *oy?* Can you see the part in the word *toy* which says *oy?* (Write word and have some child draw a line under *oy.*)

Final sounds. Listen as I say *rabbit, coat, boat.* My ears tell me that these words end with the same sound. Listen again. (Repeat words.) Is that what your ears tell you? Let's see if we are right. (Write the three words on board and call attention to final *t.*) If I wanted to add another word which ends like *rabbit,* would the word be *go* or *get?* Let's prove that you are right. (Add *get* to list on board.) I will write *just,* all but the last letter. Who can finish the word? (Write *jus____* and have some child add the *t.*)

SUPPLEMENTARY ACTIVITIES

1. *Workbook for Day In and Day Out,* pages 31, 32.
2. Bulletin board. Have the following caption on the bulletin board: *I know the word that begins like "fly." Do you?* Read caption for children. Underneath have this text.

In My Garden

Independent
word attack

I have a bird house in my garden.
One day I saw a red bird fly away.
Then I looked down at my garden.
I saw pretty blue flowers in my garden.
I saw red flowers, too.

3. Independent reading.
   My Little Green Story Book, pages 19-24. (Give help with
   words *chair,* page 19; and *Bunny,* page 21.)
   Time to Play, pages 34-41.
   We Come and Go, pages 9-12.

Pp. 54-55 Unit 14: Something for Mother (*cont.*)

PREPARATION

Have the following materials ready for use:

Pocket Card Holder
Word Cards

| 92 is | 133 have | 152 got | 460 happy | 472 Then |
| 94 It | 140 pretty | 457 just | 467 for | 492 will |

INITIAL PROCEDURE

Vocabulary review. (Have the following sentences on board. Add
underscored words to card holder as soon as each sentence is read.)

> It is a surprise.
> It is pretty.
> Alice got it just for Mother.
> Mother will like it.
> Then Alice will have a happy look.

I won't give away the secret and tell what the *something for Mother*
is. But I will tell you this much about it. (Sentences 1-5.) How quickly can someone read and remove the cards from the card holder?
(Have another child read and return cards.) How quickly can you
turn to page 54?

SILENT READING

Page 54. It isn't Mother who is surprised on this page. Who is it? Why is she surprised? These lovely flowers didn't grow overnight or in one day. Read three lines. Find out how I know they didn't.

Now read six more sentences. Alice talks, and she is as surprised as her eyes show she is. Who can read what she says and be just as surprised as Alice? Now finish the page. Help Alice pick the bouquet and find out what she does with it.

Expressing mood of characters

Page 55. Alice makes up a jingle. Read four sentences. Can you read the jingle just as Alice would say it? Now finish the page and be ready to show by your voice how much Mother likes the flowers.

Predicting outcomes. From this time on, what might you see if you visited Alice's house? What might she do with some flowers she did not need at home?

ORAL READING

Rereading by page units (Pages 50-55). I like the page which tells about Mother's garden. So suppose you give me a turn to read that. Who likes the one which tells about Jip and the hole? (Continue in similar way until story has been reread.)

VOCABULARY ENRICHMENT AND EXTENSION

Synonymous meanings

Extending speaking vocabulary. Alice was astonished when she saw the flowers in her garden. What do you suppose "astonished" means? Can you suggest two or three words which tell how Mother felt when she saw the flowers?

WORD RECOGNITION TECHNIQUES

Auditory-visual perception. *Phonetic parts.* How quickly can you read the word I write, draw a line under the part you see in the word, and then tell me what the part says? (Write *boy, toy, house, out, stay, away, day.*)

Phonics

Initial sounds. (Write *jump—Jump.*) Watch how *jump* begins. (Trace *j—J;* then erase words.) Show me how *just* begins; then I will finish the word for you. (Continue with *Jip* and *Jerry,* emphasizing fact that names of people or animals begin with capital letters. Then continue with *but, came, day, for, garden, had, me, name, puppy, ran, so, will.*)

Phonics

Final sounds. What did we find out about the words *rabbit, coat, boat?* If I write the word *rabbit,* all except the last letter, can you put the letter on for me? (Continue with *coat* and *boat.*) If I wanted to add another word which ends like *rabbit,* would I add *went* or *will?* Let's prove that *went* is the right choice. (Write *went* and draw attention to final *t.* Do not allow pupils to suggest words, as they might suggest words ending in silent *e.*)

SUPPLEMENTARY ACTIVITIES

1. *Workbook for Day In and Day Out,* pages 33-34. Be sure to discuss picture sequence on page 33. Be sure that directions are understood.

2. Bulletin board. Have the following on the bulletin board. After children have read it for themselves, read it for them to set the rhythmic pattern.

Independent word attack

My Garden

I like gardens
in the rain.
I stay by my window
and look
At the flowers in my garden.
The blue flowers,
The red flowers,
And the green, green leaves.
My garden looks
so pretty in the rain.

3. Independent reading.
   Ned and Nancy, pages 29-36. (Give help with the word *bigger* on page 33.)
   Time to Play, pages 42-51.

4. Textfilm for *Day In and Day Out,* Frames 15-16. See Textfilm manual for directions.

Unit 15: A Good Wish

Pp. 56-59

NEW VOCABULARY: Jack   pony   wish

PREPARATION

Have the following materials ready for use:

Pocket Card Holder
Phrase Cards

252 He saw	275 I had	446 You may have
253 He went	356 One morning	450 You want
272 I do	436 You can not	

Word Cards: 51 And   459 So   472 Then   499 Jack
148 What   468 But   498 wish

INITIAL PROCEDURE

Vocabulary review. (Have all word and phrase cards except *Jack* and *wish* in card holder.)

Drill on sentence beginnings

When we read, the sentence beginnings also steer us in the right direction. Suppose we each take a sentence beginning, read it, and then finish the sentence. The one I take is *And*. (Remove word card *And*.) *And* then someone else may have a turn. (Have cards removed, exchanged, reread, and returned to card holder.)

Introducing new vocabulary. (Have the following sentences on board. Add each underscored word to card holder as soon as the sentence containing it is read.)

Jack is a new name.
I will wish for something.
I will wish for this.
I will wish for that.
Is he going to get one wish?

Guidance in
methods of
word attack

This morning we need this new word. (Indicate *Jack.*) It begins like—, and it rhymes with *back*. *Back—J!* (Give sound.) The new word is *Jack,* and in our book—(sentence 1). I wonder if there will be a boy called Jack in the story.

You remember Alice's birthday cake in *Skip Along.* As soon as Alice saw the candles, she said—(sentence 2; use usual techniques for *wish*). Watch carefully how *wish* ends. (Trace *sh.*) When I write—(write *wish*), you will know that the word is—.

Someone in our story is wishing for all kinds of things. First he says—(sentence 3). Then he says—(sentence 4). The thing I want to know is—(sentence 5). Maybe he will because one of his wishes is—. Oh, I won't tell you. Find the title of the new story and you can find out for yourselves.

Contents pages. (Use in usual way.)

SILENT READING

Page 56. Who is going to wish and wish? Have you an idea? Will his wishes have something to do with that big airplane? Read six sentences and find out.

I know what Mother will do when she thinks about Jerry with a big airplane of his very own. What does she do, and what does she say? Read four sentences to find out.

Is Jerry through wishing? Finish the page and see.

Page 57. I suppose Mother says, "All right. After this I will call you Jack." See if she does.

Page 58. As soon as you know how many two-line sentences there are on page 58, stand. Now read the first two sentences. Who is wishing now, and what is she wishing for? Does Mother get her wish? Read until you find out. Then what happens next? Finish the page and find out.

Independent
word attack—
pony

Page 59. We don't have to be very smart to know what Jerry's next wish will be. If you think how *pony* begins, you can discover the word for yourselves. How many times can you find it? Are we right? Does Jerry wish for a pony? Read until you find out.

Alice has lots of common sense. Does she think Jerry will get his wish? Finish the page and see.

I wonder if Jerry will go on wishing tomorrow. Has he made a good wish yet, a wish that he could really get?

ORAL READING

Following
events in
sequence

Organization. *Following events in sequence.* (Have some child read the part of the story which tells about the first wish, another about the second wish, etc.)

VOCABULARY ENRICHMENT AND EXTENSION

Descriptive words. Jerry saw a little brown pony. Can you add other words to *pony* so that I will see a very different-looking pony? (*a circus pony, a bucking pony,* etc.)

WORD RECOGNITION TECHNIQUES

Auditory-visual perception. *Phonetic parts.* (Use techniques suggested in Unit 14.)

Initial sounds. You know this word. (Write *look.* Use techniques

Phonics

suggested in previous units. Have pupils show how *laughed, ball, coat, doll, for, get, home, just, man, new, pony, ride, saw, was* begin; then finish each word as soon as initial consonant is written.)

Final sounds. If I write *but,* all but the last letter, will you finish it? (Continue with *what, out, coat, eat.*)

Listen carefully. *Hop—Jip—jump!* What did your ears tell you about these words? Let's see if they do end with the same sound and letter. (Write words on board and direct attention to final *p.*) If I wanted to add another word to the list, would it be *coat* or *cap?* Let's prove that *cap* ends like *hop.* (Write *cap* and compare.)

SUPPLEMENTARY ACTIVITIES

1. *Workbook for Day In and Day Out,* pages 35, 36.
2. Bulletin board. Have the following paragraph on bulletin board. Watch carefully to see how many pupils are growing in power to work out new words through use of context and initial consonant clues.

Independent
word attack

What I Want

I want a pony.
He will not have a brown coat.
He will have a brown and white coat.
He will have 4 feet and a pretty tail.
My pony will go fast.
He will go like the wind.

3. Independent reading.
   My Little Green Story Book, pages 25-28. (Give help with the
   words *fast,* page 27; and *we,* page 28.)
   Time to Play, pages 52-63.

Pp. 60-62

Unit 16: A Good Wish (*cont.*)

PREPARATION

Have the following materials ready for use:

Pocket Card Holder

Word Cards:

but—by	go—so	the—then
came—come	had—have	this—that
did—do	is—it	want—wanted
fly—for	jump—just	will—wish
get—got	new—not	

(Nos.   54,   57,   65,   76,   92,   94, 120, 131, 132, 133, 139,
152, 155, 159, 457, 458, 459, 464, 467, 468, 469, 472,
482, 485, 486, 492, 497, 498)

INITIAL PROCEDURE

Vocabulary review. (Have word cards listed above arranged in
pairs in card holder.) Here are partner words that we will need to
know today. Suppose we each take one pair and read them. (Have
all cards removed, exchanged, reread, and returned to card holder.)

Drill on
carrier words

Guidance
in locating
page numbers

How quickly can you find page 61? If this is page 61, what is the number of this page? (Indicate 60; explain that not all pages in books necessarily have page numbers.)

SILENT READING

Page 60. One look at page 60 and I can guess what someone may be wishing for. Can you? Which toy would you want? Look carefully. How many two-line sentences can you find?

Now read the whole page with your eyes. Who is wishing? What is being wished for? Does the wish come true?

Two-line
sentences

Page 61. Which animal would you wish for? How many two-line sentences can you discover? Now read and find out who is wishing. I hope this wish comes true. See if it does.

Page 62. I hope Jerry hasn't forgotten what he came to the store to buy. Read two sentences and find out.

Jerry starts wishing again, and Alice follows. Read until you find out what their wish is this time. Do you think that wish may be the good wish? Will it come true? Finish the page and see. (Have children identify cookies and enjoy with them the "Thou Shalt Not Steal" inscription on cooky jar.)

Independent
word
recognition—
find

Page 63. Alice's cap in Mother's hand, her coat on a chair! But where is Alice? The title of the new story asks a question. How do I know? There is a new word (*Find*) in the title, but you know how it begins. Who can get it? Maybe Mother has a job for Jerry. What will that job be?

ORAL READING

Organization. *Following events in sequence.* (Pages 56-62). (Put a simple outline on board; for example: [1] *Jerry wants a big airplane.* [2] *Jerry wants a new name.* [3] *Mother wants someone to go to the store.* Etc. Have story reread to follow outline.)

VOCABULARY ENRICHMENT AND EXTENSION

Extending speaking vocabulary. In the title of the new story I heard a word which means *discover*. If the children liked the cookies, they—(*enjoyed*) them. If you get your wish, your wish comes—(*true*).

WORD RECOGNITION TECHNIQUES

Auditory-visual perception. *Phonetic parts.* (Review procedures of previous units.)

Initial sounds. You know this word. (Write *to—To.*) Watch how it begins. (Trace *t;* then *T;* erase words.) Show me how *toy* begins. Then I will finish the word. (Continue with *but, can, did, find, get, have, just, laughed, man, new, pony, rain, saw, wish.*)

Final sounds. If I write *went,* all but the last letter, will you finish it for me? (Follow with *want, boat, coat.* Repeat techniques with *hop, cap, Jip, jump.*)

Phonics

SUPPLEMENTARY ACTIVITIES

1. *Workbook for Day In and Day Out,* pages 37, 38. Be sure to discuss picture sequence and use of picture dictionary on page 37. Be sure directions on page 38 are understood.

2. Bulletin board.

Vocabulary
review in
new context

My Wish for You

I wish, I wish,
Oh, what do I wish?
Oh, what do I wish for you?
A puppy dog brown
That can jump up and down.
And that is my wish for you.

3. Independent reading.

All in a Day (American Book Co.), pages 3-11.

My Little Green Story Book, pages 29-34. (Give help with the word *stop,* on page 29.)

Ned and Nancy, pages 37-40. (Give help with word *cake* on page 37.)

We Come and Go, pages 13-16. (Give help with the word *funny* on page 15.)

4. Textfilm for *Day In and Day Out,* Frames 17-18. See Textfilm manual for directions.

Unit 17: Can You Find Alice?

Pp. 63-67

NEW VOCABULARY: find   her   now   say

PREPARATION

Have the following materials ready for use:

Pocket Card Holder

Word Cards:

159 this	464 came	477 splash	497 get
161 went	465 out	478 jumped	501 find
457 Just	468 But	479 into	502 her
459 So	469 new	486 wanted	503 now
461 Away	472 then	494 was	504 say

INITIAL PROCEDURE

Vocabulary review. (Have the following sentences on board. Add all of the underscored words to card holder as soon as each sentence is read.)

> So Jip came.
> She wanted Jip to get into it.
> But this was something new.
> Just then Jip jumped out
> with a big splash.
> Away went Jip.

Alice was at home alone. Jip came home with muddy paws. Alice thought she would give Jip a bath. She got a small tub of water. Then she said, "Come here Jip." (Sentence 1.) She pointed to the tub because—(sentence 2). Jip liked to chase sticks in the pond—(sentence 3). Finally Alice had to lift him into the tub, and—(sentences 4, 5;

Drill on carrier words

have word cards read and removed from card holder, exchanged, reread, and returned). (If a pupil has difficulty with a word, have him read the sentence in which that word appears.)

Introducing new vocabulary. When Mother held up Alice's coat, she might have said, "Here is Alice's coat." But she didn't. She said —(write *Here is her coat*). You know how the new word (indicate *her*) begins. If I tell you that this part of the word (draw a line under *er*) says—(give sound of *er*), you will know that the word is—. And this word card is—. (Add word card for *her* to card holder.)

Then Mother said this to Jerry. (Write *Please find her for me.*) Jerry said, "That won't be hard to do because—(write *I saw her just now*). You know how this new word begins. (Indicate *now*.) If I tell you that this part (draw a line under *ow*) says—(give sound of *ow*), you will know that the word is—. (Have sentence read and word card *now* added to card holder.)

Mother wasn't quite sure she heard what Jerry said. So she asked— (write *What did you say?*). You can get the new word (indicate *say*) because you know how it begins, and you also know what this part (underline *ay*) says. (Have sentence read and word cards *find* and *say* added to card holder. Have the new words in card holder read several times.) Has Jerry found Alice for Mother? Let's hurry and see.

Contents pages. (Use in usual way.)

SILENT READING

Page 63. What did Mother do when she wanted to talk to Jerry? Read the title and the first sentence to find out. Now read everything she says to Jerry. Jerry is very sure of himself. Why do I think so? Finish the page and see.

Page 64. (Identify jack-in-the-box from *Skip Along.*) If you wanted to find Alice, what would you do first? Read two sentences. Does Jerry call her? Does she come?

Sometimes when we look for someone or something, we find certain clues. Clues are things which make us know that we are on the right track. What clues does Jerry find? Read until you find out. Is he on the right track? Finish the page to see.

Page 65. Jerry sees someone and asks him a question. Whom does he see? What does he ask? Read until you find out. Read three more sentences. Is Jerry still on the right track? Evidently Jerry thinks he needs help. Read until you find out why I think so. I suppose Jack won't want to leave that new blue boat. Am I right? Finish the page and see.

Page 66. I wonder what brings the boys to the toy store. Read four sentences to find out. Is Jerry still on the right track? Finish the page and see. Will he never find Alice?

Oral language

Page 67. Now Jerry sees someone who really can help. Why? (Discuss dog's ability to scent.) I wonder if Jerry wants Jip's help. Read until you find out what he says to Jip. When dogs bark, they are trying to talk. Finish the page. Find out what Jip was trying to say. What do you think may happen in the story tomorrow?

ORAL READING

Organization. *Following events in sequence.* (Have pupils suggest the one important thing which happens on each page. Have them reread story to follow this simple outline.)

VOCABULARY ENRICHMENT AND EXTENSION

Synonymous meanings. Tell me an easy way to say *discover, enjoy, delighted, disappointed;* another way to say *after a while, a long time, all the time.*

WORD RECOGNITION TECHNIQUES

Phonics

Auditory-visual perception. *Phonetic parts.* Instead of saying "Here is Alice's coat," Mother said, "Here is— coat." (Write *her* as pupils suggest word.) Do you remember what I told you this part said? (Draw line under *er* and give sound if pupils do not remember.) How sharp are your ears? Listen as I say *Mother, Father.* Did you hear the part *er?* Can you read each word, draw a line under the part, and then tell us what the part says? (Write *Mother, Father* on board and have directions carried out. Continue with *away, boy, out.*)

Initial sounds. Remember that it takes two letters to begin the word —(write *the—The,* have words read, and then trace *th—Th*). If someone will show me how *this* begins, I will finish the word. (Continue with *that, then, but, came, doll, find, get, her, just, laughed, may, now, pony, rain, say, to, went.*)

Phonics

Final sounds. If I write *got,* all but the last letter, will you finish it? (Continue with *hop, not, cap, boat.*) Here are two new words. One says *let;* I will *let* you read. The other says *lap;* Jip jumped up onto my *lap.* (Write *let—lap* on board.) Which word says *let?* How do you know? The other word says—. How do you know?

SUPPLEMENTARY ACTIVITIES

1. *Workbook for Day In and Day Out,* pages **39, 40.**
2. Bulletin board.

The Toy Store

Independent word attack

Here is the toy store.
　Oh, what do you see?
You may look in the window.
　You may walk in to see
A pony, a rabbit,
　A kitten, a <u>duck</u>!
A little red <u>train</u>,
　And a big brown <u>truck</u>!

3. Independent reading.
   Molly, Pete, and Ginger, pages 11-16.
   My Little Red Story Book, pages 27-34. (Give help with the word *apple* on page 31.)

Unit 18: Can You Find Alice? (*cont.*)

Pp. 68-69

PREPARATION

Have the following materials ready for use:

Pocket Card Holder
Word Cards

132 do	156 home	472 then	494 was
139 not	457 just	479 into	496 surprise
148 what	461 away	480 city	501 find
150 going	467 for	485 that	504 say
151 good-by	469 new	493 again	

INITIAL PROCEDURE

Review of initial sounds

Vocabulary review. (Have in card holder all the cards listed above.) Find and bring me two words that begin like *nest;* two that begin like *sun;* two that begin like *across;* two that begin like *fun;* two that begin like *this;* the question word; the compound word; another word for *house;* a word which begins like *circle;* two that begin like *gate;* one that begins like *went;* one that begins like *dog;* the last word and tell me what it says.

Will Jip find Alice? Turn quickly to page 68 so that we may find out.

SILENT READING

Page 68. Here she is! Whose steps is she sitting on? Who found her? I am sure Jerry hasn't yet seen Alice when he talks at the top of the page. He doesn't trust Jip a bit. Read four lines to find out why I say that.

Jack has a much better opinion of Jip. Finish the page to find out what he thinks.

Page 69. Were we right when we said Alice was back home? Read two lines and find out. What a joke on Jerry to chase Alice all over town and then to find her at home!

Alice thinks she knows why Mother wants her. She asks Jerry two questions. Read until you find out what her questions are. Jerry answers Alice and talks to Jack. What does he say? How does Jack answer? Finish the page. What do Alice and Jerry do? What does Jack do?

ORAL READING

Rereading by page units. I will choose the people with the best ears and the best eyes to reread our story for us. The first one to find something in the picture on page 63 which begins like *but* (*bush*) may read the page for us. (Continue in similar fashion until the entire story has been reread.)

Audience reading

VOCABULARY ENRICHMENT AND EXTENSION

Extending speaking vocabulary. If Mother isn't going to the city, I know how Alice will feel. Do you? (*disappointed*) If she is going, and Alice has to hurry to get ready, I am sure Alice will be—(*excited*). What do we call the things Jerry found to keep him on the right track? (*clues*)

WORD RECOGNITION TECHNIQUES

Auditory-visual perception. *Phonetic parts.* Can you read the word I write, draw a line under the part you can hear and see, and then tell me what the part says? (Use *her, toy, out, say.*)

Phonics

Do you remember what Jerry kept repeating? Alice was here, but she is not here—(write *now* and have it read). This part in *now* (underline *ow*) says—. How sharp are your ears? *Bow-wow!* Did you hear the part *ow?* (Give sound.) Can you see the part? (Write *bow-wow* and have some pupil draw a line under each *ow*.)

Phonics

Final sounds. Listen as I say *man, green, rain.* What did your ears tell you about the way these words end? Let's see if we are right. (Write *man, green, rain* on board and direct attention to final *n*.) If I wanted to add another word to our list, should I add *can* or *coat?* Let's prove that *can* is the right choice. (Write *can* under words on board. Continue with *brown—blue, did—down, ran—red*.) If I write *train,* all but the last letter, will someone finish it? (Have someone finish *rabbit* and *jump*.)

SUPPLEMENTARY ACTIVITIES

1. *Workbook for Day In and Day Out,* pages 41, 42. Be sure directions are understood.
2. Bulletin board.

Vocabulary review in new context

My Store

I have a store,
A big toy store.
So come to my store and see.
In the window a train,
And a big airplane,
And red boats, one, two, three.

3. Independent reading.
   All in a Day, pages 12-19. (Give help with the word *stop* on page 15.)
   My Little Red Story Book, pages 35-44.
   We Work and Play (Scott, Foresman and Co.), pages 3-10. (Give help with the words *work,* page 3; and *Baby,* page 6.)
4. Textfilm for *Day In and Day Out,* Frames 19-20. See Textfilm manual for directions.

Pp. 70-76 # Unit 19: A Walk with Mother

New Vocabulary: mew

INITIAL PROCEDURE

Contents pages. Read the title of the new story. You will find out that Mother is not going to the city. Where is she going?

Guidance in locating page numbers

Our new story starts on page—. Page 70 is almost, but not quite, halfway through our book. How near can you come to page 70 with one turn?

SILENT READING

Page 70. Mother asks an exciting question. Read until you find out what it is. Have you any idea what the surprise might be?

Jerry and Alice answer Mother's question, and Alice asks another. Read until you find out what Alice's question is. Does Mother tell the surprise? Read three sentences and find out. Who gets tired first? Finish the page and see.

Page 71. On this page Mother gives three clues to the surprise. Can you read and find out all three?

Page 72. Remember the three clues. Now think. Could this kitten be the surprise? Why not?

Guidance in methods of word attack

You remember that Alice had this kind of coat. (Write *new*.) This part in *new* (draw a line under *ew*) says—(give sound of long *u*). Today the kitten says something which rhymes with *new*. (Write *mew*.) Think how the word begins. Remember that this part (draw a line under *ew*) says *ū*. All kittens say—.

When Jip said *bow-wow,* he was trying to say something else. Read four sentences. What was the kitten trying to say? Is Alice as smart as you are? Does she know why the kitten can't be the surprise? Finish the page and see.

Page 73. Is this Mac? Turn back to page 48 and see if you think it is. Now read two sentences and see if you were right. Now finish the page. Does Jerry think the dog is the surprise? Why not?

Page 74. Mother doesn't give away the surprise, but one of the pictures does. Read three sentences. I want to know exactly where the walk stops and why it stops there. The man tries to keep the surprise as long as he can. Read five sentences. What does he say? Now come the questions. What are they, and how does the man answer them?

Page 75. Remember the three clues to the surprise. Is the pony the answer? Do Alice and Jerry agree with you? Read six sentences and find out. Now finish the page. I want you to tell me how you think the children got up onto that pony. Be ready to read the line which gives the clue.

Look at the children's eyes. Can you think of two words which tell how the children feel? (*scared, frightened*) Which one is the more frightened? How can you tell? I hope they get over being frightened before the next page.

Page 76. On this page Jerry remembers something he saw on the day that he was making wishes. What did he remember? Read the whole page and see.

Will Alice and Jerry go on riding forever? What will happen?

Page 77. Can you tell the name of everything you see in this picture? What do we call cows and pigs and goats when they are all together? *Animals,* of course! Maybe that is why the title of the next part of our book is—.

ORAL READING

Organization. Mother, Alice, and Jerry start out for a walk. Who will read the page which tells about that? Mother gives three clues to the surprise. Who will read that page? (Continue to have story reread to follow a simple outline.)

Following
events in
sequence

VOCABULARY ENRICHMENT AND EXTENSION

Extending speaking vocabulary. Look carefully at the picture of the pony on page 76. What do we call the strap Jerry is holding?

(*reins* or *lines*) What do we call the straps on the pony's head? (*bridle*)

WORD RECOGNITION TECHNIQUES

Auditory-visual perception. *Phonetic parts.* This word (indicate *new*) says—, and the part (indicate *ew*) says—. (Repeat with *mew.* Then continue with *her, say, boy, now, out.*)

Phonics

Initial sounds. Two letters begin the word *she.* (Write *She—she;* trace the *sh* in each; then erase.) What do your ears tell you about *she* and *shell*? If someone will show me how *shell* begins, I will finish the word. (Continue with *sheep, shake, show;* then with *this, that, then.*)

Final sounds. Ran—red—rain! Which two words end with the same sound? Let's prove that you are right. (Write *ran—rain* and direct attention to final *n*. Repeat with *on—in—it.*) If I write *again,* all but the last letter, who will finish it?

Here are two new words. (Write *top—ten.*) One says *ten.* One says *top.* Which says *ten*? How do you know? Then the other word says—. (Repeat with *fat—fan.*)

SUPPLEMENTARY ACTIVITIES

1. *Workbook for Day In and Day Out,* pages 43, 44, 45, 46. Be sure directions on pages 44 and 46 are understood.
2. Bulletin board.

Independent word attack

Surprises

I like surprises.
Do you? Do you?
I want a surprise
That is blue, blue, blue.
A new blue coat
And a pretty blue <u>hat</u>!
The surprise I want
Is just that, that, that.

3. Independent reading.
   All in a Day, pages 20-29. (Give help with *we,* page 26.)

Molly, Pete, and Ginger, pages 17-24. (Give help with the sound word *Wuff* and the word *no* on page 22.)

My Little Red Story Book, pages 45-48.

We Work and Play, pages 15-18. (Give help with the word *funny* on page 18.)

4. Textfilm for *Day In and Day Out,* Frames 21-22. See Textfilm manual for directions.

5. Tests. Before beginning the next story, give the two informal tests in the Workbook. Pupils in average groups should make a score of at least 20 on the vocabulary test, page 47; and a score of at least 4 on the sentence-meaning test, page 48. At this point each child should be tested individually with the word cards for the new Primer vocabulary that has been introduced so far. (See page 159 of *Day In and Day Out.*)

Individual check on sight vocabulary

Unit 20: Little Goat

Pp. 77-83

NEW VOCABULARY:

am	are	goat	started
animals	ate	old	stopped

PREPARATION

Have the following materials ready for use:

Pocket Card Holder
Word Cards

508 stopped	509 ate	510 old	511 started	512 am	513 are

INITIAL PROCEDURE

Introducing new vocabulary. One morning Jerry and Father went away in the car. All at once the car—(write *stopped*). I know one thing about this word. It begins like—(write *store,* have the word read, trace *st,* and then erase). All at once the car st——. *Stopped,* of course! Watch how it begins. Watch the twin letters. Then when I write— (write *stopp*____), you will tell me to finish—.

Father was near a garage. So he went in for help. Before long the car—(write *started*). I know two things about this word. It begins

like—(pause for suggestion *stopped*). This part (draw a line under *ar*) says—(give sound of *ar*). Before long the car star——. *Started,* of course! If I write—(write *st*____) and add this part (add *ar*), you will know that the word says—. I discovered something. *Stopped* and *started* have very different meanings. They are—(*opposites*). Find the two word cards which are opposites, read them, and put them into the card holder.

While the garage man was working, he said to Jerry, "Who are you?" Jerry said—(write *I am Jerry*). Jump over the new word and let the sentence help you. Now find the word card *am* and put it into the card holder. If you forget the word *am* when it is all by itself, what can you do to help yourself? (*Read sentence.*)

Then the man said—(write *So you are Jerry*). In *started* this part said—(give sound of *ar* and draw a line under the *ar* in *are*). That is all there is to this new word. It says—. So if I write—(write *ar*) and add this letter (add *e*), the word will say—. Remember the part, and you will remember the word. (Put *are* in card holder and have the word card read.)

The man in the garage had white hair. So I know that—(write *He was old*). The name of this letter is ō. Think of the name of the letter, and you can get the new word. (Add word card *old* to card holder.)

By this time Jerry was hungry. He went into a restaurant with Father, and—(write *He ate and ate*). The name of this letter (indicate *a* in *ate*) is ā. Think of the name of the letter, and you can get the word. (Add word card *ate* to card holder.)

Bring me the two words which are opposite in meaning, and tell me what they say; the word in which you hear and see the part *ar;* the word in which the letter *o* says its name; the word in which the letter *a* says its name. Read the sentence in which you find the last word and tell me what the word says.

Do you remember the animals we saw in the last picture in our book? (Allow time to recall animal names.) The one we will read about today has a name which begins like—(write *go*), and it rhymes with—(write *coat*). It is a—(write *goat*).

Contents pages. (Use in usual way.)

SILENT READING

Page 78. (Allow time for enjoyment of picture.) Little Goat gets into mischief. Read three sentences. What is the first wrong thing he does?

I never knew a goat that didn't like to do this. (Write *eat* and have the word read.) Finish the page. Is this little goat like that?

Page 79. Little Goat won't eat that cap, will he? The first sentence is a—. Who will read the question aloud? I want to read the second

Purpose of a comma

sentence. Do you notice the comma? (Indicate comma and make one on board.) That comma tells me to pause just a little. Listen and see if I do. Will someone else read that sentence?

Now finish the page. What becomes of the big brown cap?

Pages 80-81. (Use procedures similar to those on page 79.)

Page 82. And now what have we behind the tree? Is Little Goat as smart as we are? Does he know that this is a kitten? Read three sentences and see.

I hope you know the word which is the opposite of *stopped*. You will need it. Now finish the page. How does Little Goat get along with eating that big ball?

Page 83. I hope you can read this sentence (indicate *I am Jerry*) because you will need this word. (Indicate *am*.) Maybe this kitten can't talk, but her "mew, mew, mew" means something. What is she trying to say? Read four lines and find out.

Does Little Goat give up, or is there a fight? Finish the page and see. This was certainly a joke on Little Goat, wasn't it? What do you think will happen the next time he sees a sleeping kitten? When he sees one awake?

ORAL READING

Setting standards for oral reading

Fluency-expression. (The rhythm of many of the lines in this story is apparent. Read a page or two for the children, to set the rhythmic pattern. Then have one of the best readers choose a page to set the standard for fluent phrase reading. After a good reader has read a page, have a less fluent reader try also.)

VOCABULARY ENRICHMENT AND EXTENSION

Descriptive words. The goat in our story was a frisky white goat. Can you add some other words to the word *goat* to make me see a very different kind of goat? (*old brown goat, big billy goat,* etc.)

WORD RECOGNITION TECHNIQUES

Phonics

Auditory-visual perception. *Phonetic parts.* (Write the following words on board, one at a time. Have a word read, have a line drawn under the phonetic part, and have the part named: *are, started, day, out, now, boy, her, new, garden.*)

Initial sounds. If I want to write the word *kite,* I write it this way (write *kite*), and it begins like this. (Trace *k;* then erase word.) If someone will begin *kitten* for me, I will finish the word. (Continue with *ball, came, duck, find, goat, her, Jack, laughed, mew, new, puppy, rain, say, too, will, that, she.*)

Final sounds. If I write the word *goat,* all but the last letter, who will finish it? (Continue with *cap, garden, rain, Jip, went.*)

Here are two new words. (Write *nap—nut.*) One says *nut;* I ate a *nut.* One says *nap;* I took a *nap.* Which says *nap?* How do you know? The other word says—. (Repeat procedure with *bun—bat.*)

SUPPLEMENTARY ACTIVITIES

1. *Workbook for Day In and Day Out,* pages 49, 50, 51, 52. Be sure directions on page 52 are clearly understood.
2. Bulletin board.

Vocabulary review in new context

Little Goat

Little Goat started out
For a walk one day.
He stopped at my house
And wanted to play.

He ate my doll
And my little red boat.
And then he started
On my old brown coat.

"Here, Mac! Here, Mac!"
I started to say.
Little Goat stopped eating
And ran away.

3. Independent reading.
All in a Day, pages 30-41. (Give help with *fun*, page 30.)
Molly, Pete, and Ginger, pages 25-28. (Give help with the words *cakes*, page 25; and *has*, page 28.)
My Little Blue Story Book (Ginn and Co.), pages 3-12. (Give help with the words *we* and *fast* on page 7.)
We Work and Play, pages 23-26.

4. Textfilm for *Day In and Day Out*, Frames 23-24. See Textfilm manual for directions.

Unit 21: The Little Duck

Pp. 84-89

NEW VOCABULARY: cluck could quack talk
cock-a-doodle-doo hen rooster tweet

PREPARATION

Have the following materials ready for use:

Pocket Card Holder
Word Cards

96 kitten	505 mew	517 cluck	521 quack
463 bird	514 talk	518 tweet	
466 duck	515 could	519 rooster	
484 walk	516 hen	520 cock-a-doodle-doo	

INITIAL PROCEDURE

Introducing new vocabulary. (Have the following sentences on board.)

He <u>could</u> not walk.

He could not <u>talk</u>.

One day Jerry hurt his foot. It was hurt so badly that—(sentence 1; use usual techniques for *could*). Take a good eye picture of *could*. Only smart people remember the word *could*. Are you one of those people? Then when I write—(write *coul*_____), you will tell me to finish—. And if you forget what this word says (add word card *could* to card holder), you will have sense enough to read the sentence and find out that it says—.

Jerry was crying so hard that when Mother asked him how the accident happened—(sentence 2). You know how this word begins. (Indicate *talk*.) It rhymes with—(indicate *walk*). *Walk, t*—! *Talk,* of course! If I begin my word this way (write *t*_____), you will tell me to finish—. But if I begin like this (write *w*_____), you will tell me to finish—. (Add *talk* and *walk* to card holder.)

Contents pages. Find out from the title what animal we will read about today. On what page will our story begin? Who can write 84 on the board? We are halfway through our book. Which will you be, a forward or a backward turner?

Guidance in methods of word attack

Guidance in locating page numbers

SILENT READING

Page 84. (Allow time for enjoyment of pictures.) Read the title and the first two sentences. Find out what the little duck did and what he saw. The little duck—(write *stopped* and have the word read). Read two more sentences. Find out why he stopped. What do you notice about the next sentence? Read with your eyes first. Now who can read that sentence as if it were all on one line? Now the little duck makes a—(write *wish* and have the word read). Read until you find out what the wish is. Does his wish come true? Finish the page and see. Now suppose you give me a chance to read the page for you. (Read to bring out rhythm.)

Independent
word attack—
hen, cluck

Page 85. Whom does the little duck see now? You know how *hen* begins. How many times can you find the word? What does a hen say? Can you find the word *cluck?* How many times? Now read the page. Does the little duck make another wish? Does his wish come true?

Page 86. Of course, you know this word. (Write *two.*) Here is a new word, and it says *sweet.* (Write *sweet.*) The new word we have

Guidance in
methods of
word attack

on this page begins like *two* and rhymes with *sweet.* (Write *Tweet.*) Now think! *Sweet, tw——*! *Tweet,* of course! Who do you think will say *tweet?* Now read the page. Does the little duck wish again? Does he get his wish?

Page 87. And who is this crowing? Can we find the word *rooster?* How many times? What does a rooster say? How many times can

Independent
word attack—
rooster, quack,
cock-a-doodle-doo

you find the long word *cock-a-doodle-doo?* I hope the little duck doesn't wish to say that. Read the page to see if he does.

Page 88. The little duck is sad. Read the page and find out why.

Page 89. I hope you know what sound a duck makes. Can you find the word *quack?* I wonder if the little duck can learn to say that. Read and see. Why do you think the little duck could not say *quack* when he started out on his walk?

ORAL READING

Rereading by page units. The one who can read the name of this animal (put the word card *kitten* in card holder) and can find the word card which tells what this animal says, may read the page in the story that tells about it. (Continue in the same way with other animal names.)

VOCABULARY ENRICHMENT AND EXTENSION

Extending speaking vocabulary. What is another name for a baby duck? (*duckling*) What kind of feet has a duck? (*web*) A baby duck is not covered with feathers, but with—(*down*).

WORD RECOGNITION TECHNIQUES

Accurate word recognition. Are you ready to play "Magic"? What does this word say? (Write *walk.*) Close your eyes. The word has

changed. What does it say now? (Change *walk* to *talk*. Continue with
*eat—ate, started—stopped, goat—coat, mew—new, say—stay, get—got,
here—her*.)

Auditory-visual perception. *Initial sounds.* (Have pupils show how
kitten, duck, hen, rooster, bird, goat begin. Then finish each word.)

Phonics

Final sounds. If I write *goat*, all but the last letter, who will finish
it for me? (Continue with *hen, jump, garden, cap, tweet*.)

Listen as I say *old, could, rooster*. My ears tell me that two of those
words end with the same sound. Which two are they? Let's prove
that you are right. (Write *old* and *could* on board and call attention
to final *d*.) If I want to add a word to our list, shall I add *find* or *wish*?
bird or *duck*? (Add *find* and *bird* to list.) If I were to write *did*, all
but the last letter, could you finish the word?

SUPPLEMENTARY ACTIVITIES

1. *Workbook for Day In and Day Out*, pages 53, 54, 55, 56.
2. Bulletin board.

**Vocabulary
review in
new context**

What Can He Say?

You like little ducks
That say, "Quack, quack!"
   And kittens that say, "Mew, mew!"
But the little brown rabbit
That lives in a hole,
   What can HE say to you?

3. Independent reading.
    All in a Day, pages 42-51.
    Molly, Pete, and Ginger, pages 29-34. (Give help with the words
        make, page 31; and *bigger*, page 33.)
    My Little Blue Story Book, pages 13-16. (Give help with the
        words *pie*, page 13; *funny* and *apple*, page 16.)
    Ned and Nancy, pages 41-45. (Give help with the word *school*
        on page 41.)
    We Work and Play, pages 35-38.
4. Textfilm for *Day In and Day Out*, Frames 25-26. See Textfilm
manual for directions.

Unit 22: Little Jack Rabbit

Pp. 90-93

NEW VOCABULARY: all   nest   run
                  lived   played   white

PREPARATION

Have the following materials ready for use:

Pocket Card Holder
Word Cards

159 this	464 came	492 will	522 lived	526 white
161 went	468 but	494 was	523 nest	
459 so	472 then	512 am	524 Run	
461 away	490 stay	513 are	525 all	

INITIAL PROCEDURE

Vocabulary review. (Have all word cards, listed above, in card holder, except *all, lived, nest, Run,* and *white.*)

Drill on carrier words

How quickly can you read and take from the card holder three words which begin like *window?* two which begin like *the?* two in which you hear this part (write *ay*)? one in which you hear this part (write *ar*)? one that ends like *rabbit?* one that begins like *coat?* one that rhymes with *go?* the last word and tell me what it says? Now how quickly can you use in a sentence the word or words you hold in your hand and return them to the card holder?

Introducing new vocabulary. (Have the following sentences on board. Add underscored words to card holder as each sentence is read.)

> You are all here.
> She saw a nest.
> A mother bird lived in that nest.
> Run away, Jip, run away.

Everyone is here this morning. I can say that in another way, I might say—(sentence 1). Jump over the new word and let the sentence help you. The new word is—. Watch the twin letters. Then if I write—(write *all*), the word will say—. If I begin with a capital letter (write *All*), it will still say—.

One morning Alice was in the garden. She looked up into a tree, and—(sentence 2; use usual techniques for *nest*). If I write—(write *ne*____), you will tell me to finish—. Of course, that nest belonged to someone. (Sentence 3. Use usual techniques for *lived*.) Take a good eye picture of this letter. (Indicate *v*.) Then when I write—(write *liv*____), you will tell me to finish—.

Several days later Alice saw Mother Bird trying to teach her baby birds to fly. Jip came into the garden, and Alice said—(sentence 4; use usual techniques for *run*). Take a careful eye picture of this letter. (Indicate *u*.) Then when I write—(write *Ru*____), you will tell me to finish—.

Find and read the word in the card holder which means "everyone"; the word which is the name for a bird's home; the word which begins and ends like *ran,* but doesn't say *ran,* the word which tells what Mother Bird did in the nest.

Contents pages. (Have title read, and page number read and written on board. Explain that a jack rabbit is a large, wild rabbit with long ears and strong hind legs.) I have given you two clues. How quickly can you turn to page 90 and be ready to prove that the rabbit you see is a jack rabbit?

SILENT READING

Page 90. It looks to me as if someone else lives in the—(indicate the word card *nest* and have it read) besides Mother Rabbit. (Discuss the making of a rabbit nest, how it is lined with fur from the mother rabbit, etc.)

The first two sentences tell the same story as the picture. Read and see if you agree with me.

Have you discovered the one little rabbit who is hanging his head? Read the next two sentences and find out what is the matter. What does he want? Will he get it? Finish the page and see. Will he mind

(marginal notes:)

Guidance in methods of word attack

Building background

his mother? I think the picture on the next page answers that, don't you?

Page 91. How did Jack Rabbit get away without Mother Rabbit's seeing him? Find the answer in the first sentence. The minute his mother is gone, what does he say? Read until you find out. How did he go, and where did he go? Finish the page and see. What a lovely garden! But that picture makes me know that something unpleasant may happen. Do you see the clue that I see? (*sky*)

Page 92. (Discuss difference in size between the tame rabbits and the baby jack rabbit. Identify the hutch, etc.) How many two-line sentences can you discover on this page? Now read five sentences. Will Jack Rabbit stay in the garden? Now finish the page. In the last sentence there is a color word which is new. But you can get it. It begins like *what*. (Add word card *white* to card holder.) Be sure to keep your eye on the clue I told you about. How does the sky look now? on the next page?

Page 93. Jack Rabbit was not quite sure he liked the two white rabbits. What does he do first? Read until you find out. Then what does he say to them?

This word (write *look*) says—. And now it says—(add *ed*). So, of course, this word says—(write *play*). And now it says—(add *ed*). Finish the page. How did the three rabbits spend the rest of the morning? I hope Jack Rabbit knows enough to go home before the storm. Don't you?

ORAL READING

Rereading by page units. The one who can read these two cards (hold up word cards *lived* and *nest*) may read the page of the story on which you find them. The one who can read this card (hold up *run*) may read the next page. The one who knows another word for *everyone* (hold up word card *all*) may read page 92. And the one who knows this word (indicate *played* on board) may read page 93.

VOCABULARY ENRICHMENT AND EXTENSION

Descriptive words. Suppose I say just the word *rabbit*. Can you add some words to the word *rabbit* to turn my rabbit into a jack rabbit? (*a big rabbit with very long ears, a brown rabbit with strong back legs,* etc.)

WORD RECOGNITION TECHNIQUES

Verbs ending in s, ed, ing

Word structure. Can you make words grow? This word (write *play*) says—. Who can make it say *plays? played? playing?* (Repeat with *walk* and *jump.*)

Auditory-visual perception. *Initial sounds.* The question word is— (write *what—What* on board). It takes two letters to begin the word *What.* (Trace *wh,* then *Wh,* and erase words.) Then how does the word *white* begin? If someone will show me, I will finish the word for you. (Continue with *run, lived, nest, goat, talk, could, she, that.*)

Phonics

Final sounds. Listen as I say *old, nest, find.* Which words end with the same sound? (Continue as in previous units. Write the following words on board, omitting the last letter in each; have pupils add the last letter as soon as you say each word and write it on board: *run, nest, could, hop, rain, just, jump, good.*)

SUPPLEMENTARY ACTIVITIES

1. *Workbook for Day In and Day Out,* pages 57, 58. Work out with children one or two rhymes on page 58 if necessary.

2. Bulletin board.

Independent word attack

Rabbits

I like rabbits,
The tame white rabbits
That live in a house
In my garden.
And the wild brown rabbits
That live in holes
In the green grass.
I like all rabbits
With fur coats
And tails
Like little balls.

3. Independent reading.

All in a Day, pages 52-61. (Give help with the word *make,* page 58.)

My Little Blue Story Book, pages 17-22. (Give help with the words *Bunny,* page 18; *cakes* and *dinner,* page 20.)

We Come and Go, pages 17-22.

Unit 23: Little Jack Rabbit (cont.)

Pp. 94-97

NEW VOCABULARY: gate   his   night   open

PREPARATION

Have the following materials ready for use:

Pocket Card Holder
Word Cards

51 And	459 So	503 Now	524 Run
76 The	461 Away	508 stopped	526 white
94 It	468 But	509 ate	528 gate
103 Little	483 eat	511 started	529 open
123 You	485 That	513 are	530 his
148 What	490 stay	515 could	

INITIAL PROCEDURE

Drill on carrier words

Vocabulary review. (Have all capitalized words, listed above, in two columns in card holder.) Here are words we have known for a long time, but this morning they begin with capital letters. Suppose we play "One, Two, Three! How Many for Me?" to see how well you know them. (Repeat game several times until capitalized forms become familiar.)

I know these two words because they are opposites. (Add *started—stopped* to card holder and have them read.) I can read these two words because I know the name of the first letter in each word. (Add *eat—ate*.) I know this word because I hear and see the part—(write *ay* on board and put word card *stay* in card holder). I know this word because I hear and see the part—(write *ar* and add word card *are* to card holder). I know this color because it begins like *what*. (Add *white*.) And here is the word which only smart people remember. (Add *could*.) I wish you could be one of those people. If you heard my clue, you could be. Who can read all the cards?

Introducing new vocabulary. (Have the following on the board.)

a garden <u>gate</u>
The garden gate was <u>open</u>.
He ran in at the open gate.
It was not <u>his</u> house.

Around the garden to which Jack Rabbit came, there was a fence. In the fence there was a—(write *gate*). You know how the word begins, but did you discover the little word inside the bigger word? (Draw a line under *ate* in *gate*.) So, of course, the big word says—. Because the gate opened into a garden, it was—(have phrase *a garden gate* read). The garden gate was supposed to be closed, but this morning—(sentence 1). If you remember that the name of this letter is—(indicate *o*), you won't have any trouble with the new word. When Jack Rabbit saw the open gate, he did this—(sentence 2). Of course, he saw the rabbit hutch, but he knew that—(sentence 3). You know how this word begins. (Indicate *his*.) Did you discover the little word inside? (Draw a line under *is* in *his*.) Of course, the word is—, and the sentence says—. (Add word cards for *gate, open,* and *his* to card holder. Have words and sentences reread.)

Will Jack Rabbit play until the storm comes, and he is cold and wet? Turn quickly to page 94 and see.

SILENT READING

Page 94. Will that dog have rabbit for dinner? Read until you find out what happens the minute the dog begins to bark. The two white rabbits do all the talking. What do they say? They know how to take care of themselves. Finish the page to see what they do. (Have pupils decide why Jack Rabbit doesn't run into the hutch, too.)

Page 95. The white rabbits ran home. I suppose Jack will look for his home, too. Will he find it? Read four sentences to see. No rabbit can keep running forever. What happens when Jack Rabbit cannot run any longer? Finish the page to see. One danger is over. What danger is that? Another danger has started, the danger we have been expecting. What is that? What do you think may happen to Jack Rabbit now?

Page 96. We might have known that Mother Rabbit would be looking for her baby. How does Jack feel at the top of the page? at the bottom? Is the danger over? How can you tell?

Independent word attack— night

I think I know what time it is now. How can you tell? Then the first word on page 96 says—. Can you find *night* again when it begins with a small letter? The first three sentences tell about that unhappy rabbit at the top of the page. Has he found his mother yet? Read and see.

There are three clues by which Jack Rabbit knows that it is his mother hopping toward him. Read until you find how he knew it was his mother. Now can you read the last sentence and be as surprised and happy as Jack?

Page 97. Think what your mother might do if you ran away. Then read the first sentence. Be ready to show us what Mother Rabbit did and how she did it.

Is Mother Rabbit so happy to see Jack that she forgets to scold? Read four sentences to find out.

Even with such a scolding, how does Jack Rabbit feel? Read two sentences to find out. I think Jack Rabbit has learned a lesson. Finish the page and find out what may happen from this day on.

ORAL READING

Organization. (Have pupils suggest a page-by-page outline such as the following. Have entire story reread to follow outline. Page 90: *Jack wants to run away.* Page 91: *Jack runs away.* Page 92: *Jack comes to a garden.* Page 93: *He plays with the white rabbits.* Page

Following events in sequence

94: *The dog comes.* Page 95: *Jack is lost.* Page 96: *He finds his mother.* Page 97: *Jack and Mother run home.*)

VOCABULARY ENRICHMENT AND EXTENSION

Descriptive words. This morning we read about two kinds of gates. (*the garden gate, the open gate*) How many other kinds of gates do you know about? (*barnyard gate, railroad gates, swinging gate,* etc.)

WORD RECOGNITION TECHNIQUES

Little words
in big words

Word structure. I will write a word. Can you read the word? Can you discover a little word inside the big word? Can you read the little word and draw a line under it? (Use the following words: *ball, gate, his, into, that.*)

Auditory-visual perception. *Phonetic parts.* I will write a word for each of you. Can you read the word, draw a line under the part you hear and see in the word, and then tell us what the part says? (Use the following words: *play, rooster, are, new, now, boy, out.*)

Phonics

Final consonants. If I write *night,* all but the last letter, will you finish it? (Continue with *open, nest, old, hop.*)

I will write two new words. One will say *help;* you can *help* Mother. The other will say *held;* I *held* your coat for you. Watch carefully as I write. Which word says *help?* How do you know? What does the other word say? (Repeat with *pan* and *pat.*)

SUPPLEMENTARY ACTIVITIES

1. *Workbook for Day In and Day Out,* pages 59, 60. Be sure directions are understood. Supervise one or two items on each page if necessary.

2. Bulletin board.

Independent
word attack

One Night

I ran down to the garden gate.
Night had come,
And it was late.

I looked up, and what did I see?
The moon and the stars,
Looking down at me!

3. Independent reading.
   All in a Day, pages 62-71.
   Molly, Pete, and Ginger, pages 61-66. (Give help with the word
   we on page 64.)
   My Little Blue Story Book, pages 23-32.
   We Work and Play, pages 39-42. (Give help with the words
   makes, page 39; and *yellow,* page 41.)

4. Textfilm for *Day In and Day Out,* Frames 27-28. See Textfilm
manual for directions.

Unit 24: A Good Breakfast   Pp. 98-104

NEW VOCABULARY: barnyard   cow   pig
                breakfast   moo   wee

PREPARATION

Have the following materials ready for use:

Pocket Card Holder
Word Cards

465 out	493 again	506 animal	511 started	532 breakfast
490 stay	497 get	508 stopped	525 All	537 barnyard

INITIAL PROCEDURE

Vocabulary review. (Have all word cards listed above, except
barnyard and *breakfast,* in card holder.)

Find and read for me the two words in the card holder which have opposite meanings; the word which means "everyone"; another name for a cow, a pig, or a horse; a word from the title of our book; the one which means the opposite of *go;* the one which begins and ends like *got,* but doesn't say *got.* I washed my hands; then I washed them over. Show me the word I might have used instead of *over.* Now how quickly can you climb up and down the word ladder?

Word concepts

Introducing new vocabulary. (Have the following sentences on the board.)

I had a good <u>breakfast</u>.
This is a <u>barnyard</u>.

This morning—(sentence 1). I know something about this new word. It takes two letters to start this word (trace *br*), and it begins like *brown.* I had a good br——. *Breakfast,* of course! If I begin my word this way (write *br;* then add *eak*), you will tell me to finish the word—. But if I begin like this (write *br*) and then add the part which says *ow* (give sound and add *ow*), you will tell me to finish—(*brown*).

Guidance in methods of word attack

I know a man who lives on a farm. Behind his house he has a big red *barn.* (Write *barn.*) Can you find a part you know in that word? Can you draw a line under the part and tell what it says? Now you know everything there is to know about the word *barn.* You know the sound with which it begins. You know what the part says. You know the sound with which the word ends.

Compound words

The barn is in the middle of a big *yard.* (Add *yard* to *barn.*) So the man says—(sentence 2). *Barnyard* is two words put together. So it is a—(*compound word*). Now watch as I put word cards for the two new words into the card holder. Which word begins like *brown?* What does it say? Which is the compound? What does it say?

Contents pages. (Use in usual way.)

SILENT READING

Independent word attack— pig

Page 98. Of course, you know this animal. You know how the word *pig* begins and ends. How many times can you find it? Where do you think his good breakfast will come from?

Maybe that little pig won't get into mischief. Maybe he will stop at the gate. Read the title and four sentences and see. Finish the page. Did things turn out the way we thought they would?

Page 99. I hope you remember what a hen says. (Write *cluck.*) Now read four sentences. What happens when the white hen comes to the gate?

You know how this word begins. (Write *wee.*) Now make it rhyme with—(write *see* under *wee*), and you can find out for yourselves what sound the little pig makes. Will the little pig chase the hen from the garden? Finish the page and see.

Page 100. (Call attention to the page number and have *100* written on board by some child.) There won't be much left of this garden if this keeps on, will there? You know all there is to know about this word. (Write *cow.*) You know the sound with which it begins, and you know that this part says—(draw a line under *ow*). So the word is—. How many times can you find it? You know this word. (Write *too.*) Now make this word rhyme with it, and you will know what sound a cow makes. (Write *moo* under *too.*)

Guidance in methods of word attack

Now read the whole page. What happens when the cow comes to the gate?

Page 101. (Follow usual procedure.) What do you suppose may happen before long? Turn the page and see if you are right.

Page 102. (Allow time for enjoyment of picture.) When the man looked into that garden, he didn't miss a thing. Read five lines. See if you agree with me. What would you say to those animals? What does the man say? Finish the page to see if you would both say the same things.

Page 103. I don't believe those animals intend to mind. Read the page. Why do I think so? In the meantime, what do you think the man will do? Turn and see if he does.

Page 104. No more good breakfasts! Read until you find out what the pig says; the pony; the hen; the cow. Has the farmer learned a lesson? Finish the page and see.

Page 105. It isn't hard to tell what the next part of our book will be about. I hope you have discovered something interesting on that doll's cap. If you have, I will tell you her name. It is Betsy Lee. Now can you read the title? Do you like that name for a doll?

ORAL READING

Following
events in
sequence

Organization. (Have pupils suggest a simple outline, as in Unit 23. Have story reread to follow simple outline.)

VOCABULARY ENRICHMENT AND EXTENSION

Extending speaking vocabulary. The man who left his garden gate open was—(*careless*). I am sure he has learned to be—(*careful*). The animals in the garden felt—(*happy*). When the gate was closed, they felt—(*unhappy*). What is another way of saying "everyone" (*all*)? "after a while" (*by and by*)? "all the time" (*day in and day out*)?

Opposites

Word concepts. I will write a word. Read the word and tell me a word opposite in meaning. (Use *night, he, her, open, play, run, started, old, find, stay.*)

WORD RECOGNITION TECHNIQUES

Phonics

Auditory-visual perception. *Phonetic parts.* This word says—(write *too*). And this part in the word says $\bar{oo}$. (Draw a line under *oo* as you give sound.) Can you hear and see a part in this word? (Write *moo;* then *rooster.* In *rooster,* have pupils also find the part *er.*) Here is another new word we had today. Read the word; then draw a line under the part and tell me what it says. (Write *cow.*)

Compound
words

Word structure. We found out that *barnyard* was a—(*compound word*). Watch me draw a line between the word *barn* and the word *yard* to show that there are two words in the big word *barnyard.* (Carry out directions.) Let's have fun making more compound words. If I put—(write *run*) and—(write *away*) together, the compound word will say—. Who can draw a line between the two words which make *runaway?* (Continue with *greenhouse, dollhouse,* etc.)

SUPPLEMENTARY ACTIVITIES

1. *Workbook for Day In and Day Out,* pages 61, 62, 63, 64. Be sure the first two pictures on page 61 are identified as an auto *jack* and a *jug;* pictures 4, 8, 9 on page 62 as *May, pan,* and *plate.*

2. Bulletin board.

Animals

Independent
word attack

I like animals
That live in barnyards.
Cows and pigs and goats,
    And mother sheep
With all the little lambs!

    At night
I like to see the cows
Walk into the big red barn.
        One by one,
        Two by two!
The cows have good milk for me.
Milk for my breakfast!

3. Independent reading.
    Molly, Pete, and Ginger, pages 35-40. (Give help with the
        words *there,* page 39; and *car,* page 40.)
    My Little Blue Story Book, pages 33-40. (Give help with the
        words *chair,* page 34; and *work,* page 35.)
    Under the Tree (Silver Burdett Co.), pages 9-13. (Give help
        with the word *stop* on page 12.)
    We Work and Play, pages 47-50.
4. Textfilm for *Day In and Day Out,* Frames 29-30. See Textfilm
manual for directions.
5. Tests. Before beginning the next unit, give the two informal
tests on pages 65 and 66 of the Workbook. Pupils are to be given a
score of 1 for each item marked correctly. Pupils in average groups
should make a score of at least 20 on the vocabulary test; 4 on the
sentence-meaning test. It is important at this point that each child
be tested individually with the word cards for the new vocabulary
that has been introduced so far in the Primer. (See pages 159-60 of
Day In and Day Out.)

Individual check
on sight
vocabulary

Pp. 105-9 Unit 25: The New Doll

NEW VOCABULARY: Betsy   Lee   very   word

PREPARATION

Have the following materials ready for use:

Pocket Card Holder
Word Cards:

131 did	472 Then	504 say	514 talk
161 went	494 was	509 ate	515 could
459 So	498 wish	512 am	540 very
465 out	502 her	513 are	541 word

INITIAL PROCEDURE

Vocabulary review. (Have the following sentences on board. Add underscored words to card holder as soon as a sentence is read.)

Drill on
carrier words

This morning
Mother ate her breakfast.
Then she went out to the garden.
I wish I could talk to her.
So here you are.
She did not say a word.
I am so happy to see you.
It was a very, very pretty garden.

Mother had a big surprise today. This is the way it happened. (Sentences 1, 2.) As she worked among her flowers, Mother thought of Grandmother, and she said to herself—(sentence 3). Just then someone said—(sentence 4). Mother looked up, and there was Grandmother.

Introducing new vocabulary. For a minute Mother was so surprised that—(sentence 5; use usual techniques for *word*).

Of course, when Mother recovered from her surprise, she said—(sentence 6). Then Mother showed Grandmother her garden. (Sentence 7.) A word in this sentence begins like *valentine* and *vacation*. I see it two times. Mother's garden was more than pretty. It was v—— pretty. *Very,* of course! Now read the sentence. If I write—(write v——), you will tell me to finish the word—. (Have each card in the card holder matched with the identical word in the sentence on board. Have each word and sentence reread.)

Guidance in
methods of
word attack

The title of the next part of our book is the name of a doll. Do you remember her name?

Contents pages. I know something more about Betsy Lee when I read the title of the next story. Do you? What page will the story begin on? Who can write *106* on the board? Remember that 106 is more than halfway through our book. Your first turn must be a big one. How close can you come to page 106?

Guidance in
locating page
numbers

SILENT READING

Oral language

Page 106. (Allow time for discussion of postman's uniform, etc.) The first two sentences remind me of something Mother did this morning. Read and see why. Read until you find out what the man did and what he said. Who is Alice White? Finish the page and see. We have been reading about Alice all this time, and we didn't even know her last name! What is Jerry's whole name? Mother's real name? Father's?

Page 107. Alice knew enough to show Mother the box before she opened it. Read until you know what Alice said when she saw that lovely doll. Now finish the page. Be ready to tell exactly how that doll looked. Do you think the doll has a name?

Page 108. Alice has two different ideas on this page. Read four sentences. What was her first idea? Now read four more sentences. What is her second idea? Finish the page. What does Mother think of the name?

Page 109. Alice talks to Betsy Lee as if she were another little girl. Read four sentences. What does she say? Can Betsy Lee talk?

You won't have to read far to find out. Alice tried again. Finish the page and find out what happens. Well, Betsy Lee may be a nice doll, but she certainly doesn't seem to be a talking one. What do you think may happen in the story tomorrow?

ORAL READING

Rereading by page units. Who will read the page where we discover Alice's whole name? the one on which we find this new word (indicate *very*)? the one where the new doll gets a name? the one where Alice wishes that Betsy Lee could talk?

WORD RECOGNITION TECHNIQUES

Drill on
carrier words

Accurate word recognition. (With this unit, begin a systematic review of carrier words in both the Preprimer and the Primer vocabularies. Watch carefully for any carrier words not automatically recognized; give extra attention to these words. Play "Magic" as in previous units with the following words: *walk, walked, want, wanted, went, will, wish, with, was, wee, word.*)

Auditory-visual perception. *Initial sounds.* (With this unit, begin a consistent review of initial consonant sounds. Diagnose pupil ability to write the letter or letters which represent initial consonant sounds.) If someone will show me how *Betsy* begins, I will finish the word for you. (Continue with *barnyard, coat, doll, find, very, big, cap, did, father.*)

Phonics

Final sounds. Listen as I say *Jerry, puppy, happy.* My ears told me that these words end with the same sound. Let's see if they do. (Write the three words on the board, directing attention to the final *y.*) If I want to add another word which ends like *Jerry,* shall I add *started* or *pretty*? Let's prove that *pretty* is the right choice. (Write *pretty* on board. Continue with *Betsy, city, very.*)

If I write *word,* all but the last letter, will you finish it? (Continue with *goat, old, green, jump.*)

I will write two new words on the board. One says *pet.* One says *pen.* Which one says *pen*? How do you know? Then the other word says—. (Repeat procedure with *ship* and *shed.*)

SUPPLEMENTARY ACTIVITIES

1. *Workbook for Day In and Day Out,* pages 67, 68, 69, 70.
2. Bulletin board.

In the Box

I like surprises in boxes.
Do you?
Here is a box with surprises
One, two.

Open the box,
And what do you see?
Two bird houses
For one big tree!

Vocabulary
review in
new context

3. Independent reading.
   Molly, Pete, and Ginger, pages 41-46. (Give help with the words *honk,* page 44; and *our,* page 46.)
   Under the Tree, pages 20-25. (Give help with the word *Baby* on page 20.)
   We Come and Go, pages 23-28. (Give help with the word *work* on page 25.)

Unit 26: In the Garden

Pp. 110-12

NEW VOCABULARY: gave

PREPARATION

Have the following materials ready for use:

Pocket Card Holder
Word Cards: 494 was   540 very   542 gave

INITIAL PROCEDURE

Vocabulary review. (Have these phrases on the board.)

By and by	Do you see	Alice walked
I will not	Her coat	You can
Alice went	His home	Away went
He lived	Just then	I wish
You have	She did not	Come again

Drill on sentence beginnings

Here are ways in which sentences often begin. Who can come to the board, draw a line under one of the sentence beginnings, read it, and then use it to begin a sentence of his own?

Introducing new vocabulary. (Have the following sentences on the board.)

I gave her a book.
It was a very pretty book.

Guidance in methods of word attack

(Give an attractive book to some girl in the group.) This sentence (indicate sentence 1) tells exactly what I did. You know how this word begins. (Indicate *book*.) It rhymes with *look*. So it says—. You know that this word (indicate *gave*) begins like *go*. This letter says its name, as it does in *ate*. (Indicate *a* in *gave*.) Now think. I ga—— her a book. Of course, the new word is—. (Put word card *gave* in card holder.) If I write—(write *ga*____), you will tell me to finish—. Now tell me what kind of book it was. (Sentence 2.) Here are two more words we must remember. (Add word cards for *was* and *very* to card holder. Have the three words read several times.)

Contents pages. (Use in usual way.)

SILENT READING

Page 110. What a pretty garden! It looks as if Betsy Lee can walk almost as well as Alice, doesn't it?

Read the title and the first two sentences. I think I know how long it was before Alice made up her mind to leave the house. See if you can find out.

Working for fluency

Alice makes up a jingle. Can you jingle off the next two sentences just as she does? I don't believe she intended to make up that jingle.

It was an accident. But after she said it once, how did she feel about it? Read four lines and find out. Now finish the page and get her into the garden.

Page 111. Here is a visitor I wouldn't want in my garden. Or maybe she isn't a visitor. Read the first sentence to see if she is. What does Alice say to Mother Rabbit? Read until you find out. Does Mother Rabbit like Betsy Lee's blue coat so well that she will stay to play with her? Read until you find out.

Alice is sure she knows why Mother Rabbit hopped away. Finish the page and find out the reason.

Page 112. I hope you know what birds say. (Write *tweet* and have the word read.) Is this bird a visitor to the garden? Read until you find out. Alice praises, or compliments, Brown Bird. Read until you find out what she praises him for. Does Brown Bird stay to hear what she says? Read the next sentence to see. Alice is a bit disappointed in Betsy Lee. Finish the page to find out why.

Page 113. The picture and the title give away a secret. Where will Alice and Betsy Lee go next?

ORAL READING

Organization. (Write this simple outline on board.)

Following events in sequence

_____Alice saw Brown Bird.
_____Alice went to the garden.
_____Alice saw Mother Rabbit.

Which sentence tells what happened first? Will someone number that sentence *1* for us? Who will read the page which goes with that sentence? (Continue using the same procedure with the other two sentences.)

VOCABULARY ENRICHMENT AND EXTENSION

Extending speaking vocabulary. Alice compliments Brown Bird on being able to sing and fly. What do you do when you compliment someone? (*praise*) But she is disappointed in Betsy Lee. How do you feel when you are disappointed?

WORD RECOGNITION TECHNIQUES

Accurate word recognition. (Play "Magic" with the following words, watching carefully for words which cause trouble: *the, three, this, that, then; said, saw, see, something, so, surprise, say*.)

Auditory-visual perception. *Initial sounds.* (Have pupils show how each of the following words begin; finish each word for them as soon as initial consonant is written: *garden, her, just, kitten, laughed, very*.)

Phonics

Final sounds. Listen as I say *very, pretty, word*. Which two words shall I write on the board because they end with the same sound? (When *very* and *pretty* have been written, direct attention to final *y*.) If I want to add another word which ends like *very*, shall I add *Alice* or *Betsy*? If I write *Betsy*, all but the last letter, will you finish it? (Continue with *Jerry, again, went, hop, word*.)

I will write two new words. One will say *merry*. One will say *mad*. Which one says *merry*? How do you know? The other word says—. (Continue with *chin—chop, hat—hand*.)

SUPPLEMENTARY ACTIVITIES

1. *Workbook for Day In and Day Out*, pages 71, 72, 73 ,74.
2. Bulletin board.

Independent word attack

Morning

Cock-a-doodle-doo!
Cock-a-doodle-doo!

The rooster
Up on the barnyard gate
Is saying, "Get up!
It is <u>late</u>, late, late."

I run down to breakfast
And then out to play.
"Good morning,
Red Rooster!
<u>How</u> are you today?"

3. Independent reading.
   Molly, Pete, and Ginger, pages 67-69. (Give help with the word *school* on page 67.)

Under the Tree, pages 26-31.
We Come and Go, pages 29-32.
4. Textfilm for *Day In and Day Out,* Frames 31-32. See Textfilm manual for directions.

Unit 27: In the Barnyard   Pp. 113-19

PREPARATION

Have the following materials ready for use:

Pocket Card Holder

Word Cards:	466 duck	520 cock-a-	534 wee
	516 hen	doodle-doo	535 cow
	517 cluck	521 quack	536 moo
	519 rooster	533 pig	

INITIAL PROCEDURE

Word associations

Vocabulary review. (Have the word cards listed above in the card holder.) Bring me a card which tells the name of an animal and the card which tells the sound he makes. Read both cards for us.

Contents pages. (Use in usual way.)

SILENT READING

Page 113. Here is that jingle again. Read until Alice is through with her jingle. Now read until Red Rooster begins to crow. Is he a visitor to the barnyard? Find out. Has Alice stopped wishing? Finish the page and see.

Page 114. Read three sentences and find out something interesting about that cow. Does the red cow talk to Alice and Betsy Lee? Read until you find out. Maybe Betsy Lee can do something. Finish the page and see.

Page 115. I think Alice must have had something in her pocket. Read two sentences and find out why I think so. Maybe the hens are so busy eating that they do not say a thing. Read until you find out whether that is so. Poor Betsy Lee! What question does Alice ask her now, and how does Betsy Lee answer? Finish the page and see.

Page 116. Have these baby ducks learned to talk? Read until you are ready to prove your answer. Has Betsy Lee improved? Finish the page and see.

Page 117. Read until you find out what Alice did when the pigs began to talk. Maybe Betsy Lee improves this time. Finish the page and see.

Oral language

Page 118. (Allow time for enjoyment of picture.) Maybe Betsy Lee is so surprised and frightened that she says "Oh!" before these two pages are over.

Read three sentences and get that goat into the barnyard as fast as he seems to be coming. Read four sentences. Find out exactly which animals are afraid and run away.

One animal is not afraid. Which one is that? Why doesn't she run? Finish the page and see.

Page 119. Alice is afraid that goat may do something. Read until you find out what she is afraid of. Now finish the page and see if Alice and Betsy Lee get home safely. And Betsy Lee didn't even say "Oh!" I don't believe she will ever talk. Do you?

ORAL READING

Following events in sequence

Organization. (Write *pigs, ducks, hens, rooster, cow, goat* on board. Have pupils close books and number the animals in the order in which Alice saw them in the barnyard. Then have the pages reread to follow the numbered outline.)

WORD RECOGNITION TECHNIQUES

Accurate word recognition. (Use the "Magic" game with the following words: *started, stay, stopped, store, what, white.*)

Phonics

Auditory-visual perception. *Phonetic parts.* (Write the following words on board: *garden, moo, cow, day, her, new, boy, out.* Have a pupil read a word, draw a line under the part he sees and hears, and tell what the part says.)

Phonics

Initial sounds. (Have pupils write the letter with which each of the following words begin; finish the word for them as soon as a letter is written: *man, name, pig, rooster, saw.*)

Final sounds. If I write *very,* all but the last sound or letter, will someone finish it? (Continue with *word, breakfast, run, nest, open, Betsy, could, jump, Jip.*)

Here are two new words. (Write *bed—berry.*) One says *berry;* I see a ripe berry on the bush. The other says *bed.* Which says *berry?* How do you know? Then the other word says—. (Continue with *sheep—shut, thin—thought.*)

SUPPLEMENTARY ACTIVITIES

1. *Workbook for Day In and Day Out,* pages 75, 76, 77, 78.
2. Bulletin board.

Independent word attack

Words I Like

Jack and quack,
And <u>pack</u> and <u>sack</u>,
Are words I like.
Do you?

Jerry and <u>merry</u>,
And <u>berry</u> and <u>cherry</u>,
I can say all the words.
Can you?

3. Independent reading.
   Under the Tree, pages 44-47. (Give help with the word *Daddy* on page 44.)
   We Come and Go, pages 47-52. (Give help with the words *cars* on page 47; and *yellow* on page 48.)

Pp. 120-22 # Unit 28: Betsy Lee Talks

NEW VOCABULARY: hug   Ma-ma

PREPARATION

Have the following materials ready for use:

Pocket Card Holder   **Word Cards:** 543 hug   544 Ma-ma

INITIAL PROCEDURE

Vocabulary review. (Have the following words and phrases on board.)

You are	All the animals	I could	But
She gave	You can not	That night	Then
I wish			

Drill on sentence beginnings

We must be sure we can get our sentences started on the right track. Who will draw a line under one of these sentence beginnings, read it, and then use it to start a sentence?

Contents pages. I am afraid the title of the new story will give away the surprise. See if it does. If Betsy Lee talks, we want to find out about it in a hurry. How quickly can you turn to page 120?

SILENT READING

Page 120. Safe in the house at last! I know how much Alice likes Betsy Lee. How can I tell? What is she saying to her doll? Read the whole page and see.

Page 121. Sometimes when we sit and think about something that happened to us, we say we are daydreaming. Alice must be day-dreaming about these animals. What is she thinking? Read the page and find out. Alice doesn't know the secret yet. Will she find out on the next page? Turn and see.

Page 122. (Allow time for enjoyment of picture.) Look at Alice's face. Has she discovered the secret? I wonder whether she knows the secret when she talks in the first two lines. Read and see.

Independent word attack— hug

There is a new word in the next sentence. (*hug*) You know how it begins and ends. Who will be the first to find out what it says? You can't find out about the secret without that word.

What happens when you give a talking doll a big hug? What does a talking doll say when she talks? Then what do you suppose this card says? (Hold up word card *Ma-ma.*) Does Betsy Lee say that? How many times? Finish the page and see. Do you think Alice goes right to sleep? What do you think happens? I do hope she doesn't— (put word card *hug* in card holder) Betsy Lee so much that she wears out her talking machine.

Guidance in methods of word attack

Page 123. Of course, you know the boy on this next page. Maybe if I told you that this (write *Mr.*) says *Mister,* you could get the other word for yourselves. (Write *Carl.*) You know how the word begins. You know this part. (Draw a line under *ar.*) You know how the word ends. Who is smart enough to get the whole word? Mr. Carl, of course! Do you think you will like him? Why? Does Jack? Who is ready with the title of the new part of our book?

ORAL READING

Audience reading

Expressing feelings of story characters. (Since Alice talks all through the story "Betsy Lee Talks," have some girl read the three pages, trying to show, as she reads, Alice's change in mood. In this or another period have all the "Betsy Lee" stories reread. Children may dress a doll to represent Betsy Lee and may read the stories for some other group who have not heard them.)

VOCABULARY ENRICHMENT AND EXTENSION

Extending speaking vocabulary. Can you tell me an easy way to say "delighted"? "discover"? "enjoy"? How did Alice feel when Betsy Lee could not talk? when she could talk?

WORD RECOGNITION TECHNIQUES

Establishing
sight
vocabulary

Accurate word recognition. How high can you climb? (Begin at the bottom of the board and write the following words, one at a time, to form a word ladder: *am, at, all, are, a, away, again, ate, animals.* As you write, have some child read the words until he misses. Let another child carry on from there. When all words have been written and read, have some child see how quickly he can climb down the ladder, reading and erasing as he goes.)

Auditory-visual perception. *Initial sounds.* (Have pupils show how *talk, very, will, she, what, that* begin. Complete each word as initial letter or letters are written.)

Phonics

Final sounds. Listen as I say *hug, pig, big.* What did your ears tell you about these words? Let's see if you are right. (Write the words on board, calling attention to the final *g.*) If I wanted to add another word to the list, should I add *dog* or *puppy?* (Write *dog* to prove that the choice is right.)

(Write the following pairs of new words on board, one pair at a time. Read each pair and have children discover which word is which by using their knowledge of the final sound: *tag—tan, dirt—dip, mud—muddy.*)

SUPPLEMENTARY ACTIVITIES

1. *Workbook for Day In and Day Out,* pages 79, 80, 81, 82.
2. Bulletin board.

Vocabulary
review in
new context

What Will He Say?

Oh, I have a pretty doll,
    And her name is Betsy Lee.
She can say, "Ma-ma, Ma-ma!"
    So come to my house and see.

Now I want a boy doll
    To go with Betsy Lee.
Will he say, "Pa-pa, Pa-pa"?
Oh, what will he say to me?

3. Independent reading.
    Under the Tree, pages 32-37. (Give help with the word *we* on
    page 36.)

We Come and Go, pages 33-42. (Give help with the words *help,*
   page 33; *we,* page 37.)

   4. Textfilm for *Day In and Day Out,* Frames 33-34. See Textfilm
manual for directions.

   5. Tests. Before beginning the next unit, give the two informal
tests on pages 83 and 84 of the Workbook. In each test pupils are to
be given a score of 1 for each item marked correctly. Pupils in average groups should make a score of at least 20 on the vocabulary test;
of 4 on the sentence-meaning test. It is important at this point that
each child be tested individually with the word cards for the new
vocabulary that has been introduced so far in the Primer. (See pages
159-60 of *Day In and Day Out.*)

*Individual
check on sight
vocabulary*

Unit 29: My Little Girl   Pp. 124-29

NEW VOCABULARY: Carl   girl   hello   liked   Mr.

PREPARATION

Have the following materials ready for use:

Pocket Card Holder
Word Cards:

123 You	483 eat	510 old	545 Mr.
134 he	493 again	525 all	546 Carl
145 she	502 her	530 his	547 girl
162 Yes	509 ate	540 very	549 Hello

INITIAL PROCEDURE

Vocabulary review. (Have the following phrases on board.)

Alice lived	One morning	Do you like	So she stopped
He was	He had	She saw	Then she went

We are going to become acquainted with—(add word cards for *Mr. Carl* to card holder) this morning. So we must be sure we start our sentences right. Who will draw a line under one of the sentence beginnings, read it, and then use it to begin a sentence of his own?

Of course, you know this word. (Write *look.*) And now it says—(add *ed*). So this word says—(write *like*). And now it says—(add *d*). Who will read this sentence beginning (write *He liked*) and use it to begin a sentence?

I hope you remember these partner words (add *Yes—You* to card holder; then *eat—ate*); and these opposites (add *he—she;* then *his—her*). In the picture you saw of him, Mr. Carl looked—(add cards for *very* and *old*). I know that—(add *all*) of you will like him. When you read about him once, you will want to read about him—(add *again*). If these words were the fence around Mr. Carl's garden, how fast could you read the words and climb the fence?

Introducing new vocabulary. Sometimes when I meet friends, I say, "Good morning." Or I may say, "How do you do?" But generally, if I know them very well, I just say—(add *Hello* to card holder). You know how the word begins. You see the letter *o* on the end. Think what you say when you see a friend. The new word is—.

(Write *Alice is a girl.*) Think how the new word begins. Let the sentence help you. The new word is—(add *girl* to card holder). If *girl* begins with a capital letter, it looks like this. (Reverse the word card.)

Contents pages. Now use your contents pages to find out three things: the name of the new part of our book, the name of the first story, and the page number on which the story begins. *My Little Girl.* Do you suppose that means that Mr. Carl has a little girl? Turn quickly to page 124 so that we may find out.

SILENT READING

Page 124. I knew from his picture that Mr. Carl was very old. But this picture tells me some other things about him. What does it tell you?

Read the page and find out one way in which Alice and Mr. Carl are just alike.

Page 125. These pictures tell me something more about Mr. Carl. What do they tell you?

Read until you find out whether Mr. Carl has a little girl of his very own.

Are these birds that Mr. Carl is looking at in a bird store? Read until you find out. Now finish the page. Find out what kinds of birds Mr. Carl had in his house. Did you find out one reason Alice is Mr. Carl's little girl?

Page 126. What other things can you find out about Mr. Carl from this picture?

How does Alice happen to be in Mr. Carl's garden? Read until you find out. I hope you know what she will say to him. (Indicate word card *hello*.) Now finish the page. Ask the question and answer it, just as Alice does.

Page 127. I am sure Betsy Lee is trying to say—(indicate word card *Yes*). But what does she really say?

Will Mr. Carl, Alice, and Betsy Lee spend the morning in the garden? Finish the page and see.

Oral language   **Page 128.** (Allow time to identify items in pictures: perches, swings, water cups, packages of birdseed, etc.)

I really believe these birds are very smart. They know that Alice is a big girl and Betsy Lee is a little doll. I can tell by what they say. Read and see if you can.

Alice makes a discovery. Continue reading until you find out what it is.

Page 129. I know why Mr. Carl likes to have Alice visit him. See if you would like to have her for a visitor.

Do the birds still know the difference between Alice and her doll? Be ready to read the sentences which prove that they do. What may happen next in the story?

ORAL READING

Rereading by page units. One picture in our story tells me that Mr. Carl lives in a white house and likes flowers. Which picture is that? Now who will read the page which goes with that picture? (Continue in similar fashion.)

202 <small>Average Group</small>

VOCABULARY ENRICHMENT AND EXTENSION

Word associations. When I hear the words *Mr. Carl,* many nice things come to my mind. Each of you tell me one nice thing you think of when I say *Mr. Carl.* Of course, you won't copy what someone else says.

WORD RECOGNITION TECHNIQUES

Auditory-visual perception. *Phonetic parts.* Can you read this word and then draw a line under the part you see and hear in it? (Write *Carl;* then continue with *brown, house, garden, toy, moo, Mother, new, say.*)

Mr. Carl liked—(write *birds*). This part says—(draw a line under *ir* and give the *r* sound). Listen as you say the word. Can you hear the *r* (give sound) sound? Now what do you discover about this word? (Write *girl.*) Can you draw a line under the part?

Phonics

Final sounds. If I write *hug,* all but the last letter, will you finish it? (Continue with *happy, jump, bird, nest, green.*)

(Write the following new words on board in pairs, one pair at a time. As in previous units, read each pair and have pupils determine which word is which through the final consonant sound: *candy—cart, map—mug, ten—toad.*)

SUPPLEMENTARY ACTIVITIES

1. *Workbook for Day In and Day Out,* pages 85, 86, 87, 88.
2. Bulletin board.

Independent
word attack

My Garden

I have a pretty garden,
With a bird house in a <u>tree.</u>
A brown bird saw the <u>bird</u> house.
"Tweet, tweet," he said,
"I see
A home
For me."

One day I saw a blue bird
Fly in at the garden gate.
He can not stay in my bird house.
He came
Too late,
Too late.

3. Independent reading.
   Under the Tree, pages 48-51. (Give help with the words *make*
   and *thank* on page 50.)
   We Come and Go, pages 43-46. (Give help with the words
   cookies, page 44; and *where,* page 45.)
   We Work and Play, pages 27-30.

Unit 30: The Big Green Bird   Pp. 130-33

NEW VOCABULARY: help

PREPARATION

Have the following materials ready for use:

Pocket Card Holder

Word Cards:	139 Not	493 again	501 find	525 all
	474 laughed	494 was	513 are	550 help

INITIAL PROCEDURE

Drill on
sentence
beginnings

Vocabulary review. (Have the following words and phrases on
board. Use techniques suggested in previous unit.)

Just then	She could not	That is	I gave
It said	Yes	But	Please
What	Then	Now	And

Drill on
carrier words

I hope you know this word when it begins with a capital letter. (Put word card *Not* in holder.) Can you read these other cards as quickly as I add them to the card holder? (Add *again, all, are, find, laughed, was.*)

Introducing new vocabulary. One morning Alice was trying to tie the sash on her apron. She just couldn't reach it. So she went to

Guidance in
methods of
word attack

Mother and said—(write *Please help me;* use usual techniques for *help* and place word card in holder). Watch how *help* begins. (Trace *h.*) Watch how it ends. (Trace *p.*) Listen as you say *help.* Do you hear the last sound? When I write—(write *help*), you will know that the word says—.

Contents pages. Do you remember the color of Mr. Carl's birds? The title of the new story makes me know that he may have a bird we have not read about. Why do I think that? Who can read and then

Guidance in
locating page
numbers

write on the board the page number on which our story begins? We can tell by looking at the contents page that there are not many more stories in our book. Then what kind of turn will your first turn be?

SILENT READING

Page 130. Do you see a big green bird anywhere? Alice begins her sentences like this. (Indicate *Now, I gave* on board.) She is very sure of something. Read two sentences. What is she sure of?

Mr. Carl is going to play a joke. He begins with this word. (Indicate word card *Not.*) Read three sentences. What do you think the joke will be? Now finish reading the page. How does everything turn out?

Page 131. Can you guess from the picture what Alice is trying to do? Maybe she is trying to get some—(indicate the word card *help;* allow time for discussion of Mr. Carl's carving and for identification of

Oral language

all items in picture). Now read the page. See if we were right when we said Alice might be asking for help.

Page 132. Can you find the green bird? (Allow time for discussion of parrots and what they can do.)

On page 131 Mr. Carl was sitting down. What does he do now, and what does he say? The first two sentences will tell. The strangest thing happens in the next sentence. Find out what it is. Alice doesn't know who is talking because she asks the same question twice. What is her question?

Now Alice does something; she sees something; she hears something. What does she do? What does she see? What does she hear? Read until you find out. I don't blame Alice for doing what she did in the last sentence. Do you? (Bring out the idea that Mr. Carl has had the parrot for some days and has taught it to say "Alice.")

Page 133. I know how excited Alice is by the way she talks. Read four sentences silently. Then we will let someone read them for us and show by his voice how excited Alice is.

Of course, Betsy Lee has to share the fun. What does she do? Read until you find out.

I hope that big green bird talks again. Finish the page to see if it does. What do you think will happen when Alice goes home?

ORAL READING

Setting standards for oral reading

Fluency-expression. (The rhythmic pattern of several sections of this story is very apparent. Suggest that you like certain sections particularly well, so well that you like to read them over and over. Read these sections to set the pattern. Then have the children reread the story by pages.)

VOCABULARY ENRICHMENT AND EXTENSION

Word associations. What new things come to your mind today when I say *Mr. Carl?* What did his eyes do when he played that joke on Alice? Can you make your eyes twinkle?

WORD RECOGNITION TECHNIQUES

Drill on carrier words

Accurate word recognition. (Play the "Magic" game with these words: *oh, on, one, out, old, open; in, is, it, into.*)

Auditory-visual perception. *Initial sounds.* Some words need two letters to begin them. If you will show me how *this* begins, I will finish the word. (Continue with *she, what, white, that.*)

You are sitting on a chair. (Write *chair*.) Two letters begin *chair*. (Trace *ch* in colored chalk; then erase word.) If someone can show me how *chimney* begins, I will finish the word. (Continue with *chalk, child, chicken*.)

Phonics

Final sounds. If I write *help*, all but the last letter, can you finish it? (Continue with *word, went, pony, big, man*.)

(Write the following new words on board in pairs; have pupils identify each word through final sound as in previous units: *sorry—sad, wag—win, shop—shirt*.)

SUPPLEMENTARY ACTIVITIES

1. *Workbook for Day In and Day Out,* pages 89, 90, 91, 92.
2. Bulletin board.

Vocabulary review in new context

Hello

Do you like to say, "Good morning"?
Do you like to say, "Good night"?
I like to say, "Hello, hello!"
Hello, hello,
And away I go.
Hello, hello, hello!

I was playing ball this morning.
I saw Jack going by.
I did not say, "Hello, hello!"
But I did say, "Hi, Jack, hi!"

3. Independent reading.
My Little Green Story Book, pages 35-42.
Under the Tree, pages 2-7.
We Work and Play, pages 31-34.

4. Textfilm for *Day In and Day Out,* Frames 35-36. See Textfilm manual for directions.

Unit 31: The Best Store

NEW VOCABULARY: best

PREPARATION

Have the following materials ready for use:

Pocket Card Holder
Word Cards:

116 store	455 toy	506 animal
155 had	485 that	551 best
159 this	493 again	

INITIAL PROCEDURE

Drill on
sentence
beginnings

Vocabulary review. (Have the following words and phrases on board. Use techniques suggested in previous units.)

In the morning	You are	I could have	He was
One day	I wish	He wanted	Jack came
Just	Then	But	He liked

It is a long time since we have read about a—(put word card *store* in card holder). You won't find a single—(add *toy*) in this store. But someone likes it so well that he comes to it over and over—(add *again*). He looks at—(add *this*), and he looks at—(add *that*). I don't know how much money he—(add *had*). But I do know that he liked almost every kind of—(add *animal*). Now I wonder if you know all these words. Show me that you do.

Guidance in
methods of
word attack

Introducing new vocabulary. Jerry had three coats. One was his old coat to play in. One was his everyday coat to wear to school. And—(write *One was his best coat;* use usual techniques for *best*). Watch the way *best* begins. It rhymes with *nest*. So if I begin my word this way (write *b*_____), you will tell me to finish—. But if I begin it like this (write *n*_____), you will tell me to finish—.

Contents pages. You aren't going to hear about Jerry's best (add word card *best* to card holder) coat this morning. Find out from the title what the best "something" in today's story is. Then turn quickly to the page on which the story begins.

SILENT READING

Oral language

Page 134. (Allow time for full discussion of picture. Have pupils discover what the kittens are doing, the color of the dog, etc.) Jack certainly seems to like this store. I know two names for it. Do you? (*pet,* or *animal, store*) I hope you know what this word (write *store*) will say when I add this. (Add *s*.)

I find out something very interesting about Jack on this page. Read and see what you find out. Do you agree with Jack? Which store do you like best?

Page 135. I think I know what Jack liked to do again and again. Read until you come to the question mark and see if you can find out.

Read two more sentences. Can you see what Jack saw? Do the next two sentences tell the right story? Read and see. Now finish the page. What is the best pet in the best store?

Page 136. Where were all these puppies in the other picture? Jack starts to make friends. What does he say and what does the puppy do? Read two sentences to see.

I wonder if you would feel as Jack feels. Read what else he says to the puppy and see. What does the puppy's "bow-wow" mean? Read until you find out.

Page 137. Why does Jack have a questioning look on his face? Why is his hand in his pocket? Can you tell by the look on the face of the storekeeper whether he likes boys?

I wonder whether that dog will be gone when Jack comes again. Read two sentences and find out. Now find out the name of the man who runs the store. If Mr. Green sees Jack at his window day after day, what may happen? (If children suggest that he may give Jack the dog, remind them that dogs in pet stores are too expensive to give away.)

ORAL READING

Rereading by page units. I will ask a question. Who will read the page which answers my question? *What stores did Jack like?* (Continue with *What animals did Jack see in the window? What did Jack say to the dog? How long did the dog stay in the window?*)

WORD RECOGNITION TECHNIQUES

Plurals in s

Word structure. Can you read this word? (Write *kitten.*) Can you make this word mean more than one kitten? (Have some child add *s;* then continue with *store, stores; rabbit, rabbits;* etc.)

Verbs ending in s, ed, ing

This word says—(write *like*). And now it says—. (Add *d*. Continue with *open, opens; say, saying; find, finding, finds;* etc.)

Phonics

Auditory-visual perception. *Initial sounds.* Show me how *best* begins. Then I will finish the word for you. (Continue with *help, girl, liked, Carl, gave, very.*)

SUPPLEMENTARY ACTIVITIES

1. *Workbook for Day In and Day Out,* pages 93, 94. Be sure directions on page 93 are understood.
2. Bulletin board.

Independent word attack

One Day

What did I have in my house?
What did I see today?
Something little, something gray!
A little gray mouse
In my house!

3. Independent reading.
   My Little Green Story Book, pages 43-54.
   We Work and Play, pages 11-14.

Pp. 138-39 # Unit 32: The Best Store (*cont.*)

NEW VOCABULARY: Snap

PREPARATION

Have the following materials ready for use:

Pocket Card Holder
Word Cards: 162 Yes   468 But   474 laughed   552 Snap
        459 So   472 Then   543 hug

INITIAL PROCEDURE

Drill on
sentence
beginnings

Vocabulary review. (Have the following phrases on board. Use procedures suggested in previous units.)

For three days	By and by	Out jumped	Jack gave
He will not	I will open	What is	He is not
He started	Do you like	His name	

I hope that you remember what Alice gave Betsy Lee. (Add word card *hug* to card holder.) Now can you read these other words as quickly as I can put the cards into the card holder? (Add *laughed, But, Then, So, Yes.*)

Guidance in
methods of
word attack

Introducing new vocabulary. This word (write *snow*) says *snow*. Say it and listen to the way it begins. Of course, this word (write *cap*) says—. This morning we will have a word (write *snap*) which begins like *snow* and rhymes with *cap*. It tells what a dog does sometimes when he is not friendly. *Cap, sn——*! The new word is—. And if I add this (add *s* to *snap*), the word will say—. What does this card say? (Add word card *Snap* to card holder.) If I were to write—(write *sn____*), what word would you tell me to finish? I hope that dog in the window doesn't snap at Jack. Turn quickly to page 138 so that we may find out.

SILENT READING

Page 138. If you saw a boy looking at the same dog in your store window day after day, what would you think? What would you do? Is Mr. Green like you? Read to the first question mark and find out.

Jack answers Mr. Green's question and then asks one of his own. Find out what Jack wants to know.

Does Mr. Green agree that that dog is the best pet in the store? Read until you find out all he says.

Jack is very sure, very confident, about something. What is he confident about? I hope Jack is right.

Page 139. Sometimes when a person is too sure about something, we say, "All right! I'll show you." Mr. Green says this in a nicer way. What does he say? What does he do? What happens? Read three sentences to find out.

Who will be right about that puppy, Jack or Mr. Green? The next three sentences will prove who is right.

Does Mr. Green give in? Does he admit that he was wrong? How does everything turn out? Finish the page and find out.

ORAL READING

Rereading by page units. These are big long pages. But good readers like you can read long pages. Who wishes to try page 138? page 139?

VOCABULARY ENRICHMENT AND EXTENSION

Extending speaking vocabulary. Jack was confident that Snap would not snap at him. What does it mean to be confident? What are you confident that you can do?

WORD RECOGNITION TECHNIQUES

Auditory-visual perception. *Phonetic parts.* Will you read this word? (Write *girl*.) Will you draw a line under the part you hear and

Phonics

see in the word, and then tell us what the part says? (Repeat with *her*.) What did you discover about this part (indicate *ir*)? and this part (indicate *er*)? (Repeat procedure with *out* and *cow*.)

Final sounds. If I write *Snap*, all but the last sound, will you finish the word? (Continue with *best, hug, word, very, open*.)

Here are two new words. (Write *bag—bad*.) One says *bad*. One says *bag*. Which says *bag*? How do you know? Then the other says—. (Continue with *carry—corn, mop—meat*.)

Drill on carrier words

Accurate word recognition. *Watch Me Go.* (Write each of these words on the board, one at a time: *like, liked, little, look, laughed, lived*. Erase each word as soon as it is written. Have pupils tell what was written.)

SUPPLEMENTARY ACTIVITIES

1. *Workbook for Day In and Day Out,* page 95.
2. Bulletin board.

The Dog for Me

Independent word attack

Mac was a pretty good dog.
Jip was a good dog, too.
But the best dog in town
Had a coat white and brown.
So he was the dog for me
You see.
Snap was the dog for me.

3. Independent reading.
   My Little Blue Story Book, pages 41-48. (Give help with the word *make* on page 43.)
   My Little Green Story Book, pages 55-63. (Give help with the word *cake* on page 59.)

Unit 33: The Best Store (*cont.*) Pp. 140-43

PREPARATION

Have the following materials ready for use:

Pocket Card Holder

Word Cards:

139 Not	484 walk	511 started	540 very
159 this	493 again	514 talk	543 hug
162 Yes	503 Now	525 all	550 help
467 for	506 animal	530 his	551 best

INITIAL PROCEDURE

Drill on sentence beginnings

Vocabulary review. (Have the following phrases on board. Follow techniques suggested in previous units.)

Are you	I will stay	He did not	You are
I am	He saw	He gave	That is

Drill on difficult words

I hope you remember these partner words when they begin with capital letters (add word cards for *Not—Now* to card holder); and these two words (add *talk—walk;* continue to add the rest of the word cards listed above). How long will Jack continue to play with Snap? Turn quickly to page 140 so that we may find out.

SILENT READING

Page 140. By the time I have read two sentences, I know Mr. Green is right. Snap is not the best pet in the store. Why do I know? Read and see.

A strange thing happens in the next three sentences. What is it? See if you can figure out why it happened.

Mr. Green has the best plan. Read until you come to the question mark and find out what the plan is.

I know without reading what Jack will say to that plan. But when will he begin working? Finish the page to see.

Page 141. (Allow time for thorough discussion of picture: kinds of dogs, feeding bowls, types of food used, etc.)

Oral language

Jack plays favorites on this page. Read to find out why I think so. I wonder if Jack will become so interested in working that he will forget to go home to eat his lunch. Turn to the next page and see if he does.

Page 142. I am glad Mr. Green is holding onto Snap. What might happen if he didn't?

Is Jack's work over for good? Does Mr. Green pay him off? Read until you find out.

The rest of the page prepares me for the picture on the next page. Where did Alice and Jerry come from? Read to find out.

Page 143. What is going on here? What can the quarrel be about? Read until the children stop talking, and find out what has happened. I am glad Jack does what he does in the last sentence. Are you? Why does each child think his dog is best?

I wonder what Mother will say when she hears about Jack's **job**. Will she let him keep it? We will find out tomorrow.

ORAL READING

Expressing mood of characters

Rereading by page units. Who wants to read the page which tells about Mr. Green's plan? the page where Jack plays favorites? the page where Jack goes home for lunch? the page where the children quarrel? I hope you will read just the way those quarreling children talked to each other.

VOCABULARY ENRICHMENT AND EXTENSION

Extending speaking vocabulary. Jack played favorites with Snap. What does that mean? What is your favorite toy? color? pet? Alice, Jerry, and Jack are very confident about something. What are they confident about?

WORD RECOGNITION TECHNIQUES

Establishing sight vocabulary

Accurate word recognition. *Watch Me Go.* (Use techniques suggested in previous unit with *have, had, he, here, her, house, home, hop, hole, happy, help, hen, his, hug, hello.*)

Auditory-visual perception. *Initial sounds.* Remember that it takes two letters to begin some words. If you will show me how *this* begins, I will finish the word. Maybe, just maybe, you can finish it. (Continue with *that, she, sheep, white, what, child, chair.*)

Phonics

Final sounds. Here are two new words. (Write *tent—ten* on board and proceed as in previous units. Continue with *pup—penny, sand—sun, rag—rat.*)

SUPPLEMENTARY ACTIVITIES

1. *Workbook for Day In and Day Out,* page 96.
2. Bulletin board.

Independent word attack

My Wish

I wish, I wish,
Oh, what do I wish?
Oh, what do I wish for you?
Three little kittens
With little red <u>mittens</u>!
Oh, that is my wish for you.

3. Independent reading.
   My Little Blue Story Book, pages 49-52. (Give help with the word *stop* on page 52.)
   Under the Tree, pages 58-63.
   We Come and Go, pages 53-60. (Give help with the word *make* on page 54.)

Pp. 144-46 # Unit 34: A Dog for Jack

INITIAL PROCEDURE

Drill on
sentence
beginnings

Vocabulary review. (Have the following phrases on board. Follow procedure suggested in previous units.)

Jack came	He could not	Out jumped	I will find
Now you are	I will help	It is not	May he go
He was	You did not	Can you	Jack gave

I am sure Mother will tell Jack that, if he is to work for Mr. Green, he must be a good workman. He cannot come to work one day and stay home the next. He cannot come—(write *Now and then*). He will have to go to work—(write *Day in and day out*). If he is a good workman, if Mr. Green gives him some money, and if he saves his money, what might happen?

Contents pages. There is a big surprise in the title of the next story. Find out what it is. Do you suppose the dog for Jack is Snap? To what page must we turn to find out?

SILENT READING

Page 144. I think Jack was a good workman. Read three sentences and find out why I think so. Why did he play with Snap only now and then?

Mr. Green asks two very important questions. Find out what they are. If you were Jack, how would you answer?

Page 145. What does Jack say? Read two sentences and see.

Does Mr. Green really mean what he said? Prove it by reading the next two sentences. I suppose Jack said, "Oh, thank you! Thank you!" Read and see if he did. Do you suppose his eyes said, "Thank you," even if he couldn't talk? Now Mr. Green does something to show that he means what he said. What does he do?

Page 146. It looks as if Jack can't wait to get home to give that puppy a big hug. How is the puppy saying, "I like you"?

Once upon a time Snap would not mind Mr. Green. Read three sentences to see if he minds now. The next sentence goes with the picture. Why?

Jack has some important work for the rest of the day. Find out what it is. What name would you choose if you were Jack?

Page 147. Alice and Jerry in—(*pajamas*) on their way to—. What do you think they are saying as they look over the bannister? Then what is the title of the next part of our book?

ORAL READING

Rereading by page units. Who wishes to read the page which proves that Jack was a good workman? the one on which he says, "Thank you," with his eyes? the one where the puppy says, "I like you," by licking Jack's face? (In this or another period have the entire story of *The Best Store* and of *A Dog for Jack* reread by pages.)

VOCABULARY ENRICHMENT AND EXTENSION

Word
concepts

Extending speaking vocabulary. When the puppy licked Jack's face, what was that puppy confident of? When Jack hugged the dog, what was Jack confident of? I am confident Jack was a good master. Each of you tell me your favorite name for a dog.

WORD RECOGNITION TECHNIQUES

Accurate word recognition. *Watch Me Go.* (Use procedure, outlined in previous units, with *big, blue, boat, brown, ball, but, bird, box, by, boy, breakfast, barnyard, best.*)

Verbs ending
in s, ed, ing

Word structure. (Write *play* four times in a column on the board.) This word says—(indicate top word in column). If I want it to say *plays,* I add—(add *s* to second word). If I want it to say *played,* I add—(add *ed* to third word). And if I want it to say *playing,* I add—(add *ing* to fourth word). Are you as smart as I am? (Write *help* four times in a column on board.) Can you make this second *help* say *helps?* this third *help* say *helped?* (Continue in similar fashion with *open* and *talk.*)

Phonics

Auditory-visual perception. *Final sounds.* If I write *happy,* all but the last letter, will you finish it for me? (Continue with *bird, Snap, dog, brown, goat.*)

(Write the following new words in pairs, one pair at a time on the board: *log—let, town—top, sled—slip, fairy—first.* Tell what each pair of words says and have pupils discover which word is which by using the final sound.)

SUPPLEMENTARY ACTIVITIES

1. *Workbook for Day In and Day Out,* pages 97, 98, 99, 100.
2. Bulletin board.

Girls and Boys

Independent word attack

Girls like to play
With kittens and cats.
Boys like dogs,
And balls and bats.

But now and then

A boy likes a kitten,
A boy likes a cat,
And a girl likes to play
With a ball and a bat.

3. Independent reading.
   Molly, Pete, and Ginger, pages 47-52. (Give help with the words *cat,* page 51; and *kitty,* page 52.)
   My Little Blue Story Book, pages 53-63.
   Under the Tree, pages 14-19.
   We Work and Play, pages 19-22.
4. Textfilm for *Day In and Day Out,* Frames 37-38. See Textfilm manual for directions.
5. Tests. Give the informal tests on pages 101 and 102 of the Workbook. Pupils should be given a score of 1 for each item marked correctly. Pupils in average groups should make a score of at least

Individual
check on sight
vocabulary

20 on the vocabulary test and of 4 on the sentence-meaning test. At this point pupils should be tested individually with the word cards for the entire Primer vocabulary. (See pages 159-60 of *Day In and Day Out.*)

Unit 35: A Happy Day   Pp. 147-49

INITIAL PROCEDURE

Vocabulary review. (Have the following sentences on board.)

> I am going to help you.
> I am going to help you get
> something good to eat.
> So Alice ran to find Jerry.

Alice ran into the kitchen. Mother was just beginning to get lunch. So Alice said—(sentences 1, 2). When everything was ready, Mother said, "It is time for Jerry to come in and clean up." (Sentence 3.)
Contents pages. (Use usual procedure.)

SILENT READING

Page 148. Evidently part of Jerry's happy day is spent with Jack. Read the title and the first two sentences and find out how the day starts. In the next two sentences Jack tells Mother what he is going to do next. What is that? How does Jerry spend the rest of the morning? Finish the page and see.

Page 149. How does Alice's day start? Read two sentences and see. How does Alice spend the rest of the morning? The next three sentences tell that. I think both Alice and Jerry knew enough to come home for lunch. See if you think they did. Find out what happened in the afternoon.

Would you call this a happy day? Why?

ORAL READING

Two-line sentences

Rereading by page units. The first boy to find out how many two-line sentences there are on page 148 may read about Jerry's happy day. The first girl to find out how many two-line sentences there are on page 149 may read about Alice's day.

VOCABULARY ENRICHMENT AND EXTENSION

Word associations. What do you think about when I say *a happy day?* Suppose someone starts by telling what he would like to do on a happy day. We will each add something. By the time we are through, we should have a very, very happy day.

WORD RECOGNITION TECHNIQUES

Auditory-visual perception. *Phonetic parts.* Alice and Jerry had a happy—(write *day*). Read the word, draw a line under the part you see and hear, and then tell us what the part says. (Continue with *boy, girl, new, house, cow, Carl, her, moo.*)

Phonics

Final sounds. I will write *nest,* all but the last letter. Will you add the last sound or letter? (Continue with *pony, old, help, big, man.*)

I will write two new words (*win—wild*). One says *wild;* Little Rabbit was wild. One says *win;* he will win the race. Which word says *wild?* How do you know? Then the other word says—. (Continue with *top—town, leg—let, lady—load.*)

SUPPLEMENTARY ACTIVITIES

1. *Workbook for Day In and Day Out,* pages 103, 104, 105, 106.
2. Bulletin board.

A Happy Day

Independent word attack

I wish I could have a boat ride.
I wish I could ride on a train.
I wish I could fly
Up into the <u>sky</u>
In a big, big airplane.

I wish you could come to my house
To play with my new red ball.
Then I could say,
"I had the best day,
The very best day of all."

3. Independent reading.

   Molly, Pete, and Ginger, pages 53-56. (Give help with the sound word *Meow* on page 53.)
   Under the Tree, pages 38-43. (Give help with *cake,* page 38.)
   We Come and Go, pages 61-64.
   We Work and Play, pages 43-46. (Give help with the word *cars* on page 43.)

Unit 36: Good Night

Pp. 150-57

INITIAL PROCEDURE

Drill on sentence beginnings

Vocabulary review. (Have the following sentence beginnings on the board.)

Now it was	In my barnyard	Just then	This
Mother came	I have had	I do not want	Not
She gave	That is	I want	What

You will need to know these sentence beginnings. Draw a line under a sentence beginning, read it, and then use it to start a sentence of your own. Suppose you give me the first turn. (Draw a line under *I have had.* Then say, "I have had the best time." Have several pupils read that particular sentence beginning; then proceed as in previous units.)

Contents pages. Suppose we say, "Good night," to the contents pages by using them for the last time. Find the title of the last story. Be ready to read the page number on which it begins. Be ready to write that number on the board. Can you find page 150 without a forward or a backward turn?

Guidance in locating page numbers

Creating
story
background

Page 150. (Allow time for identification of two-bunk bed. Then show page 122. Discuss the possibility that this is a new bed for Jerry; so Alice has to have the fun of sleeping in it for one night. Since it is Jerry's new bed, he has the fun of climbing to the top. Have pupils decide what may happen to Jip before Mother leaves.)

Alice is getting a big hug now. But I am sure Jerry got one, too. Read four sentences and see if I am right.

Alice uses this sentence beginning. (Indicate *I have had.*) I hope you remember it. Finish the page to see what happens when the hugs are over. Where do you think Jip was when Mother went away?

Page 151. Now the mischief starts. Who do you think started it? Do you think that is where Mother left Jip?

I think the mischief concerns a game. Read three sentences. Find out if we were right about the one who started the mischief. Find out the name of the game.

I suppose Jerry says, "No, Alice. I am going to be good and go right to sleep." Does he? Read two more lines and see. Now finish the page and get the game started.

Page 152. What does Alice add to that barnyard? Read until you find out. What does Jerry add? Finish the page and see.

Pages 153-55. (Use procedure suggested for page 152.)

Page 156. Is this going on forever or will someone put a stop to this nonsense? Read nine lines and find out what happens. I think Mother means business. Does Alice intend to mind? Read until you find out. Does Jerry? Finish the page and see.

Oral language

Page 157. (Allow ample time for discussion of picture. Identify the *F V* on banner as the initials for Friendly Village, where the children live. Remark that Mother allowed Jip to stay.)

I don't believe Alice and Jerry can say, "Good night," to you. Read the page and find out why. I hope they wake up in another book, don't you?

Dramatization. (Have one child be Alice, another Jerry, and have the game part of the story reread from the bottom of page 151. Have someone read what Mother says on page 156.)

VOCABULARY ENRICHMENT AND EXTENSION

Word associations. (Play a game similar to the one suggested in story; e.g., "I packed my grandmother's suitcase, and in it I put—"; or "I want a toy store. In my toy store I will have—."

WORD RECOGNITION TECHNIQUES

Verbs ending in s, ed, ing

Word structure. What is this word? (Write *go.*) Who can come to the board and make it say *going?* (Continue with *help—helps, talk—talked, look—looking.*)

Little words in big words

What does this word say? (Write *gate.*) I see a little word in *gate.* Can you draw a line under the little word and tell what it says? (Continue with *all* in *ball, in* and *to* in *into, at* in *that, barn* and *yard* in *barnyard.*)

Auditory-visual perception. *Initial sounds.* (Have pupils show how *that, she, white, what,* and *child* begin. Finish each word for them as soon as initial letters are written.)

Phonics

Final sounds. (Using techniques suggested in previous units, have pupils finish the following words: *said, want, pretty, ran, big, Jip.*)

Here are two new words. (Write *read—rug.*) One says *read;* you can read a book. The other says *rug.* Which one says *read?* How do you know? Then the other word says—. (Continue with *sorry—sun, flat—flap, bill—bat.*)

SUPPLEMENTARY ACTIVITIES

1. *Workbook for Day In and Day Out,* pages 107, 108, 109, 110.
2. Bulletin board.

Independent word attack

Good Night

Good night, rabbit,
In your little dark hole.
Good night, little bird,
On your nest.

Out in the barn
Is the one I like best.
Good night, brown pony,
Good night.

3. Independent reading.

Molly, Pete, and Ginger, pages 57-60.

Under the Tree, pages 52-57. (Give help with the words *bed,* page 52; and *sleep,* page 57.)

We Come and Go, pages 65-70.

We Work and Play, pages 51-62.

4. Textfilm for *Day In and Day Out,* Frames 39-40. See Textfilm manual for directions.

5. Tests. Give the informal tests on pages 111 and 112 of the Workbook. Scores on vocabulary test should be at least 20; on sentence-meaning test, 4. Test with word cards as in Unit 34.

6. *My Own Book,* Nos. 5, 6, 7, 8. If possible, give pupils copies of each of these books to take home to read to their fathers and mothers. See page 100 for explanation.

STANDARDIZED ACHIEVEMENT TEST

A Reading Achievement Test for use at the end of the Primer can be bought from Harper & Row, Publishers. The test should be given before beginning the Basic First Reader, *Round About.*

PARALLEL PRIMER

The Parallel Primer, *Wishing Well,* can be read with a minimum of vocabulary difficulty upon the completion of *Day In and Day Out.*

Diagnosis of Pupil Growth

(Upon completion of *Day In and Day Out*)

1. Are pupils having an enjoyable experience learning to read? Can they enter into story experiences so that the characters and events come alive to them as they read? Do they turn to reading as an enjoyable leisure-time activity?

2. Have they mastered the 180 words in the Primer vocabulary so well that they can use these words in context other than the Primer with ease and confidence? DO THEY RECOGNIZE AUTOMATICALLY ALL CARRIER WORDS (all words except nouns) IN THE PRIMER VOCABULARY?

3. Are they using their reading ability throughout the school day: reading bulletin boards, library books, other primers and preprimers, announcements? Is there evidence of home reading?

4. Have certain fundamental reading habits become well established? Do pupils read silently before reading orally without being reminded to do so? Do they read without evidences of head and lip movement? Can they read two-line sentences without breaking the sentence at the end of the first line? Can they interpret common marks of punctuation: the period and the question mark?

5. Is oral reading fluent, rhythmic, and expressive?

6. Have auditory and visual acuity developed to the degree that pupils are able to:

   a) associate initial consonant sounds with the letters which represent them?

   b) combine initial consonant sounds with picture clues to unlock new words?

   c) combine initial consonant sounds with context clues for the same purpose?

   d) use the above techniques independently?

7. Are you, the teacher, constantly diagnosing the reading needs of individuals in the group and adapting the unit plans to meet the needs of these pupils before rushing on to new text material?

8. Are you having a thoroughly enjoyable time, also? Have you a feeling of confidence in the firm foundation for reading development which your pupils are acquiring?

PROGRAM FOR IMMATURE GROUP

Unit 1: Little Rabbit (Introduction)

NEW VOCABULARY: oh   rabbit

PREPARATION

Have the following materials ready for use:

Pocket Card Holder
Word Cards

49	Alice	128 brown
62	Jerry	146 too
67	look	161 went
103	little	451 rabbit
124	a	452 Oh

Rebus Card: 37 rabbit
Phrase Cards

252 He saw
362 said Alice
385 She saw
389 something brown
391 something little

INITIAL PROCEDURE

Introducing new vocabulary. (Have the following sentences built in the card holder.)

> Alice went too
> He saw something little
> She saw a little brown (*rebus* rabbit)
> Oh look Jerry said Alice

Guidance in methods of word attack

Jerry ran to his favorite place high on the hill. Of course,—(indicate sentence 1). This word begins like *window*. (Indicate *went*.) Think how it begins. Then jump over it. Alice w——, too. (Form lips for *w* sound, but do not give sound.) The word is—. Watch how *went*

226

begins. Watch this letter carefully. (Indicate *e*.) When I write—(write *we*_____), you will tell me to finish the word—.

All at once Jerry looked down and—(sentence 2; substitute *something brown* for *something little* and have new sentence read). Of course, he called Alice. She came running up and—(sentence 3; rebus card may be added at last moment to sustain suspense).

Boys and girls who can read as well as you do not need to use the picture for *rabbit*. (Turn rebus card to show word; then substitute word card *rabbit* for rebus card. Direct attention to the way the word begins and show capitalized form.)

When Alice saw the rabbit, she was so surprised that she said, "Oh!" (Write *Oh*.) Make your mouth look just like the beginning of this word as you say, "Oh!" If Alice had not been quite so surprised, her mouth might not have been so big and round. Then the word *oh* might have looked like this. (Write *oh*.) Alice said more than *oh*. (Indicate sentence 4. Have all sentences reread.)

See how quickly we can clear the card holder. Suppose you each take one card and read it.

WORD RECOGNITION TECHNIQUES

Building sight vocabulary

Accurate word recognition. (Add word cards *went, rabbit, Oh* to card holder.) Find and read the word which begins like *window;* the name of the animal; the surprise word.

Auditory-visual perception. *Initial sounds. Saw, Jerry, said!* Which two words begin with the same sound? If I wanted to write *saw*, would I begin it like this (write *h*) or like this (write *s*)? (Have some child indicate correct beginning; then complete the word *saw*.) If someone will show me how *said* begins, I will finish the word. (Continue with *something*.)

Phonics

I will write two new words for you. One will say *sand;* it is fun to play in the sand. The other word will say *hand;* I have chalk in my hand. If you have very sharp eyes, you can tell me which word says *sand*. (REMEMBER THAT THESE TWO WORDS ARE NOT PART OF PRIMER VOCABULARY. PUPILS ARE NOT EXPECTED TO REMEMBER THEM. They are used simply for directed training in the use of initial consonant clues.)

SUPPLEMENTARY ACTIVITY

Guidance in
Workbook
activities

Vocabulary Primer Workbook, pages 1, 2. Give whatever guidance is necessary so that all similar pages in this Workbook can be done independently.

Pp. 5-9 # Unit 2: Little Rabbit

NEW VOCABULARY: hole   hop

PREPARATION

Have the following materials ready for use:

Pocket Card Holder
Word Cards: 51 and   451 rabbit   453 hop
                 161 went   452 oh   454 hole

INITIAL PROCEDURE

Vocabulary review. (Have these sentences on board.)

Alice went, too.
A little brown rabbit hole!

When Jerry went to the hillside—(sentence 1). I hope you remember this word. (Draw a line under *went*.) On this chair are three words we need when we read our new books (*went, rabbit, oh*). As you pass by, read the three words for me.

Introducing *Day In and Day Out*. Each day you are growing taller. Each day you are growing to be better readers. The books you read must grow, too. How is this book more like the books Father and Mother read? (Hold up a copy of *Day In and Day Out,* directing attention to hard covers and to the thicker book.) Alice and Jerry have fun all day long and every day. They say that they have fun *Day In and Day Out*. (Move your hand under title as you read. Have several children read title.) Now look closely at the cover. Where are Alice and Jerry? What do they see?

Alice and Jerry have fun with a little brown rabbit. The story begins on page 5. How quickly can you turn to page 5?

Frontispiece and page 5. Who will read the names on page 5? Remember the joining word. (Add *and* to card holder.) Were these two pictures taken on the same day? What things would you enjoy most on this hilltop?

Oral language

Telling story from pictures. Suppose we tell this story from the pictures before we read it. Turn to page 6, and I will begin.

Page 6. One lovely spring day Alice and Jerry were playing on the hilltop. All at once Jerry saw something. He called softly to Alice and said—. Who will go on?

Page 7. Then what happened? Use some good words to tell about the animal the children saw.

Page 8. When boys and girls want to get somewhere in a hurry, what do they do? What does a rabbit do? Now tell what is happening in the picture. I hope I hear the words *ran* and *hop*.

Page 9. Good for Little Rabbit! She knows how to take care of herself. Finish the story and tell what she did.

Guidance in
methods of
word attack

Introducing new vocabulary. You remember how *here* begins. (Write *here—Here* on board, directing attention to *h—H*. Then erase words.) *Hop* begins like *here*. How many times can you find *hop* on page 8? How many times does it begin with a capital letter? with a small letter? What does this card say? (Add *hop* to card holder.)

Hole begins like *here*. How many times can you find *hole* on page 9? Then what does this word say? (Add *hole* to card holder.) Who can read all three words in the card holder?

SILENT READING

Page 6. Read the whole page silently. Be ready to tell exactly what Jerry said when he saw the rabbit.

Page 7. The first sentence tells exactly what Alice did. What was that? The next three sentences tell exactly what she saw. What was that? The last sentence tells exactly what she said. Be ready to tell why you know she was surprised.

Page 8. I hope you remember what Little Rabbit did. (Indicate word card *hop*.) But first she saw something. Read two sentences and find out what she saw. Read two more sentences and find out what Little Rabbit did. Now finish reading the page. What did Alice and Jerry do?

Page 9. I think that hole belongs to Little Rabbit because it is— (indicate sentence 2 on board). The first three sentences tell what Little Rabbit saw. What was that? The next sentence tells what she did. Find out what that was. Someone is surprised in the last sentence. Who is surprised, and how do I know?

ORAL READING

Working for fluency

Rereading by page units. (Have two fluent readers and two who need practice alternate in rereading the story by pages.)

WORD RECOGNITION TECHNIQUES

Accurate word recognition. (Put *went, rabbit, oh, hop, hole* in the card holder.) Be ready to bring me the word I need to finish my sentence. (Say aloud the following sentences: Little gray mouse lives in a—. Hold up one foot and try to—. I was so surprised I said—. Jerry saw a little brown—. Hop, hop it—.)

Building sight vocabulary

(Return cards to card holder. Have pupils hop down the rabbit hole by reading the column of cards from top to bottom.)

Auditory-visual perception. *Initial sounds.* If someone will show me how *said* begins, I will finish the word for you. (Continue with *see, saw, something*.)

Phonics

(Write *here—Here,* directing attention to *h—H*. Then erase words.) If someone will show me how *hop* begins, I will finish the word. (Continue with *hole*.)

I will write again the two words *hand* and *sand*. Which says *hand*? How do you know? What does the other word say? How do you know? (PUPILS ARE NOT SUPPOSED TO REMEMBER THESE WORDS. See caution in Unit 1.)

1. *Vocabulary Primer Workbook,* pages 3, 4.

Guiding
Workbook
activities

2. *Workbook for Day In and Day Out,* pages 1, 2. On page 1 give sufficient guidance so that similar pages can be done independently. On page 2 read text with pupils; be sure directions are understood.

Unit 3: (Supplementary) *reviec*

1. Textfilm for *Day In and Day Out,* Frames 1-2. See Textfilm manual for directions.

2. Additional reading. In the following preprimers the pages noted may be used as supplementary reading under teacher guidance. New vocabulary (aside from character names, which should be told to children) is indicated the first time a new word appears in each book.

  Bill and Susan (Silver Burdett Co.), pages 2-7. (Give help with the word *stop* on page 4.)

  Here and There (Harper & Row, Publishers), pages 2-6.

  Molly, Pete, and Ginger (D. C. Heath and Co.), pages 1-6.

  My Little Red Story Book (Ginn and Co.), pages 2-8.

  Ride Away (American Book Co.), pages 2-9.

  We Look and See (Scott, Foresman and Co.), pages 3-6.

Unit 4: Toys   Pp. 10-13

NEW VOCABULARY: ball   just   toys

PREPARATION

Have the following materials ready for use:

Pocket Card Holder
Word Cards

69 one	118 train	161 went	453 hop	456 ball
86 boat	159 this	451 rabbit	454 hole	457 just
94 it	160 this	452 Oh	455 toy	

Phrase Cards: 252 He saw   298 I want
                   278 I like   446 You may have

INITIAL PROCEDURE

Building sight
vocabulary

Vocabulary review. Little Rabbit lived in a—(put word card *hole* in card holder). Can you hop down the rabbit hole by reading each card I add? (Add *went, Oh, hop, rabbit*. Reverse order of cards continually and have each child read.)

Introducing new vocabulary. (Have the following sentences ready in the card holder.)

He saw just one boat
I like this
I want this
You may have it

Guidance in
methods of
word attack

It was Jerry's birthday. Father took him to a store where there were kites, tops, and other things boys like to play with. Jerry called each one of these things a—(write *toy*). The new word begins like *to*. It rhymes with *boy*. *Boy, t——*. (Put lips, teeth, and tongue in position to form *t* sound. Wait for some child to suggest *toy*.) When Jerry looked around, he said, "Oh, see all the—(write *toys*). Show me the word which means one toy; the word which means more than one. What does this word say? (Add word card *toy* to card holder.)

Jerry saw many toy animals, but—(sentence 1). This word begins like *jump*. (Indicate *just*.) Think how it begins. Then hop over it and read the rest of the sentence. He saw j—— one boat. (Wait for some child to suggest *just*. Substitute *train* for *boat* and have new sentence read.) Next Jerry saw something that could roll and bounce. It begins like *big* and *boat*. So you know that Jerry saw—(substitute *ball* for *train*).

Adding meaning
to carrier words

Sometimes when I point to something, I use the pointing word *this*. (Write *This*.) I say, "This is Jane." (Point to Jane.) I may say, "See this chair." (Point to chair.) As Jerry pointed to one toy after another, he used the pointing word. He said—(sentences 2, 3). I hope when Jerry finds the toy he really wants, Father will say—(sentence 4).

(Have all cards read and removed from card holder, except *toy, just, ball, this.* Have pupils play "One, Two, Three! How Many for Me?" reversing order of cards continually.)

I know you wish you were in that toy store. You will think you are if you turn to page 10.

SILENT READING

Oral language

Page 10. (Allow time for identification of all toys.) If you were to choose a toy, which one would it be? Can you read the title? Why is it a good title for this story? Does it mean one thing or more than one?

The minute Jerry walked into the store, what did he see? Read one sentence and find out. How many toys does Jerry want? Read two more sentences and be ready to tell me how you know. (word *a*) What toy is Jerry pointing to? What is the pointing word? (Hold up word card *this.*) Finish the page and see if you chose the right toy.

Page 11. I wonder if Jerry will be satisfied with just one toy. Read three sentences and see. I wonder if two toys will satisfy him. Finish the page and find out.

Page 12. Can you discover any new toys? Father looks as if he is about to buy something. How do I know? I hope Jerry tells him what to buy. Read the page and see if he does.

Page 13. Will Father have money enough to buy three toys, or will he buy—(put word cards *Just one* into card holder)? Read six sentences and find out.

Has Jerry made up his mind what to buy? Finish the page and see. I am sorry he is so slow. We must wait until tomorrow to find out what he wants. But maybe you can guess.

ORAL READING

Following events in sequence

Organization. What was the first toy Jerry thought he wanted? Who will read the page which tells about that? What did he want next?

Read just the part of page 11 which tells about the ball. (Continue in similar fashion.)

WORD RECOGNITION TECHNIQUES

Phonics

Auditory-visual perception. *Initial sounds.* If someone will show me how *hop* begins, I will finish the word for you. (Continue with *saw, said, have, hole.* Have pupils play "See Me Go" to read and erase words from board.) I will write two new words. One will say *hat.* One will say *sat.* If you have sharp eyes, you can tell which says *sat.* How do you know? Then the other word says–. How do you know?

Watch how *big* begins. (Write *big–Big,* directing attention to *b–B.* Then erase words.) What do your ears tell you about the words *big* and *ball?* If someone will show me how *ball* begins, I will finish the word for you. (Continue with *boat.*)

SUPPLEMENTARY ACTIVITIES

1. *Vocabulary Primer Workbook,* page 5.
2. *Workbook for Day In and Day Out,* pages 3 and 4. Read text with pupils. Be sure directions are understood.

Pp. 14-15 # Unit 5: Toys (*cont.*)

NEW VOCABULARY: fly   happy   so

PREPARATION

Have the following materials ready for use:

Pocket Card Holder
Word Cards

68 my	159 this	452 Oh	456 ball	460 happy
92 is	161 went	453 hop	457 Just	
94 it	162 Yes	454 hole	458 fly	
148 What	451 rabbit	455 toy	459 so	

Phrase Cards: 231 He looked 294 It is
272 I do 390 something good

INITIAL PROCEDURE

Vocabulary review. (Have the following sentences on board. As each sentence is read, have word card for underscored word added to card holder.)

Father <u>went</u>, too.
See <u>this</u> <u>ball</u>.
<u>Just</u> one <u>toy</u>!

When Jerry went to the toy store—(sentence 1). As Jerry walked around, he said—(sentence 2). Father reminded Jerry that he could have—(sentence 3). The best toys are always on the top shelf. Can you climb the word ladder to the top shelf? (Add *Oh, hop, hole, rabbit* to card holder. Have pupils read up and down the word ladder. Then remove cards.)

Establishing sight vocabulary

Introducing new vocabulary. (Have these sentences ready in card holder.)

He looked so happy
Yes I do
What is it
It is something good

Guidance in methods of word attack

When your birthday comes, you feel very—(write *happy;* remind pupils that the word begins like *here;* wait for suggestion *happy*).
On his birthday morning Jerry hopped out of bed, and—(sentence 1; suggest that *so* begins like *see* and rhymes with *go*). "Do you like birthdays?" asked Mother. Of course, Jerry said—(sentence 2).

There was a box by Jerry's plate. Alice said—(sentence 3). Jerry could tell by feeling that it was a box of candy. So he said—(sentence 4).

My, but I am eager to find out what Jerry buys at the toy store. Turn quickly to page 14.

SILENT READING

Page 14. Maybe you know without reading what Jerry wants now. But you had better check. Read three sentences to see if you are right.

Father will not want to waste money. He will want Jerry to get—(indicate phrase *something good*). If that airplane is a good one, it can—(put word card *fly* into card holder; if pupils do not immediately suggest *fly*, suggest that the word begins like *floor* and tells what airplanes can do). Now finish the page. Find out if the airplane is worth buying.

Page 15. If you can read this sentence (indicate sentence 1 in card holder), you can read the first sentence on page 15. If Jerry gets that airplane, I am sure he will begin using this word. (Add word card *my* to card holder.) Read the next three sentences and see if he does. Now if you know this word, you can finish the page. (Indicate word card *it*.)

Guidance in methods of word attack

ORAL READING

Rereading by page units. This is such a good story that it will be fun to read it right through from the beginning. The one who knows this word may read page 10. (Hold up word card *toy*. Continue in similar way, holding up *ball* for page 11, *Oh* for page 12, *just* for page 13, *Yes* and *fly* for page 14, *so* and *happy* for page 15.)

WORD RECOGNITION TECHNIQUES

Auditory-visual perception. *Initial sounds. Happy—here!* What do your ears tell you about these words? If someone will show me how *happy* begins, I will finish the word. (Continue in same way with *so—see, big—ball*.)

Phonics

I will write three new words. One will say *bat*. See me *bat* the ball. One will say *hat,* and one will say *sat.* Which word says *bat?* How do you know? (Continue in similar way with *hat* and *sat.*)

Word structure. If Jerry has one airplane, we might say he has one—(write *toy*). If he has two or three, he has—(write *toys*). Which word means one? Which means more than one? You know what this word says. (Write *ball.*) Can anyone make it say *balls?* (Repeat with *train, boat, rabbit,* etc.)

Plurals in s

SUPPLEMENTARY ACTIVITIES

1. *Vocabulary Primer Workbook,* pages 6, 7, 8.
2. *Workbook for Day In and Day Out,* pages 5 and 6. On page 6, have text read and be sure directions are understood.

Unit 6: (Supplementary)

1. Textfilm for *Day In and Day Out,* Frames 3-4. See Textfilm manual for directions.
2. Additional reading. In the following preprimers the pages noted may be used as supplementary reading under teacher guidance:

Bill and Susan, pages 8-15.

Molly, Pete, and Ginger, pages 7-10.

My Little Red Story Book, pages 9-12. (Give help with the word *fast* on page 11.)

Ride Away, pages 10-15.

We Look and See, pages 7-10. (Give help with the word *funny* on page 10.)

Pp. 16-17 # Unit 7: Jip

NEW VOCABULARY: away   bow-wow

PREPARATION

Have the following materials ready for use:

Pocket Card Holder

Word Cards:	51 And	162 yes	459 so
	155 had	453 hop	460 happy
	159 this	457 just	461 away
	161 went	458 fly	462 Bow-wow

Phrase Card: 356 One morning

INITIAL PROCEDURE

Vocabulary review. (Have the following word cards in a column in the card holder: *so, happy, fly, hop, this, yes, just, went.*)

Drill on carrier words

Find and read two cards which tell how Jerry felt when Father said he might have the airplane; the word which tells what a kite can do; what a rabbit can do; the pointing word; the opposite of *no.* Father might have said, "You may have *only* one toy." But he didn't. Show me the word he used. What does the last word say? Who can climb one step up the word ladder? two steps? (etc.)

Introducing new vocabulary. (Have the following sentences on the board.)

> She had a happy look.
> Jip ran away.
> Up and away went Alice.
> She did not have a happy look.
> She did not want to play.
> Not with a puppy like Jip!
> Bow-wow!

Guidance in
methods of
word attack

When Alice was cross, she had a cross look. But most of the time the look on her face was—(draw a line under *a happy look* in sentence 1 and have the phrase read). Now read the whole sentence. This word begins like *here.* (Indicate *had.*) Think how it begins. Then jump over it. Alice h—— a happy look. (Wait for suggestion *had.*) Of course, the word is *had.* Watch how it begins. (Trace *h.*) Watch how it ends. (Trace *d.*) Then when I write—(write *had*), you will know that the word is—. And this word card says—(add *had* to card holder and have sentence reread).

Alice was playing with her dolls. Do you know what Jip did? He took one doll in his mouth. Then—(sentence 2). If you remember this word (indicate *a* in sentence 1) and if you see it on the beginning of this new word (indicate first syllable in *away*), you can tell what Jip did. Jip ran a——. Watch this letter closely. (Trace *w.*) Then when I write—(write *aw____*), you will tell me to finish—. And this card says—. (Add *away* to card holder.) I hope you will know this word in the next sentence. (Indicate *away* in sentence 3.)

Alice jumped—(indicate *Up* in sentence 3) in a hurry! What did she do then? Read the sentence and see. (Have sentence reread until pupils sense the rhythm of phrase *Up and away.* With some groups it is advisable for the teacher to read the phrase, thus setting a pattern for rhythmic oral reading.)

I wonder if Alice had a happy look. (Sentence 4.) I wonder if she wanted to play. (Sentence 5.) Since you know this word (indicate *not* in sentences 4 and 5), you will know it when it begins with a capital letter. (Indicate *Not* in sentence 6.) Alice might like to play with a good puppy, but—(sentence 6; have this sentence reread until pupils sense rhythm and read with expression).

Working
for fluency

Of course, Alice caught Jip and got her doll back. Do you know what Jip did when she said, "You bad dog!" Jip said something which begins like *ball.* He said—(sentence 7). And this card says—(show *Bow-wow* in both lower-case and capitalized forms; add card to card holder and have all sentences reread).

In our book today, Jip gets into more mischief. If you can tell me when the story begins, we can find out what he does. (Hold up phrase card *One morning.*) Now turn quickly to page 16. Will you need to take a big turn or a little turn?

SILENT READING

Page 16. What kind of look does Jip have at the top of the page? Can you figure out why he looks that way? Read the title and the first sentence. What did he do?

Why didn't Alice and Jerry stop Jip? Read until you find out. What kind of look does Jip have at the bottom of the page? If you remember the joining word, you can finish the page and find out what Jip intends to do when he runs away. (Hold up *And.*)

Page 17. Now the mischief begins. If you remember this word, you can read four sentences and find out what Jip said to that kitten. (Hold up *So.*)

Will the kitten play with Jip? Finish the page to see.

ORAL READING

Rereading by page units. The one who knows these words may read page 16. (Indicate word cards *had* and *away.*) The one who knows this card may read page 17. (Indicate *Bow-wow.*) Maybe someone knows all three words and can read both pages.

WORD RECOGNITION TECHNIQUES

Accurate word recognition. (Hold up a small ball.) I have a ball. (Write sentence as you say words.) This word says—(draw a line under *have;* give ball to some child). I had a ball (write words as you say them), but I do not have one now. This word says—. (Draw line under *had.* Let each child hold the ball; then give it away, each time reading the sentence appropriate to the action, until meaning has been added to *have* and *had.*)

Adding meaning to carrier words

Have and *had* are partner words. I remember which one is *have* because it is a little longer word. I also remember this letter. (Trace *v.*) Now tell me what word I have written. If you don't know, find it in the sentence and let the sentence help you. (Alternate writing *have* and *had* until recognition becomes automatic.)

Drill on carrier words

Auditory-visual perception. *Initial sounds.* Show me how *so* begins. Then I will finish the word for you. (Continue with *ball, had, bow-wow, saw, happy.*)

Phonics

(Write *band, hand, sand.*) Here are three new words. One says *band.* I want to play in the band. Which word says *band?* How do you know? (Repeat procedures with other two words.)

You remember how *jump* begins. (Write *jump—Jump;* direct attention to *j—J;* then erase words.) If someone will show me how *just* begins, I will finish the word.

SUPPLEMENTARY ACTIVITIES

1. *Vocabulary Primer Workbook,* page 9.
2. *Workbook for Day In and Day Out,* page 7. (Should be done under teacher guidance.)

Unit 8: Jip (*cont.*)   Pp. 18-19

NEW VOCABULARY: bird   came   out

PREPARATION

Have the following materials ready for use:

Pocket Card Holder
Word Cards:

155 had	162 Yes	459 so	464 came
159 this	453 hop	460 happy	465 out
161 went	457 just	461 away	

INITIAL PROCEDURE

Drill on carrier words

Vocabulary review. (Have the following word cards in the card holder: *away, had, happy, hop, just, so, this, went, Yes.*)

Who can read and take one card from the card holder? two cards? (Continue until all cards are removed.)

Introducing new vocabulary. (Have the following sentences on the board.)

> Come out, Alice, come out.
> So Alice came out.
> Do not go away.
> She had to go.
> Away went May.

May ran to Alice's house. She saw Alice at the window. May wanted her to—(draw a line under *Come out* in sentence 1 and let context suggest *out*). Now read the sentence to see what May said. Watch how this new word begins. Watch the next letter carefully. (Trace *o;* then *u.*) Then when I write—(write *ou*_____), you will tell me to finish—. This card says—(add *out* to card holder).

Alice heard May call. (Indicate sentence 2.) This new word begins like *come,* but it doesn't say *come.* (Indicate *came.*) We must make the sentence sound just as it would if we were talking. So Alice c—— out. (Wait for suggestion *came.*) Good for you! Watch this letter carefully. (Indicate *a.*) Then when I write—(write *ca*_____), you will tell me to finish—. This word card says—. (Add *came* to card holder.)

By and by May thought it was time to go home. But Alice said—(sentence 3). Before long, May heard Mother calling. So—(sentences 4-5).

Find and read the sentence in which you see this word. Then tell me what the word says. (Hold up *out.* Continue with *came, away, Away, had, went, So.*)

Now we are ready to find out what mischief Jip gets into today. Turn quickly to page 18.

**Guidance in
methods of
word attack**

SILENT READING

Independent
word attack—
bird

Page 18. Of course, you know whom Jip sees now. Think how *bird* begins. Then see how many times you can find the word *bird.* This bird is very—. Can you find the word *pretty?* Now read four sentences. What does Jip want the bird to do?

The picture at the bottom of the page makes me think that the bird did not like Jip's idea. Finish the page and see if I am right.

Page 19. More mischief! That rabbit gives Jip time to say just one thing. Read two sentences to find out what that is.

I hope you remember these words. (Indicate *came* and *Away* on board.) Now read four sentences. How does that rabbit take care of herself? Did Jip find the rabbit hole? Read the next sentence and see if he did.

If you remember this word, you can read two more sentences and find out what Jip told the rabbit to do. (Indicate *out* on board.) That rabbit is very wise. Finish the page and find out why. What do you think happens next?

Predicting
outcomes

ORAL READING

Rereading by page units. The one who knows the name of the pretty red bird on page 18 (*cardinal*) may read the page. Maybe I will have to tell you and read the page myself. The one who knows these two words may read page 19. (Hold up *out* and *came*.) The one who knows both words and also the name of the bird may read both pages.

WORD RECOGNITION TECHNIQUES

Drill on
carrier words

Accurate word recognition. Suppose you have an ice-cream cone. Use this word (write *have*) and tell us what you might say. Suppose you ate that cone. Use this word and tell us about it. (Write *had*. Alternate the writing of *have* and *had* several times.)

May wanted Alice to—(write *Come out*). This word says—(draw a line under *Come*). So—(write *Alice came out*). This word says— (draw a line under *came*). Do you know how I remember that this word is *came*? I watch for this letter. (Trace *a*.) Its name is *a*. When I see the letter *a*, I know the word is *came*. How sharp are your eyes? Which word did I write? (Alternate *come* and *came*, directing pupils to use sentences for help, if necessary.)

Noting word
details

Auditory-visual perception. *Initial sounds.* (Write *hit, bit, sit*.) Here are three new words. One says *hit;* I was hit by a ball. Which word says *hit*? How do you know? (Use similar techniques with the other words.)

Phonics   When *jump* begins with a capital letter, it begins like this. (Write *Jump;* trace *J;* then erase word.) If you will show me how *just* begins when it starts with a capital letter, I will finish the word. Jerry's name always starts with a capital letter. Show me how it begins so that I may finish it. (Continue with *Jip.*)

SUPPLEMENTARY ACTIVITIES

1. *Vocabulary Primer Workbook,* pages 10 and 11.
2. *Workbook for Day In and Day Out,* page 8. Be sure directions are understood.

Pp. 20-21

Unit 9: Jip (*cont.*)

NEW VOCABULARY: but   duck   for

PREPARATION

Have the following materials ready for use:

Pocket Card Holder
Word Cards

106 me	161 went	461 away	466 duck
126 at	162 Yes	462 Bow-wow	467 for
155 had	457 Just	463 bird	468 But
156 home	459 So	464 came	
159 this	460 happy	465 out	

INITIAL PROCEDURE

Drill on   **Vocabulary review.** (Have these word cards in a column in card
carrier words   holder: *away, came, had, happy, Just, out, So, this, went, Yes.*)

I feel *happy*. Show me the word card which says *happy*. (Continue with the following sentences, having pupils find underscored words: Alice came out. Just then Mother called. So May went home. Alice had to go to the store. Jip ran away this morning. Yes, he did.)

How far up the word ladder can you climb without "falling off"? How far down can you climb?

Introducing new vocabulary. (Have the following sentences on board.)

> May ran home to Mother.
> Mother looked at May.
> I looked and looked for you.
> But I did not see you.

Of course, when Mother called—(sentence 1). This word (indicate *home*) begins like *here*. Hop over it and let the sentence help you. May ran h—— to Mother. (Wait for suggestion *home*.) Watch this letter especially. (Indicate *m*.) Then when I write—(write *hom*___), you will tell me to finish—. And this card says—(add *home* to card holder).

When May came into the house—(sentence 2). I hope you remember this word. (Add *at* to card holder.) Then Mother smiled and said —(sentence 3). Remember that this new word begins like *father*. (Indicate *for*.) Think how it begins; then jump over it, and the sentence will help you get it. I looked and looked f—— you. (Wait for suggestion *for*.) If I write—(write *fo*___), what word will you tell me to finish? (Add word card *for* to card holder.)

You know how this word begins. (Indicate *But*, sentence 4.) Now think. Mother said, "I looked and looked for you. B—— I did not see you." (Wait for suggestion *But*.) This card says—(add *But* to card holder). When *but* begins with a small letter, it looks like this. (Reverse card.) Watch this letter especially. (Indicate *u*.) Then when I write—(write *bu*___), you will tell me to finish—. (Repeat with *Bu*___.)

Read the sentence in which you find this word; then tell me what the word says. (Indicate word card *home*. Repeat technique with *at*, *for*, *But*.) How many people can read all four words?

Does Jip get into more mischief? Turn to page 20 to see.

(margin note) Guidance in methods of word attack

SILENT READING

Independent word attack— duck

Page 20. Whom does Jip meet now? You know how *duck* begins. How many times can you find it on this page?

This is a very big duck. But what does Jip do to her? Read four sentences and see.

If you remember this word, you can finish the page and find out what the duck says as she flies. (Hold up word card *me*.)

Page 21. Does Jip have a happy look now? Can you explain why not? I think May saw Jip and Jip saw May at the same minute. Read the first sentence. Do you agree?

Predicting outcomes

May scolds Jip. If you know this word (indicate *for* in sentence on board), you can find out what she says. Read six sentences. If you know these two words, you can finish the page. (Hold up word card *So* and indicate *But* in sentence on board.) Now what do you think happens when Jip gets home?

ORAL READING

Rereading by page units. Let's have fun and reread the story. The one who knows these words may read page 16. (Put *away* and *had* in a place by themselves in card holder. Continue in similar way, using *Bow-wow* for page 17; *bird,* page 18; *came* and *out,* page 19; *duck* and *home,* page 20; *for* and *But,* page 21.)

VOCABULARY ENRICHMENT AND EXTENSION

Adding meaning to carrier word

Word concepts. (Write *But* on board in large letters.) I can ride a bicycle, *but* I cannot fly an airplane. Tell me something you can do. Then use this word and tell me something you cannot do.

WORD RECOGNITION TECHNIQUES

Building sight vocabulary

Accurate word recognition. (Repeat techniques from Units 7 and 8 for *have* and *had, come* and *came*.) Alice lives in a—(write *house*). This house is her—(write *home*). I remember which word says *home* because I remember this letter. (Trace *m*.) How sharp are your eyes?

Which word did I write? (Alternate the writing of *house* and *home* until recognition becomes accurate.)

Phonics

Auditory-visual perception. *Initial sounds.* If you will show me how *just* begins, I will finish the word for you. (Continue with *hop, but, home, bird, jump, so, saw.*)

SUPPLEMENTARY ACTIVITIES

1. *Vocabulary Primer Workbook,* pages 12 and 13. On page 13 be sure pupils understand that, in lower section of page, two sentences go with each picture.

2. *Workbook for Day In and Day Out,* pages 9 and 10. Give adequate guidance on page 9 so that similar pages may be done independently. On page 10 read text with pupils if necessary, but be sure the answer to each question is kept secret.

Unit 10: (Supplementary)

Review

1. Textfilm for *Day In and Day Out,* Frames 5-6. See Textfilm manual for directions.

2. Additional reading. In the following preprimers the pages noted may be used as supplementary reading under teacher guidance:

Bill and Susan, pages 16-23. (Give help with the word *Baby,* page 17.)

Here and There, pages 7-17.

My Little Red Story Book, pages 13-18.

Ned and Nancy (D. C. Heath and Co.), pages 1-8.

Ride Away, pages 16-23.

We Look and See, pages 11-14. (Give help with the word *Baby,* page 11.)

Pp. 22-23 # Unit 11: The New Coat

NEW VOCABULARY: coat   new   please

PREPARATION

Have the following materials ready for use:

Pocket Card Holder
Word Cards

68 My	161 went	457 just	464 came	469 new
94 it	162 Yes	459 so	465 out	470 coat
155 had	452 Oh	460 happy	467 for	471 Please
159 This	454 hole	461 away	468 But	

Phrase Card: 446 You may have

INITIAL PROCEDURE

Building sight
vocabulary

Vocabulary review. (Have the following cards in card holder: *away, But, came, for, had, happy, hole, just, Oh, out, so, This, went, Yes.*)

I see three words in the card holder which begin like *here.* Who will read and bring me the words? Bring me the pointing word; the word which means the opposite of *no;* the word which means the opposite of *in;* the surprise word; a word which begins like *window;* like *cap;* like *jump;* like *father;* like *said;* like *bird.* Now bring the last word and tell me what it says.

How many words can you read and return to the card holder?

Introducing new vocabulary. Open your books to page 22. We will read the picture first. Where is Alice? What is she doing? What is the matter with her coat? What does she need badly?

Using initial
consonant clues

Coat begins like *come.* How many times can you find it on page 22? Then what does this word card say? (Add *coat* to card holder.)

Look at page 23. What is happening now? Why does Alice have a happy smile? I see a sentence which begins like this. (Hold up phrase card *You may have.*) Can you find it? There is a new word in it which begins like *not*. Think how the new word begins. Then jump over it and let the sentence help you. You may have a n—— coat. (Wait for suggestion *new*.) Now do you know why Alice is smiling? Now do you know this word? (Add word card *new* to card holder.)

SILENT READING

Page 22. I am sure someone can read the title of the story. Do you think it may be a good title? Why? If you know this word, you can read the first sentence. (Indicate word card *had*.) When Alice sees that old torn coat, she uses this word two times. (Hold up word card *My*. Have second sentence read several times until pupils sense rhythm of phrase *My, oh, my!*)

Rereading with a purpose

I believe Alice likes her last year's coat. Read the next sentence and see what she says about it. *But* (indicate word card *But* in card holder) there are two things the matter with that coat. If you know the riddle word (hold up word card *it*), you can read the next two sentences and find out what the two things are. If you remember this word (hold up word card *so*), you can finish the page and find out what Alice decides to do.

Page 23. Does Mother see the hole? Does she think the coat is too little? Read four sentences and find out.

Guidance in methods of word attack

Alice has good manners. When she asks for something, she uses a word which begins like *play*. She says—(hold up word card *Please* and wait for suggestion *Please;* add word card to card holder). Now read two sentences. What kind of coat does Alice want? Maybe Mother thinks she should have a blue coat. Finish the page and see. Where do you think we may go in the story tomorrow? Won't it be fun to buy Alice a coat!

ORAL READING

Rereading by page units. The one who knows these two words may read page 22. (Indicate *coat, new*.) The one who knows the word to use when you ask for something may read page 23. (Indicate *Please*.) The one who knows all three words may read both pages.

WORD RECOGNITION TECHNIQUES

Building sight vocabulary

Accurate word recognition. (Review techniques from Units 7, 8, 9 for *have—had, come—came, house—home*.) Alice likes to—(write *play*). She remembers to say—(write *please*). Which word did I write? (Alternate *play* and *please*.)

Phonics

Auditory-visual perception. *Initial sounds.* I will write two new words. One will say *hill.* One will say *bill;* I paid the telephone *bill.* Which word says *bill?* How do you know? (Repeat techniques with *hill;* then with *sell* and *jell.*)

You remember how *come* begins. (Write *Come—come;* direct attention to C—c; then erase words.) Show me how *coat* begins, and I will finish the word. (Continue with *can, cap.*)

SUPPLEMENTARY ACTIVITIES

1. *Vocabulary Primer Workbook,* pages 14, 15.
2. *Workbook for Day In and Day Out,* pages 11 and 12. On page 11 give whatever guidance is necessary so that similar pages in workbook may be done independently.

Pp. 24-25 # Unit 12: The New Coat (*cont.*)

PREPARATION

Have the following materials ready for use:

Pocket Card Holder
Word Cards

133 have	157 man	459 so	469 new
140 pretty	159 This	467 for	470 coat
154 green	162 Yes	468 But	471 Please

INITIAL PROCEDURE

Vocabulary review. (Have the following sentences on the board.)

<u>This</u> is a <u>pretty</u> coat.
<u>But</u> it is too little <u>for</u> me.
<u>Yes</u>, I do.
<u>Please</u>, Mother, please.
You may <u>have</u> a <u>new</u> coat.
Alice looked <u>so</u> happy.
Good morning!

Suppose we think about what happened in the story yesterday. When Alice put on that brown coat, she said—(sentences 1-2). This word card says—. (Match word card *This* to word *This* in sentence 1; have the word read; then put word card into card holder. Use same procedure for each underscored word.)

When Mother asked Alice if she wanted a new coat, Alice said—(sentences 3-4). Then Mother said—(sentence 5). And—(sentence 6). Just then someone came to the door. Mother went to the door and said—(sentence 7).

Drill on carrier words

How many cards are in the card holder? (*10*) Who will read and bring me one card? two? three? four? Be sure you remember these cards. You will need them this morning. (Return *so, But, Yes,* and *This* to card holder. Have cards reread.)

We decided that today Mother and Alice would buy a new coat. Turn to page 24 to see if they do.

SILENT READING

Page 24. Here they are on their way to the store. If you know this word (indicate *So*), you can read two sentences and hurry them along.

Using initial consonant clues

Who will wait on Mother? *Man* begins like *me* and *my*. Can you find *man* on page 24? Now read two more sentences. What does the man say to Mother? What does Mother say to the man?

Mother wants the man to know who Alice is and what she wants. So what does she say in the next two sentences? Mother forgets something, but Alice doesn't. Finish the page to see what it is.

Page 25. Now the man starts to work. What does he do first? Read the first sentence and see.

What color is he showing Mother? Can you find the word *green* in the next sentence? in the next? How many more times? Does he think Alice wants the coat? Read the next two sentences and see.

Does Mother like that coat? Will she forget what Alice wants? Read three sentences and find out. Alice agrees with Mother. What does she say? Finish the page and see.

Predicting
outcomes

What may happen if the man cannot find a red coat? Maybe we will find Mother and Alice at another store tomorrow.

ORAL READING

Rereading by page units. The one who knows this word (put word card *man* in card holder) may read page 24. The one who knows this (add word card *green*) may read page 25.

WORD RECOGNITION TECHNIQUES

Drill on
carrier words

Accurate word recognition. (Write the following words on board, one at a time; erase as quickly as written; have pupils tell what was written: *So, went, this, just, want, had, is, at, have, Yes, But.*)

Phonics

Auditory-visual perception. *Initial sounds.* Here are two new words. (Write *bell—jell.*) One says *jell;* I like to eat *jell.* One says *bell;* hear the *bell* ring. Which word says *bell?* How do you know? What does the other word say? (Repeat procedures with *hide—side, cat— bat.*)

SUPPLEMENTARY ACTIVITY

Workbook for Day In and Day Out, page 14. Have pupils read each section silently and then aloud. Be sure directions are understood.

Unit 13: The New Coat (*cont.*)   Pp. 26-28

NEW VOCABULARY: box   laughed   then

PREPARATION

Have the following materials ready for use:

Pocket Card Holder
Word Cards

132 do	154 green	468 But	471 Please	474 laughed
133 have	157 man	469 new	472 Then	
140 pretty	457 Just	470 coat	473 box	

INITIAL PROCEDURE

Story recall

Vocabulary review. Let's recall what has happened in our story so far. Alice wanted a—(add word cards <u>new</u> and <u>coat</u> to card holder, one at a time, and have them read; continue to add underscored words as you continue talking).

The one who waited upon them in the store was a <u>man</u>. The first coat he brought out was <u>green</u>. He said, "This is a <u>pretty</u> coat. It is the prettiest coat I <u>have</u>."

Alice said, "Look for a red coat. <u>Please</u> do!" The man said, "I wish I could find a red coat. <u>Just</u> one! <u>But</u> I will look again." How fast can you climb up and down the word ladder?

Introducing new vocabulary. (Have the following sentences on board.)

Just then he saw Mother.
So then he looked happy.
Then Jerry had something good.
He laughed and laughed.

Guidance in
methods of
word attack

One day Jerry came home. Mother wasn't at home, and Jerry was feeling sorry for himself. But—(indicate sentence 1). This new word (indicate *then*) begins like *the* and *this*. Think how it begins. Then jump over it. Just th—— he saw Mother. (Wait for suggestion *then*.) Of course the new word is—. And this phrase (draw a line under *Just then*) says—.

The sad look left Jerry's face. (Sentence 2.) This word says—(indicate *then*). And this phrase says—(draw a line under *So then*). Mother had a package of ice-cream. So she opened it and—(sentence 3). This word (indicate *Then*) says—. And this card says—(add word card *Then* to card holder).

Mother gave Jip some ice-cream in a dish. Jip got the ice-cream all over his nose. When Jerry saw that—(sentence 4). Think how the new word begins. Think what you would do if you saw a dog with ice-cream on his nose. Jerry l——. (Wait for suggestion *laughed*. Have word card *laughed* added to card holder.) Now who can read all the sentences? Who can read the two new words? Remember—(indicate *Then*). It will be the first word you read this morning.

Turn quickly to page 26. Let's see what happens there.

SILENT READING

Page 26. Can you read the sign? The first sentence tells me the same thing as the picture. Read and see if it does. Don't forget this word. (Indicate *Then*.)

What does the man find? Read three sentences and find out.

Maybe Alice will say, "If you can't find a red coat, I will take one of these." Finish the page and see if she does.

Independent
word attack—
box

Page 27. If you know where that red coat is, if you know how *box* begins, you can find the word *box* in the first sentence. How many more times can you find it? Then this card says—(add *box* to card holder).

I hope you remember this phrase. (Indicate *Just then* on board.) Now read four sentences. What did the man say when he looked into the box? Now finish the page. What did Alice say and do? I hope you remember this word. (Indicate *laughed*.) Turn and see what that man finds next.

Page 28. Have you found the surprise? Where do you think that pretty red cap came from? What does the man say when he finds it? Read two sentences and see.

What does Alice say the minute she sees the cap? The next two sentences tell.

Purpose of
question mark

Now she asks Mother two questions. How do I know that she does? (Direct attention to question marks.) Read the questions. Be ready to tell how you think Mother answered them. Now I will ask you a question. Does Alice like her own coat and cap? Finish the page and see.

Page 29. Can you tell from the picture what is happening outdoors? I wonder what Jerry wants to do. Can you tell from the picture? Will Mother let him go outdoors? We will find out the next time we read.

ORAL READING

Rereading by page units. The person who knows this word (indicate *Then* in card holder) may read page 26. The one who knows these two (indicate *laughed* and *box*) may read page 27. The one who can tell me the word you use when something belongs to you (*my*) may read page 28. (In this or another period have the entire story reread. Some child with a red coat and cap may represent Alice, and the story may be read for a group from some other room.)

Audience
reading

WORD RECOGNITION TECHNIQUES

Drill on
carrier words

Accurate word recognition. What does this word say? (Write *The.*) What does it say now? (Add *n.*) Let's play "Magic." Close your eyes while I write a word. Now open them. What word did I write? (Use *the—then, come—came, had—have.*)

Auditory-visual perception. *Initial sounds. Box* begins like *ball.* If someone will show me how *box* begins, I will finish the word. (Continue with *Just, So, have, came.*)

Phonics

You remember how *look* begins. (Write *look;* direct attention to *l;* then erase word.) Now if someone can show me how *laughed* begins, I will finish the word for you.

SUPPLEMENTARY ACTIVITIES

1. *Vocabulary Primer Workbook,* pages 16, 17.

2. *Workbook for Day In and Day Out,* pages 13, 15, and 16. On page 13 give sufficient guidance so that similar pages may be done independently. On pages 15 and 16 supervise the first section on each page; then let pupils work independently.

Unit 14: (Supplementary)

1. Textfilm for *Day In and Day Out,* Frames 7-8. See Textfilm manual for directions.

2. Additional reading. In the following preprimers the pages noted may be used as supplementary reading under teacher guidance:

Bill and Susan, pages 24-33. (Give help with the words *help,* page 25; and *thank,* page 33.)

Here and There, pages 18-25.

My Little Red Story Book, pages 19-22.

Ned and Nancy, pages 9-16. (Give help with the word *no,* page 12.)

Ride Away, pages 24-29. (Give help with the word *stop,* page 24.)

We Look and See, pages 15-22. (Give help with the word *run,* page 18.)

Unit 15: The Big, Big Puddle

Pp. 29-31

NEW VOCABULARY: puddle   rain   splash

PREPARATION

Have the following materials ready for use:

Pocket Card Holder
Word Cards

54 come	132 do	161 went	476 rain
76 the	133 have	464 came	477 splash
109 play	147 walked	471 please	
120 want	149 window	472 then	
131 did	155 had	475 puddle	

INITIAL PROCEDURE

Building sight vocabulary

Vocabulary review. (Have the following words in pairs in card holder: *came–come, did–do, had–have, play–please, the–then, want–went, walked–window.*) Who can read two partner words and then use each word in a sentence?

Introducing new vocabulary. (Have the following sentences on the board.)

He ran out in the rain.
He saw a big puddle.

Guidance in methods of word attack

Do you remember what kind of day it was in the last picture we saw in our book? Jerry liked a day like that. As soon as he could— (sentence 1). Think how the new word begins. Remember what kind of day it was. He ran out in the r——. (Wait for suggestion *rain*.) Then this card says—(add *rain* to card holder). On the sidewalk—

(sentence 2). This new word (indicate *puddle*) begins like *puppy*. He saw a big p——. (Wait for suggestion *puddle*.) Then this word says—(add *puddle* to card holder). Now who will read both sentences and the two new words? Turn quickly to page—(write *29*).

SILENT READING

Page 29. If you know this word (indicate word card *puddle*), you can surely read the title.

The minute Jerry heard thunder, what did he do and say? Read four sentences and find out. Did Mother do as Jerry asked? Finish the page and see. Who can read the last two sentences and make us hear the rain come down?

What would you want to do if you were Jerry? Do you think Mother will let him go out? Turn and see.

Page 30. The picture answers our question, doesn't it? Maybe the reason Mother let Jerry go out is that he asked so courteously. Read three sentences. What did he say?

Independent word attack— splash

Have you sharp eyes? What is the water in that puddle doing? Can you find the new word *splash?* (Put word card in card holder.) How many times? Read three more sentences. What kind of puddles did Jerry find first? How many splashes did they make? Now finish the page. What kind of puddles does he find next? How many splashes do they make? Why do big puddles make more splashes?

Page 31. Alice can't let Jerry have all that fun by himself. I hope she is as polite as he is. Read three sentences. See if she is. Now finish the page. Does she do just what Jerry did or does she do something different?

We didn't hear about a big, big puddle today. Maybe that will be the surprise tomorrow.

ORAL READING

Setting oral reading standards

Fluency and expression. (Read each page for children to give pattern for rhythmic, expressive reading. Then have them try to read the pages to show by their voices the sound of falling rain and splashing puddles.)

WORD RECOGNITION TECHNIQUES

Building sight
vocabulary

Accurate word recognition. What does this word say? (Write *ran*.) What does it say now? (Change *ran* to *rain*.) What does this word say? (Write *puddle*.) Watch it change. (Change *puddle* to *puppy*. Then play "Magic" with the four words until recognition becomes accurate.)

Phonics

Auditory-visual perception. *Initial sounds.* (Write *say—lay* on board.) Here are two new words. One is *say;* what did you *say?* One says *lay;* I will *lay* the book on the table. Which says *lay?* How do you know? (Continue with *June—soon, corn—horn, butter—letter.* DO NOT OMIT THESE ACTIVITIES.)

SUPPLEMENTARY ACTIVITIES

1. *Vocabulary Primer Workbook,* pages 18, 19.
2. *Workbook for Day In and Day Out,* page 17.

Unit 16: The Big, Big Puddle (*cont.*)

Pp. 32-34

NEW VOCABULARY: into   jumped

PREPARATION

Have the following materials ready for use:

Pocket Card Holder
Word Cards

92 is	139 not	161 went	478 jumped
106 me	141 ran	465 out	479 into
108 on	144 saw	467 for	
131 did	150 going	474 laughed	

260 IMMATURE GROUP

INITIAL PROCEDURE

Drill on carrier words

Vocabulary review. (Have all words listed above, except *going, into, jumped,* in card holder. Have pupils play "One, Two, Three! How Many for Me?" Concentrate on pupils who need help in sight vocabulary.)

Introducing new vocabulary. (Have these sentences on board.)

He is going to jump.
Jerry jumped
into the puddle.

Guidance in methods of word attack

When Alice looked out the window, Jerry was about to jump into the first puddle. So Alice said to Mother—(sentence 1). If you remember what this word says—(draw a line under *go* in *going*) and then make the sentence sound just as if you were talking, the new word won't trouble you. (Wait for some child to read sentence correctly.) Of course, the word is—. If I write—(write *go*), the word says—. But now it says—(add *ing*). And this card (add *going* to card holder) says—.

Sometimes we put two little words together to make one bigger word. If I put—(write *in,* and wait for word to be read) and—(write *to*) together, the new word says—.

Two-line sentences

I hope you notice that the next sentence is a two-line sentence. But we will read it as if it were all on one line. As Alice looked at him—(sentence 2). Show me the word *into*. Then this card (add word card *into* to card holder) says—. And here is a word which grew up for you and didn't bother you. (Draw a line under *jumped.*) Read the sentence again. What does the word say? Of course, this word (draw a line under *jump* in sentence 1) says—. But the new word (add word card *jumped* to card holder) says—.

Who can read both sentences and the three words in the card holder? Who can read our page number? (Write *32.*)

SILENT READING

Page 32. What does Jerry say the minute he sees the great big puddle? Read three sentences and find out. Alice isn't so brave as Jerry. Finish the page and find out why.

Page 33. Jerry thinks it is silly to be afraid. Read four lines and find out what he says to Alice. Don't forget these two new words. (Indicate *jumped, into.*) Watch out for the two-line sentence. Now finish the page. Does Alice get over being afraid? How do you know that this puddle is bigger than the other puddles? (*four splashes*)

Page 34. (Allow time for enjoyment of picture.) Jerry thought Jip was Alice's dog. That is what fooled him. What did he think Jip would do? Read three sentences and see.

But Jip fooled Jerry. Read two more sentences. What did Jip do? Then what happened? The next two sentences tell. Would you have done what Alice did? Finish the page and see.

Page 35. Did you ever see such a cross-looking girl? What can be the matter? (Stimulate pupils to see that Jerry and Mother are going away. Evidently Alice must stay at home.) I hope you never look like that. Do you think she will cheer up tomorrow?

Predicting
outcomes

ORAL READING

Organization. (Write on board *Jerry sees the rain,* and have sentence read.) This sentence tells what happened first in the story of "The Big, Big Puddle." So I will number this sentence *1.* Now who will find and read for us the page in the story where Jerry sees the rain? (Continue with: [2] *Jerry plays in the puddles.* [3] *Alice plays in the puddles.* [4] *Alice and Jerry see a big, big puddle.* [5] *Alice and Jerry jump into the puddle.* [6] *Jip jumps on Jerry.*)

Following
events in
sequence

WORD RECOGNITION TECHNIQUES

Word structure. What does this word say? (Write *jump.*) What does it say now? (Add *s.*) And now? (Add *ed.*) (Repeat with *look, looks, looked.*)

Verbs ending
in s, ed, ing

What does this word say? (Write *go.*) What does it say now? (Add *ing;* then repeat with *play, playing.*)

Auditory-visual perception. *Initial sounds.* You remember how *rabbit* begins. (Write *rabbit;* trace *r;* then erase.) If someone will show me how *rabbit* begins, I will finish the word. (Repeat with *ran* and *rain;* then with *laughed, box, coat, home, just, so.*)

Phonics

SUPPLEMENTARY ACTIVITIES

1. *Vocabulary Primer Workbook,* page 20.
2. *Workbook for Day In and Day Out,* pages 18, 19, 20. Have

Guiding
Workbook
activities

text on page 18 read silently; then aloud. Be sure directions are understood. Give whatever guidance is necessary on page 20.

Unit 17: (Supplementary)

1. Textfilm for *Day In and Day Out,* Frames 9-10. See Textfilm manual for directions.
2. Additional reading. In the following preprimers the pages noted may be used as supplementary reading under teacher guidance:
    Bill and Susan, pages 34-37. (Give help with the word *sleep* on page 34.)
    Here and There, pages 26-33.
    My Little Red Story Book, pages 23-26. (Give help with the word *Bunny* on page 25.)
    Ned and Nancy, pages 17-20. (Give help with the word *make* on page 18.)
    Ride Away, pages 30-38.
    We Look and See, pages 23-30.

Pp. 35-37 # Unit 18: A Box for Alice

NEW VOCABULARY: city

PREPARATION

Have the following materials ready for use:

Pocket Card Holder
Word Cards

57 go	132 do	155 had	471 Please
109 play	133 have	158 name	472 then
120 want	148 What	159 This	474 laughed
122 with	150 going	161 went	480 city
131 did	151 Good-by	468 But	

INITIAL PROCEDURE

Vocabulary review. (Have the following words arranged in pairs in card holder: *did–do, go–going, had–have, play–with, want–went.*) Read and bring me two partner words. Use each one in a sentence.

Drill on carrier words

(Add the following cards to card holder: *But, laughed, Please, then, This, What.*) Show and read for me the question word; the pointing word; the word which tells a polite way to ask for something; the one which tells what you did when you saw something funny; the word you use when you tell me that you can walk but you cannot fly; the word that begins like *the*. Could anyone climb this word ladder and down again?

Introducing new vocabulary. (Have the following sentences on the board.)

> She went to the city.
> Not this morning.
> Is this Jerry?
> Just then he laughed.
> My name is Jerry.
> Good-by, good-by!

Word associations

Alice and Jerry lived in a small town. Sometimes Mother could not get what she wanted in the stores there. So she went to the big— (write *city* and tell word if not suggested by children). What do you think of when I say *city*? (Add word card to card holder and wait for suggestions, such as factories, tall buildings, etc.) Now read the first sentence and tell what Mother did.

One morning at breakfast Father said, "Are you going to the city this morning?" Mother said—(sentence 2).

Mother was at work in the kitchen when in came Jerry with a Halloween false face over his own face. Mother was astonished. She said—(sentence 3). This sentence is a question. How do you know? Jerry tried his best to fool Mother. But—(sentence 4). Then he said—(sentence 5). This word (indicate *name*) begins like *not*. Jump over it and let the sentence help you. My n—— is Jerry. (Wait for suggestion *name;* then add word card to card holder.) Jerry wanted Mother to be sure to know who he was. So he said this word in a loud voice. (Indicate *is*.) So I will write *is* in big letters. (Erase *is* and write *IS;* then have sentence reread.)

Guidance in methods of word attack

Before long Jerry wanted to go out and play. So he waved to Mother and said—(sentence 6). Since you know this word (indicate *good*), you know that Jerry said—(add *Good-by* to card holder; have sentences reread).

I remember a cross-looking girl that we were going to read about this morning. If you can read this page number (write *35*) and turn to that page quickly, we can find out what is the matter.

SILENT READING

Page 35. I hope you remember where the man found the coat for Alice. (Write *Box*.) Now read the title. We hear about another box. Whom is it for? *A box for Alice* sounds like a—. I am afraid she would have to cheer up before I would give her a present. Let's see if she does.

Read two sentences. Where is Mother going? Who is going with her? Read three more sentences. How is she going to the city? In a bus? In a car? I don't blame Alice so much, do you? I would want a train ride, too. Will Mother change her mind and let Alice go? Finish the page and see. Can you think of some good reasons why Mother might want to take Alice but can't today? If that is the case, Alice should behave herself. Turn and see what happens.

Page 36. What is Father doing for Mother? Alice is telling her troubles to Father. Read three sentences. What does she say?

I believe Father is like Mother when she saw Jerry's false face. He doesn't know who this cross girl is. He starts by saying, "What! What!" Finish the page. What else does he say?

Page 37. It must have been Father's joking which cheered Alice up. Read two sentences. What did she do? She wants Father to be sure to know that she *is* Alice. So what does she say in the next two sentences? I hope she said the next sentence in a happy voice. What did she say?

I have sharp eyes. I notice something about the next two sentences. The first one to see what I see may stand. Now read the two-line sentences silently. Who can read each sentence as if it were all on one line?

Predicting outcomes. Remember what Mother told Alice she could do. What do you expect will happen next in the story?

Two-line
sentences

ORAL READING

Rereading by page units. The one who knows this word (indicate *city* in card holder) may read page 35. I hope your voice will sound the way Alice's face looks.

Alice is still cross. Father is trying to cheer her up on page 36. So he must have a cheery voice. Who can read the page and show the difference in their voices? The one who knows these words (indicate *name* and *Good-by* in card holder) may read page 37. How does Alice's voice sound now?

Expressing
mood of
characters

VOCABULARY ENRICHMENT AND EXTENSION

Word concepts. What did Father mean when he said—(write *I like Alice*). Yes, I think he meant that he *loved* Alice. What do you mean when you say you like to go to a show? (*enjoy*) But what did Father mean when he said—(write *You do not look like Alice*)? Yes, I think he meant that this cross little girl did not look the same as Alice. We have to think what *like* means as we read.

Multiple
meanings

WORD RECOGNITION TECHNIQUES

Auditory-visual perception. *Initial sounds.* (Write *rake–bake* on board.) One of these new words says *bake;* Mother will *bake* some cookies. *Bake* begins like *but.* Which word says *bake?* How do you

Phonics

know? (Continue with *jeep—heap, lake—cake, side—hide*. DO NOT OMIT THESE ACTIVITIES.)

SUPPLEMENTARY ACTIVITIES

1. *Vocabulary Primer Workbook,* page 21.

2. *Workbook for Day In and Day Out,* page 22. Be sure directions are understood. Then page should be done independently.

Independent study habits

Pp. 38-39 # Unit 19: A Box for Alice (*cont.*)

NEW VOCABULARY: by   dolls   eat

PREPARATION

Have the following materials ready for use:

Pocket Card Holder
Word Cards

457 Just	461 Away	472 Then	482 by
459 So	468 But	481 doll	483 eat

Phrase Cards:

379 She did	383 She ran
380 She did not	385 She saw
381 She had	386 She walked
382 She is not	388 She went

INITIAL PROCEDURE

Vocabulary review. (Have all cards listed above, except *by, doll,* and *eat,* in card holder.)

It is very important that trains like the one Mother took to the city run on the track. It is very important also that we start our sen-

Drill on sentence beginnings

tences on the right track. Take a card, read it, and then start a sentence with it. (When all cards have been removed, have pupils exchange cards, repeat sentence procedure, and return cards to holder. Play "One, Two, Three! How Many for Me?" to remove cards again.)

Introducing new vocabulary. (Have these sentences on board.)

> By and by you may go.
> You may have something to eat.
> You may have something good.

Guidance in methods of word attack

Phrase meaning

One day Alice wanted to go to May's house. Mother might have told Alice that she could go "after a while." But she didn't say it that way. She used a word which rhymes with—(write *my*). Mother's word begins like *but*. Think how it begins. (Write *by* under *my*.) Make it rhyme with *my*. (Wait for suggestion *by*. Tell the word, if necessary.) Then this word card says—(add *by* to card holder, reversing card to show capitalized form). Now how did Mother say "after a while"? (Draw a line under *By and by* in the first sentence and have phrase read by several pupils.) Who is ready to read the whole sentence?

Alice said, "Oh, I am so hungry." Mother said—(indicate sentence 2). Let the sense of the sentence help you to get this word. (Indicate *eat*.) This card says—(add *eat* to card holder). When Mother remembered the cookies she had just baked, she said—(sentence 3; have sentences and new words reread).

We decided that Alice might be at May's house today. Let's see if she is. Turn quickly to page—(write *38*).

SILENT READING

Page 38. The girls are certainly enjoying themselves. But someone isn't. Who is that? Why is Jip yawning?

Independent word attack— doll

Of course, you know what the girls are playing with. You know how the word begins. How many times can you find the new word? If May had only one doll, the word would look like this. (Write *doll*.) But she has more than one. So it looks like this. (Write *dolls*.) Show me the word which means one; more than one. Then this card says— (add *doll* to card holder).

Now read two sentences. Start Alice and Jip on the road to May's house. Why would you enjoy going to May's house? Read four sentences and find out. How many big dolls has she? How many little dolls? How many all together? I know why Jip is yawning. I know what he does. Finish the page and see.

Phrase meaning

Page 39. I hope you remember how Mother said "after a while." (Indicate *By and by* on board.) By and by what happened? Read two sentences and see.

I know Alice asks Father a question. How do I know? Read and see what she asks. How did Father answer? Read two more sentences to find out. Now Father tells Alice she may do two things. Read until you find out what they are. Does Alice do them? Finish the page and see.

ORAL READING

Rereading by page units. I think we need a girl to read about that playroom. The girl who knows—(indicate word card *doll*) may read page 38. The one who knows these two words (indicate *By* and *eat*) may read page 39.

WORD RECOGNITION TECHNIQUES

Auditory-visual perception. *Initial sounds.* Show me how *rabbit* begins, and I will finish the word. (Continue with *hop, ball, just, so, came, laughed.*)

Phonics

You know how *down* begins. (Write *down;* write *d;* then erase word and letter.) If you will show me how *down* begins, I will finish it. *Doll—down!* What do your ears tell you about these two words? Show me how *doll* begins, and I will finish it. (Repeat with *duck.*)

SUPPLEMENTARY ACTIVITIES

1. *Vocabulary Primer Workbook,* pages 22, 23.
2. *Workbook for Day In and Day Out,* page 23. Be sure directions are understood.

Unit 20: A Box for Alice (*cont.*)

Pp. 40-42

NEW VOCABULARY: that   walk   wanted

PREPARATION

Have the following materials ready for use:

Pocket Card Holder
Word Cards: 90 In   152 got   484 walk
                      92 Is   457 Just   485 That
                    148 What   472 Then   486 wanted
Phrase Cards: 175 Alice looked   294 It is
                    244 Here is   399 This is

INITIAL PROCEDURE

Vocabulary review. (Have all words and phrases listed above, except *got, That, walk, wanted,* in card holder.) Take a card from the card holder, read it, and then use it in a sentence. (Continue, using the procedure that was outlined in Unit 19.)

Introducing new vocabulary. (Have these sentences on board.)

> By and by Jip ran up the walk.
> See that ball!
> So Jip got the ball.
> That is just what I wanted you to do.

Of course, you know this word. (Write *looked*.) Now it says— (erase the *ed*). Do you remember the day that Alice walked and walked? Then this word says—(write *walked*). I wonder what it would say if I did this. (Erase *ed*. Wait for suggestion *walk*.) Of course, it says *walk*. When I go from place to place, I—(add word card *walk* to

Drill on sentence beginnings

Word structure

card holder). And another word for *sidewalk* is just—(indicate word card).

When I point to something near at hand, I use the pointing word. (Write *This.*) When I point to something far away, I say—. (Point

Guidance in
methods of
word attack

and say, "See that picture. See that boy." Write *That* under *This.*) I always know which pointing word says *That* because I see the little word—(draw a line under *at* in *That*). Read the two pointing words. Which one says *That?* How do you know? Then this word card says— (add *That* to card holder).

Phrase
meaning

One day Jerry was playing ball. You will learn what happened if you read the first sentence on the board. These words (underline *By and by*) mean "after a while." Jerry threw the ball far away. He pointed to it and said—(sentence 2). Then he said, "Get it, Jip, get it!" This is what happened next. (Sentence 3.) Think how this word begins. (Indicate *got.*) Then hop over it and let the sentence help you. So Jip g—— the ball. (Wait for suggestion *got.*) Then this card says—(add *got* to card holder).

Jerry used the pointing word *That* again and said—(sentence 4). You can get this word (indicate *wanted*) because you see this little word inside it. (Draw a line under *want* in *wanted.* Have sentence

Word structure

read.) What does this word say? (Write *want.*) What does it say now? (Add *ed.*) Then this card says—(add *wanted* to card holder; have sentences and words reread).

Reading
numbers

This is the day when we find out whether Alice really gets a box. If you can read this number (write *40*) and can turn to page 40, we can find out.

SILENT READING

Page 40. (Let pupils discover the box on page 41.) Alice didn't see Mother the minute she ran out on the walk. How long was it before Mother came? Read three sentences and find out.

What did Alice say and do when she saw Mother? What did Mother say when she saw Alice? Finish the page and see. I hope you remember this word. (Indicate *got.*)

Page 41. Who has the box? I am sure, if Mother points to it, she uses this word. (Indicate *That.*) Alice asks a question. How do I know? Read and find out what she asks.

Who answers the question first? What does he say? Read and see. What can it be? (Wait for suggestions: gloves, socks, ribbons.) Does Mother tell us which guess is the right one? Finish the page and see. Alice must be puzzled. Anyway, I am.

Oral language

Page 42. (Allow time for enjoyment of picture. Have pupils decide which ribbons Alice will wear with her red coat.) I don't believe Alice knew what was in the box when she asked those questions at the top of the page. How many questions did she ask? Read three lines and find out what she asks.

I think Mother told her to do what she is doing. Read two sentences and see if Mother did. Does Alice say, "Thank you," or something else just as nice? Finish the page and find out. Watch out. She uses a pointing word, but which one does she use?

Predicting outcomes

I am going to watch Alice's braids from this time on. Are you? What are you going to watch for?

Page 43. Can you tell where Father may be going? Do you think Jerry may be going with him? Then can you explain Jip's sad look? I hope we can cheer him up when we read the story.

ORAL READING

Rereading by page units; Dramatization. You must know these words (indicate *walk* and *got*) if you want to read page 40. Maybe we can have three people read page 41. Alice can ask her question. Jerry and Mother can answer. The one who can make *want* grow into —(indicate *wanted*) may read page 42. (In some other period have the entire story reread.)

WORD RECOGNITION TECHNIQUES

Verbs ending in ed, ing

Word structure. (Write *walk* and then *walked, want—wanted, go—going, play—playing,* etc., and then have the pupils tell what you have written on the board.)

Phonics

Auditory-visual perception. *Initial sounds.* You remember how *walked* began. (Write *walked;* write *w;* then erase word and letter.) Show me how *walk* begins, and I will finish the word. (Continue with *wanted, went.*)

(Write *jacket—racket.*) John has a new *jacket.* Please do not make so much *racket.* Which of these new words says *jacket?* How do you know? (Continue with *bed—head, cap—lap, Dave—save.*)

SUPPLEMENTARY ACTIVITIES

1. *Vocabulary Primer Workbook,* pages 24, 25.

2. *Workbook for Day In and Day Out,* pages 21, 24. On page 24, do the first two items with the children.

Guiding
Workbook
activities

Unit 21: (Supplementary)

1. Textfilm for *Day In and Day Out,* Frames 11-12. See Textfilm manual for directions.

2. Additional reading. In the following preprimers the pages noted may be used as supplementary reading under teacher guidance:

Bill and Susan, pages 38-47. (Give help with the word *Daddy* on page 38.)

Here and There, pages 34-38.

My Little Green Story Book (Ginn and Co.), pages 3-10. (Give help with the word *work* on page 7.)

Ride Away, pages 39-47.

We Look and See, pages 31-38.

Unit 22: A Dog for Jerry

Pp. 43-45

NEW VOCABULARY: boy   day   dog   Mac   stay

PREPARATION

Have the following materials ready for use:

Pocket Card Holder
Word Cards

54 come	131 did	159 This	485 That	489 boy
68 my	132 do	162 yes	486 wanted	490 stay
120 want	135 house	464 came	487 dog	491 Mac
123 you	156 home	482 by	488 day	

INITIAL PROCEDURE

Building sight vocabulary

Vocabulary review. (Have the following words in pairs in card holder: *by—my, came—come, did—do, home—house, This—That, want—wanted, yes—you.*) Bring me one pair of partner words and read each word for me. (Continue until all cards are removed.) Who can read all the words as I return them to the card holder?

Introducing new vocabulary. (Have the following sentences on the board.)

One day Father said,
"I have to go to the city."
I have to stay for days and days.
I want a good big boy.
Here is that boy.
I can not have that.
I can stay home with Mother.

(Put word cards *boy* and *dog* in holder.) Here are two new words. One says *boy;* Jerry is a *boy*. One says *dog;* Jip is a puppy, but also a *dog.* Which word says *boy?* How do you know? Then the other word says—. If I begin my word this way (write *b*), you will tell me to finish—. If I begin it this way (write *d*), you will tell me to finish—.

The title of our book is—. Here is one of the words in our title. (Add *day* to card holder.) What does it say? (Reverse card to show capitalized form.) I will tell you something interesting about the word *day.* (Write *day* on board.) It begins like *do,* and this part (draw line under *ay*) says *ā*. Take a careful eye picture of that part. Then when I write—(write *d*) and add the part which says *ā* (add *ay*), the word will say—. If I add this letter (add *s*), the word will mean more than one day. It will say—.

I hope you know when the story begins. (Draw a line under phrase *One day.*) Now read the two-line sentence and find out what happened one day. "I won't be home tonight or tomorrow night," said Father. (Indicate sentence 2.) This word (indicate *stay*) begins like *store.* It rhymes with *day.* (Wait for suggestion *stay;* then add word card *stay* to card holder.) Now read the whole sentence and tell why Father won't be home that night. How long a time do you think this will be? (Draw a line under phrase *days and days.*)

"I want someone to help Mother while I am gone," said Father. (Sentence 3.) "Oh," said Jerry—(sentence 4). "Yes," said Father, "but what if that boy runs off to play when he should be helping? (Sentence 5.)" What does Father mean when he says, "I can not have that"? Jerry knew what Father meant because he said, "I don't have to run off to play. (Sentence 6.)" (Have sentences and all new words reread.)

The last time we saw Jerry, he was talking to Father. If you can read this number (write *43*) and turn quickly to that page, we can find out what he is saying.

SILENT READING

Page 43. If you know—(indicate word card *dog*), you can read the title. Do you suppose Jerry is going to have a dog of his own? Can you figure out why Jip has such a sad look?

Marginal notes:

Guidance in methods of word attack

Two-line sentences

Sentence meaning

One day Jerry happened to think of something. Read two sentences. What did he think of, and what did he do?

Read the next four sentences. What kind of dog did Jerry want? Will Father say, "All right"? Finish the page and see.

Page 44. I don't believe Father changed his mind. Read two sentences and find out. Maybe Jerry forgets about the dog. Read two more sentences to see if he does.

The next two sentences tell us exactly the same thing the picture does. Read and see if they do. Now the man asks a question. What does he ask, and how does Jerry answer? Finish the page and find out.

Page 45. The first two sentences tell me two things about that man. What are they? The next two sentences tell me two more things. What are they? Why do you think the dog cannot go to the city? (Discuss difference between city dogs and country dogs.)

Oral language

If I tell you that the man's dog was called *Mac* (add word card *Mac* to card holder), can you find his name on the page? How many times? If Mac cannot go to the city, what does his master plan to do with him? Read three sentences and you will know. What does Jerry think of that plan? Finish the page and see.

Predicting outcomes

Do you think Father will agree to this plan? If he does, what may happen in the story tomorrow?

ORAL READING

Rereading by page units. The one who can read these two new words (indicate *day* and *dog*) may read page 43. (Continue with *boy* for page 44, *stay* for page 45.)

WORD RECOGNITION TECHNIQUES

Auditory-visual perception. *Phonetic parts.* You remember that this word says—(write *day*) and the part in the word (draw a line under *ay*) says—. Then what does this word say? (Write *play*.) Can you see the part *ā* in *play*? Draw a line under it. Tell me what the word says; the part. (Continue with *away, May, stay*.)

Phonics

Initial sounds. If you will show me how *rain* begins, I will finish the word. (Continue with *dog, walk, laughed*.)

You remember how *man* begins. (Write *man—Man;* direct attention to *m—M;* then erase words.) If you show me how *morning* begins, I will finish the word. (Continue with *Mac, Mother,* directing attention to necessity for capital letters for names.)

Capitalization—names

SUPPLEMENTARY ACTIVITIES

1. *Vocabulary Primer Workbook,* pages 26, 27, 28.
2. *Workbook for Day In and Day Out,* pages 25 and 26. On page 25 do first section with pupils, if necessary. Page 26 is to be done under teacher guidance.

Guiding Workbook activities

Pp. 46-48

Unit 23: A Dog for Jerry (*cont.*)

NEW VOCABULARY: again   garden   was   will

PREPARATION

Have the following materials ready for use:

Pocket Card Holder
Word Cards

51 And	161 went	471 Please	492 will
155 had	162 Yes	482 by	493 again
158 name	460 happy	485 That	494 was
159 This	464 came	488 day	495 garden

INITIAL PROCEDURE

Vocabulary review. (Have these word cards in card holder: *And, by, came, day, had, happy, name, Please, That, This, went, Yes.*)

Read and bring me the two pointing words; the joining word; a word you find in the title of our book; the word which means the

Building sight vocabulary

opposite of *no;* a word which tells how you feel when you laugh; a word which begins like *coat;* one that begins like *but;* the partner of the word *have;* the word we use when we ask for something; a word which begins like *not;* one that is the partner of the word *want.*

Can you climb the ladder as fast as I return the words to the card holder? Can you play "One, Two, Three! How Many for Me?" and remove them again?

Introducing new vocabulary. (Have these sentences on board.)

> I can not go to the garden.
> I will go.
> It was May.
> Stay and play with me.
> But I will come again.

"Dear me," said Mother one morning. "I need lettuce for dinner, but I am so busy that—(indicate sentence 1)." If you watch how this word begins, you will know it cannot say *store.* (Indicate *garden.*) Think how it begins. Think where Mother might get lettuce. Who is ready? Then this word (add word card *garden* to card holder) says—.

Alice wanted to help Mother. So she said—(indicate sentence 2). Think how this word begins. (Indicate *will.*) Jump over it and let the sense of the sentence help you. Then this word says—(add *will* to card holder). Watch how *will* begins. Watch the twin letters. (Trace *w* and *ll.*) Then when I write—(write *will*), you will know that the word says—.

Alice was going into the house with the lettuce when she saw someone going by the gate. (Indicate sentence 3.) Think how this word begins. (Indicate *was.*) Jump over it. The sentence will help you. The new word is—(add *was* to card holder). Watch as I trace *was.* Then when I write—(write *was*), you will know that the word says—. Alice wanted someone to play with her. So she called—(sentence 4). I hope you remember how this word begins. (Indicate *Stay.*) I hope you remember that this part says—(draw a line under *ay*). Now read what Alice said.

May couldn't stay. "I have to go home now," she said—(indicate sentence 5). If you see this little word (write *a*) on the beginning of your word (draw a line under *a* in *again*), you can get that new

Guidance in
methods of
word attack

word. Who is ready? Then this word says—(add *again* to card holder; have sentences and words reread).

We decided yesterday that Father might change his mind and let Jerry have that dog. If you can read this number (write *46*) and can turn quickly to that page, we can find out.

SILENT READING

Page 46. I don't believe we were right. If you know this word (indicate *will* in sentence 2), you can read three sentences and find out why. The man wants Father to understand what kind of dog Mac is. Read two more sentences and find out what he says. Is the man going to move to the city and stay there forever? Read two more sentences, and they will tell you. Don't forget this word. (Indicate *again*.) What will happen when the man comes home from the city? The next sentence will tell you.

Will Father give in? Finish the page and see.

Page 47. (Allow time for discussion of picture. Have pupils judge from expression on Mother's face what may happen.)

What does Jerry think about Mother, and what does he do? Read two sentences, and you will know.

If I wanted anything as much as Jerry wants that dog, I would use a certain word when I talked to Mother. Does Jerry use that word? Read three sentences and find out what he says. I believe Jerry is teasing. Remember this word. (Indicate *again*.) Then read the next sentence and see if you agree. Why do you know he is teasing?

Does Mother give in? The next two sentences will tell you. Will Jerry make a bed for that dog by the fireplace? Finish the page and find out.

If that dog cannot stay in the house, maybe he can stay in the— (indicate *garden*). But what will he live in? Then what do you expect to see in the next picture? Turn and see if you are right.

Page 48. (Allow time for full enjoyment of picture. Have pupils decide why Jip stays close to Mother.)

How long was it before Mac came? The first two sentences tell. I hope you remember this word. (Indicate *was* in third sentence on board.) Now read two more sentences. Find out three things about

Mac. Could you tell all those things from the picture? I wonder how Mac feels about his change of home. Read until you find out.

Mother must know from what Jerry says how happy he is. Finish the page and find out what he says. Will Jerry be as happy when the man comes and Mac must go home again?

Page 49. Just look at those eyes! Alice and Jerry certainly look—. Maybe that is why the name of the next part of our book is *Surprise*. Can you read the title? It will be fun to find out what the surprise is, won't it?

ORAL READING

Rereading by page units. The one who knows these two words (indicate *will* and *again*) may read page 46. (Continue with *stay* for page 47, *was* and *garden* for page 48. In this or another period choose six boys to reread the story of "A Dog for Jerry" by pages.)

VOCABULARY ENRICHMENT AND EXTENSION

Multiple meanings

Word concepts. What do you mean by—(write *a good dog*)? by —(write *a good boy*)? by—(write *a good big dog*)? Yes, when Jerry wanted a good big dog, he wanted a very big dog. And Mac was big, wasn't he?

WORD RECOGNITION TECHNIQUES

Drill on carrier words

Accurate word recognition. (Erase everything from board except *I will go* and *It was May*.) This sentence says—(indicate *I will go*), and this word says—(underline *will*). I always remember *will* by these twin letters. (Trace *ll*.) Read this sentence. (Indicate *It was May*.) This word (indicate *was*) says—. Take a good picture of *was*. (Trace word; then erase entire board.) Don't let me catch you. (Write *was;* then erase quickly.) What word did I write? Use it in a sentence. (Repeat with *will*. Continue until words are recognized with ease.)

Auditory-visual perception. *Phonetic parts.* I hope you remember what this part says. (Write *ay*.) Then this word says—(write *play;* then *day, away, stay*).

Phonics

Initial sounds. You remember how *not* begins. (Write *not—Not;* trace *n—N;* then erase words.) *New* begins like *not*. Show me how *new*

begins. Then I will finish the word. (Continue with *name, was, will, man, Mac, dog, doll.*)

(Write *west-nest.*) Here are two new words. One says *west;* I am going out *West.* One says *nest;* I saw a *nest* in a tree. Which word says *west?* How do you know? (Continue with *much* and *dish.*)

SUPPLEMENTARY ACTIVITIES

1. *Vocabulary Primer Workbook,* pages 29, 30.

Independent study habits

2. *Workbook for Day In and Day Out,* pages 27, 28. Supervise the reading of text on page 28, but have each incomplete sentence marked independently.

3. Tests. Give the informal tests in the *Workbook for Day In and Day Out,* pages 29, 30. A score of 1 is given for each item correctly marked. Pupils should make a score of at least 16 on the vocabulary

Individual check on sight vocabulary

test and a score of at least 3 on the sentence-meaning test. At this time, check each pupil individually with the word cards for the new Primer vocabulary. (See page 159 of the Primer.)

Unit 24: (Supplementary)

1. Textfilm for *Day In and Day Out,* Frames 13-14. See Textfilm manual for directions.

2. Additional reading. In the following preprimers the pages noted may be used as supplementary reading under teacher guidance:

Here and There, pages 39-47.

My Little Green Story Book, pages 11-18. (Give help with the words *apples,* page 11; and *dinner,* page 18.)

Ned and Nancy, pages 21-28. (Give help with the word *has* on page 27.)

Time to Play (American Book Co.), pages 3-9.

We Come and Go (Scott, Foresman and Co.), pages 3-8. (Give help with the word *Baby* on page 5.)

We Look and See, pages 39-47.

Unit 25: Something for Mother

Pp. 49-53

NEW VOCABULARY: get   surprise

PREPARATION

Have the following materials ready for use:

Pocket Card Holder
Word Cards

155 had	464 came	475 puddle	493 again
161 went	465 out	476 rain	494 was
457 just	467 for	488 day	496 surprise
461 away	472 Then	490 stay	497 get

INITIAL PROCEDURE

Vocabulary review. (Have the following words in card holder: *away, came, day, had, just, puddle, rain, stay.*) I will say a sentence.

Building sight vocabulary

The first one to see in the card holder a word which I used in my sentence may read the card and take it from the card holder. Who will have the most cards? (Use the following sentences: I went away. Sally came to see me. One day I had a cold. I walked in a rain puddle. I had to stay at home just one morning. Have pupils use the words they took from the card holder in sentences and then return cards to card holder. Have pupils who took no cards play "One, Two, Three! How Many for Me?" to remove the cards a second time.)

Introducing new vocabulary. (Have these sentences on board.)

It was Jerry.
That was a big surprise.
Will you get it for me?
I will get it.
Then he went out to play again.

Guidance in
methods of
word attack

Jerry had gone to Jack's house. Mother didn't expect him home for another hour. All at once someone came in at the door. (Sentence 1.) Mother's eyes opened wide because—(indicate sentence 2). Think how this word begins. (Indicate *surprise*.) Remember that Mother didn't expect to see Jerry. That was a big s——. (Wait for suggestion *surprise*.) Then this word (add *surprise* to card holder) says—. What a long word it is! Watch how it begins. (Trace *s*.) Do you like surprises? What kind of surprises?

When Mother recovered from her surprise, she said, "Oh, Jerry! I want my thimble." (Indicate sentence 3.) Think how this word begins. (Indicate *get*.) Think what Mother wanted Jerry to do. Now read the sentence. The new word is—(add *get* to card holder).

Of course, Jerry said—(sentence 4). After that what happened? (Sentence 5. Have sentences and new words reread.)

Today we start a new part of our book, and the title of this part is our new word. (Indicate *surprise*.) Turn quickly to page 50 so that we may find out what the surprise is.

SILENT READING

Page 50. I believe it is springtime. What makes me think so? The title makes me think that Mother is going to get a present. Read it and see if you think so, too. The first sentence tells me the same thing that the picture does. Read it and see.

The picture makes me think that Alice is talking, but it doesn't tell me what she is saying. Read the next three sentences and find out. How does Mother answer? The next sentence tells. What does Mother mean by "come with me"? Finish the page and prove that she meant that Alice could have a garden.

Page 51. I believe Jip has been into mischief. What does Alice seem to be covering up? Now read four sentences. Are we right about that hole?

If Jip did that to my garden, I am sure I would use this word. (Indicate *get;* then reverse card to show capitalized form.) Finish the page. Does Alice use this word? What does she say?

Page 52. Why do you think Alice looks so happy? What two things did her garden have to have before it could grow that way? The

Two-line sentence

sun seems to be shining today, but I wonder if it did rain on that garden. Read three sentences and see. One is a two-line sentence. Watch out for it.

The next sentence tells me how long after the rain the garden turned green. How long was it?

Alice wants someone to see her garden. Finish the page. Whom does she want to come? What does she say?

Page 53. I see someone I wouldn't want in my garden. Who is it, and why wouldn't I want him? I wonder if Alice wants that rabbit. Read five sentences and find out. Now read another sentence. Does the rabbit hop away?

Two-line sentence

Someone plays a trick on Alice. Finish the page and see who it is. Who will be the first one ready to read that two-line sentence as if it were all on one line?

Predicting outcomes. I hate to leave that little rabbit in the garden, don't you? What may happen before we get back to the story tomorrow?

ORAL READING

Rereading by page units. The one who knows these words (add word cards *went* and *for* to card holder) may read page 50. The one who can read the new word (indicate *get*) and also these cards (add *was* and *out* to card holder) may read page 51. (Continue in same way, using *came* for page 52; *Then* and *again* for page 53.)

WORD RECOGNITION TECHNIQUES

Accurate word recognition. Alice said this to Jip. (Write *Get out, get out!* and have sentence read.) Take a careful eye picture of this word. (Indicate *get.*) Watch this letter. (Indicate *e.*) Then when I write (write *Get*), you will know the word says—. (Repeat the procedure with *get.*)

Drill on carrier words

This is what happened when Alice said that. (Write *Jip got out.*) What does this word say? (Indicate *got.*) Watch this round letter. (Indicate *o.*) Then when I write—(write *got*), you will know that it says—. Watch carefully. Which word will I write? Check with the sentence if you don't know. (Alternate with *get* and *got* until recognition becomes automatic. Repeat sentences and word procedure with *was, will*.)

Phonics

Auditory-visual perception. *Initial sounds.* You remember how *good* begins. (Write *good—Good;* trace *g—G;* then erase words.) Show me how *garden* begins; then I will finish the word for you. (Continue with *get, will, was, day, dog, me, may, name, not*.)

SUPPLEMENTARY ACTIVITIES

1. *Vocabulary Primer Workbook,* pages 31, 32.
2. *Workbook for Day In and Day Out,* pages 31, **32.**

Pp. 54-55

Unit 26: Something for Mother (*cont.*)

PREPARATION

Have the following materials ready for use:

Pocket Card Holder
Word Cards

51 And	461 away	482 by	492 will	496 surprise
152 got	467 for	488 day	493 again	497 get
457 just	472 Then	490 stay	494 was	

INITIAL PROCEDURE

Vocabulary review. Can you read each word as I put it into the card holder and then use the word in a sentence? (Add each of the words listed above to form two columns. Have pupils hop down Jip's hole in the garden by reading one column; down the rabbit hole by reading the other.)

Reading page numbers

Is Little Rabbit still eating away in Alice's garden? If you can read this number (write *54*) and can turn quickly to that page, we can find out.

SILENT READING

Page 54. I really believe Jip must have chased Little Rabbit away, don't you? Alice looks as if she had had a big—(indicate word card *surprise*). I wonder if those flowers grew overnight. Read the first sentence and see. How long do you think it means when your book says, "The days went by and by"?

Read the next sentence and find out what Alice did then. When she gets over her surprise, she begins to talk. Read six sentences. What does she say? Now I would like to read that part aloud for you. I think I can sound as surprised as Alice looks. (Set pattern for expressive reading.)

I know what I would do if I saw flowers like that in my garden. What would you do? What does Alice do? Finish the page to see. What do you think the "something green" was?

Page 55. Alice makes up a little rhyme as she talks to Mother. Read four sentences and see what she says. I would like to read her rhyme also. Listen as I read. Then I will let you try.

Does Mother enjoy the surprise? Does she say, "Thank you," or something else just as nice? Finish the page and see.

ORAL READING

Rereading by page units. (Have the group choose six girl readers, who in turn may choose one page of the story. In this or another period have the story "Something for Mother" reread by these children.)

WORD RECOGNITION TECHNIQUES

Auditory-visual perception. *Initial sounds.* You remember how *father* begins. (Write *Father—father;* trace *F—f;* then erase.) *Father, for!* What do your ears tell you about these words? If you will show me how *for* begins, I will finish the word. (Continue with *find, garden, name, man.*)

One day we wanted to eat outdoors. We wanted to have a—(write *p_____,* wait for suggestion *picnic,* then complete word; continue in

Margin notes: Sentence meaning · Setting standards for oral reading · Audience reading · Phonics the same manner). So we took our s—— (*supper*) in a b—— (*basket*) and went to the p—— (*park*). We found a t—— (*table*). Then we made a f—— (*fire*) so that we could c—— (*cook*). After we ate, we had a ride on a p—— (*pony*). When it grew d—— (*dark*), we went h—— (*home*).

SUPPLEMENTARY ACTIVITIES

1. *Vocabulary Primer Workbook,* page 33.

Guiding
Workbook
activities

2. *Workbook for Day In and Day Out,* pages 33, 34. Give whatever guidance is necessary on page 33.

Unit 27: (Supplementary)

1. Textfilm for *Day In and Day Out,* Frames 15-16. See Textfilm manual for directions.

2. Additional reading. In the following preprimers the pages noted may be used as supplementary reading under teacher guidance:

My Little Green Story Book, pages 19-24. (Give help with the words *chair,* page 19; and *Bunny,* page 21.)

Ned and Nancy, pages 29-36. (Give help with the word *bigger* on page 33.)

Time to Play, pages 10-17. (Give help with *we,* page 11; and *stop,* page 16.)

We Come and Go, pages 9-12.

Unit 28: A Good Wish

Pp. 56-57

NEW VOCABULARY: Jack   wish

PREPARATION

Have the following materials ready for use:

Pocket Card Holder
Word Cards

132 Do	159 this	468 But	485 that	499 Jack
139 Not	455 toy	469 new	497 get	
155 had	458 fly	474 laughed	498 wish	

INITIAL PROCEDURE

Building sight vocabulary

Vocabulary review. (Have all cards listed above, except *Jack* and *wish,* on a chair.) On this chair, find a word you know, read the card, use the word in a sentence, and then put the card into the card holder. How many steps up the word ladder can you climb without falling off?

Introducing new vocabulary. (Have these sentences on board.)

> My name is Jack.
> I will wish for one.

Guidance in methods of word attack

A new boy has moved into our neighborhood. I met him the other day, and he said—(indicate sentence 1). You know how this word begins. (Indicate *Jack.*) It rhymes with *back. Back, J——*! (Wait for suggestion *Jack.*) Read the sentence and tell us what he said. This word (add *Jack* to card holder) says—.

While Jack was talking to me, a boy went by on a bicycle. "I want a bicycle," said Jack. "When my birthday comes—(indicate sentence 2). Think how this word begins and ends. (Indicate *wish.*) Think what you do when you blow out birthday candles. Who is ready to tell what Jack said? Then this word says—(add *wish* to card holder and have sentences and new words reread).

Reading page numbers

We are going to read about someone this morning who makes all kinds of wishes. If you can read this number (write *56*) and can turn quickly to that page, we can find out who it is.

SILENT READING

Page 56. I think I know who is making wishes. Do you? I think I know what day it is, too.

Can you find the new word *wish* in the title? What kind of wish will Jerry make? Read the title to see.

Jerry asks a question; then he answers it. Read until you find out what the question and the answer are. Now what does he wish for first? Read until you find out. Do you think he will get that wish?

Setting oral reading standards

Mother must think a little boy with a real airplane would be very funny. Does she think that wish will come true? Read four sentences and see. (Read these sentences aloud for pupils to set the pattern for similar sentences which recur throughout the story.)

What is Jerry's second wish? Finish the page and see. Do you agree with Jerry? Do you think he should change his name?

Page 57. What does Mother think about changing names? Read the whole page and find out. Jerry doesn't seem to have very good luck with his wishes, does he? Maybe he will have better luck tomorrow.

ORAL READING

Rereading by page units. The one who knows this word (indicate word card *wish*) may read the part of page 56 which tells about Jerry's first wish. The one who knows this word (indicate *Jack*) may read about the second wish. The one who knows both words may read page 57.

WORD RECOGNITION TECHNIQUES

Phonics

Auditory-visual perception. *Initial sounds.* You remember how *puppy* begins. (Write *puppy—Puppy;* direct attention to *p—P;* then erase words.) If you will show me how *pet* begins, I will finish the word. (Continue with the words *new, name, wish, will, garden, got, for, Father.*)

Here is something hard, but you can do it. I know four boys. Here are their names. (Write *Ned, Walter, Paul, Fred.* Do not use names of pupils in group.) One boy's name is Paul. Can you find the name *Paul?* (Continue in similar way.)

SUPPLEMENTARY ACTIVITIES

1. *Vocabulary Primer Workbook,* pages 34, 35.
2. *Workbook for Day In and Day Out,* pages 35, 36. Be sure directions on page 36 are understood.

Unit 29: A Good Wish (*cont.*)   Pp. 58-59

NEW VOCABULARY: pony

PREPARATION

Have the following materials ready for use:

Pocket Card Holder

Word Cards:	51 And	468 But	485 That
	459 So	472 Then	500 pony
Phrase Cards:	177 Alice saw	446 You may have	
	304 Jerry went		

INITIAL PROCEDURE

Drill on sentence beginnings

Vocabulary review. (Have all cards listed above, except *pony,* in card holder.) Jerry was making wishes. I am wishing, also. I am wishing that our sentences may get started on the right tracks. Take a card from the card holder, read it, and then use it in a sentence. (When all cards have been removed, have them exchanged, reread, and returned to card holder.)

Reading page numbers

If you can read this number (write *58*), we can turn to that page quickly and find out if Jerry makes a wish which comes true.

SILENT READING

Page 58. Where do you think Alice, Jerry, and Jip are going? Alice may have the bag, but I think Jerry has the money. Do you?

Is Jerry still wishing, or is he giving someone else a chance? The first two sentences tell.

Will Mother get her wish? Read until you find out. Now finish the page. Does it tell you anything about Jip? Where do you think he came from?

Independent word attack

Page 59. I know what Jerry will wish for now. You know how *pony* begins. How many times can you find it?

The first two sentences tell just what the picture tells. Read them and see if they do.

Don't forget this word. (Indicate word card *That.*) What does Jerry say the minute he sees the pony? Read until you find out. Will he get that wish? What does Alice think about it? Finish the page and see.

ORAL READING

Rereading by page units. The one who can tell me how many two-line sentences there are on page 58 and can read those sentences as if they were each on one line, may read the page. The one who knows this word (add word card *pony* to card holder) may read page 59.

WORD RECOGNITION TECHNIQUES

Phonics

Auditory-visual perception. *Initial sounds.* You remember how *too* begins. (Write *Too—too;* direct attention to *T—t;* and then erase words.) Show me how *toy* begins, and I will finish the word. (Continue with *puddle, pony, new, name, good, get, for, Father.*)

You have sharp eyes. Here are four new words. (Write *paint, girl, nest, fast.*) Which one of these words says *paint?* I like to *paint.* (Continue in similar way with other words.)

SUPPLEMENTARY ACTIVITIES

1. *Vocabulary Primer Workbook,* pages 36, 37. Do first item on page 36 with the children.

2. *Workbook for Day In and Day Out,* page 37 (to be done under teacher guidance).

Unit 30: A Good Wish (*cont.*)

Pp. 60-62

PREPARATION

Have the following materials ready for use:

Pocket Card Holder
Word Cards

133 have	159 this	457 Just	468 But	492 will
155 had	455 toy	464 came	485 that	498 wish

INITIAL PROCEDURE

Vocabulary review. (Have all word cards listed above in card holder.)

Drill on
sentence
beginnings

I hope you know this sentence beginning. I hope you can use it to begin a sentence. (Write *Alice came;* then continue with *I wish, I want, I had, But, Just, I will have, This is, That is, Not one.*) Since *not one* (indicate phrase) of you had any trouble, I am sure we can play "One, Two, Three! How Many for Me?" and remove the cards from the card holder in a hurry.

If you can read this number (write *61*) and can find that page quickly, we can find out whether Jerry gets a wish today.

SILENT READING

Page 60. (Have pupils notice that there is no page number. Have them decide that since 60 comes before 61, this page must be 60.

Locating pages   Emphasize that not all pages have page numbers.)

I know one name we can use for each thing we see on this page. Do you? Find the word I am thinking of. (Have word card *toy* returned to card holder.)

I wonder if Mother sent Alice and Jerry to the toy store. I wonder who is wishing this time. Read the first four sentences and find out. Now read until you find out what Alice wants in her store. Did she get her wish? Finish the page and see.

Page 61. What name could you give to everything you see on this page? Could someone be wishing for an animal store? Read two sentences and see. Now find out what Jerry wants in his store. Does he get his wish? Finish the page and see.

Two-line sentence   **Page 62.** I see a two-line sentence. Do you? Now read two sentences. Did the children forget what Mother wanted?

The minute Jerry walked into the house, what did he say? What did Alice say? Read until you find out. Do you suppose they might get that wish? Why could that wish come true and not the wish for a pony? Let's see if you are right. Read two sentences and find out what Mother says.

Now finish the page. What did Alice and Jerry say then? What

Oral language   did they get? (Enjoy with the children the inscription on cooky jar "Thou shalt not steal.")

Page 63. Mother with her gloves on, and Alice's cap in her hand! What do you suppose that means? When we read again, we will learn whether you have figured out the right answer. I wonder if Jerry will go away, too.

ORAL READING

Following events in sequence   **Organization.** This is such a good story. The first thing that happens is that Jerry wishes for an airplane and talks to Mother about it. Who wants to read just that much of the story? (Continue suggesting sequence of events in similar fashion.)

WORD RECOGNITION TECHNIQUES

Phonics

Auditory-visual perception. *Initial sounds.* You know how *kitten* begins. (Write *kitten,* direct attention to *k;* then erase word.) Show me how *kite* begins, and I will finish the word. (Continue with *king, pony, man, for, toy.*)

I like cookies. I like to help Mother m—— cookies. (Write *m;* wait for suggestion *make;* then complete word.) (Continue as in previous units.) She puts them into a p—— (*pan*). Then she puts them into the oven to b—— (*bake*). She keeps her cookies in a j—— (*jar*). The kind I like best are ch—— (*chocolate*) cookies. I could eat s—— (*six* or *seven*) at a time.

SUPPLEMENTARY ACTIVITIES

Guiding Workbook activities

1. *Vocabulary Primer Workbook,* pages 38, 39, 40. On page 38 give help with the marking of first item. Page 39 should be done under teacher guidance.

2. *Workbook for Day In and Day Out,* page 38. Supervise marking of item 1.

Unit 31: (Supplementary)

1. Textfilm for *Day In and Day Out,* Frames 17-18. See Textfilm manual for directions.

2. Additional reading. In the following preprimers the pages noted may be used as supplementary reading under teacher guidance:

My Little Green Story Book, pages 25-28. (Give help with the words *fast,* page 27; and *we,* page 28.)

Ned and Nancy, pages 37-40. (Give help with the word *cake* on page 37.)

Time to Play, pages 18-25.

We Come and Go, pages 13-16. (Give help with the word *funny* on page 15.)

Pp. 63-65 # Unit 32: Can You Find Alice?

NEW VOCABULARY: find   her   now

PREPARATION

Have the following materials ready for use:

Pocket Card Holder
Word Cards

51 And	155 had	457 just	469 new	501 find
131 did	159 this	461 away	471 Please	502 her
152 got	161 went	464 came	472 Then	503 now

INITIAL PROCEDURE

Drill on
carrier words

Vocabulary review. (Have all words listed above, except *find, her,* and *now,* in card holder. Have pupils play "One, Two, Three! How Many for Me?")

Introducing new vocabulary. (Have these sentences on board.)

> I can not find her.
> She was here.
> But she is not here now.

Guidance in
methods of
word attack

When you came into the room, I heard someone say, "Oh, look at Janet's new dress." I know another word you might have used instead of *Janet's.* You might have said—(write *her*). You know that the word begins like *here.* These two letters (underline *er*) say—(give sound). *H—er!* The new word is—(add *her* to card holder). When we talk about something which belongs to a girl or a woman, we often use the word—(indicate *her*). Use the word and tell us about Mary's new shoes.

Jerry came home from school. There on the table was a basket which he knew belonged to Grandmother. He looked for—(indicate *her*) everywhere. Then he ran out to Mother in the garden. He said, "Where is Grandmother?" (Indicate sentence 1.) Remember that this word (indicate *find*) begins like *Father*. Jump over it and let the sentence help you. I can not f—— her. (Wait for suggestion *find*.) Then this card says—(add *find* to card holder).

Mother looked up and said—(sentence 2). Then Mother went on to say—(indicate sentence 3). This word (indicate *now*) begins like *not*. The next two letters (underline *ow*) say—(give sound). But she is not here n—ow. The new word is—(add *now* to card holder; have sentences and new words read).

Someone in our story is trying to—(indicate word card *find*) some-one else. If you can read this page number (write *63*) and turn quickly to that page, we can find out who seems to be lost. Perhaps we can even (indicate word card *find*) her.

Reading page numbers

SILENT READING

Page 63. I discover two things about the title. It is a question. How do I know? This new word is in the title. What does it say? (Indicate *find*.) Who will read the question? Do you suppose Alice is lost?

What did Mother do when she wanted to talk to Jerry? Read the first sentence and see. If you remember this word (indicate *her*), you can read and find out what she said to Jerry. Can Jerry help Mother? Finish the page and see.

Page 64. What was the first thing Jerry did, and how did it turn out? Read two sentences and see. The next two sentences tell me the same thing as the picture. Read and see if they do. The box and the train are like Grandmother's basket. Finish the page and find out why.

Page 65. Read two sentences. To whom does the boat belong? Jerry asks a question, and Jack answers. Read the question and Jack's answer. Maybe Jerry thinks he needs help. Read two sentences and find out what he says to Jack. I wonder if Jack will help. Finish the page and see.

ORAL READING

Rereading by page units. The one who knows these two new words (indicate *find, her*) may read page 63. The one who knows this word (indicate *now*) may read page 64. The one who knows all three new words may read page 65.

VOCABULARY ENRICHMENT AND EXTENSION

Understanding
the meaning
of pronouns

Word concepts. When I talk about Alice's coat, I often use this word. (Write *her*.) Instead of saying *Alice is going,* I may say—(write *She*). *She* and *her* are two words I use when talking about a girl or a woman. What words do I use when I am talking about myself? (*I, me, my*)

WORD RECOGNITION TECHNIQUES

Drill on
carrier words

Accurate word recognition. (Write *Here is Alice.*) This word (underline *here*) says—. (Write *See her cap.*) This word says—(underline *her*). I always remember which word says *here* because it is the longer word and I see this letter on the end. (Indicate *e.*) Let's play "Magic." (Alternate writing *her, here* until recognition becomes accurate.)

Phonics

ay

Auditory-visual perception. *Phonetic parts.* Do you remember this word from the title of our book? (Write *day.*) It begins like *do,* and this part (underline *ay*) says *ā.* What does this word say? (Write *May.*) Can you find the part which says *ā?* Draw a line under it. (Continue with *play, stay, away.*)

SUPPLEMENTARY ACTIVITIES

1. *Vocabulary Primer Workbook,* page 41.
2. *Workbook for Day In and Day Out,* pages 39, 40.

Unit 33: Can You Find Alice? (*cont.*)

Pp. 66-67

NEW VOCABULARY: say

PREPARATION

Have the following materials ready for use:

Pocket Card Holder
Word Cards

51 And	161 went	461 Away	501 find	504 say
147 walked	457 Just	468 But	502 her	
159 This	459 So	494 was	503 now	

INITIAL PROCEDURE

Vocabulary review. I will tell what has happened in the story so far. You help me out by reading the words I put into the card holder.

Drill on carrier words

Mother could not—(add find to card holder and have card read; continue to add each underlined word) Alice. So she sent Jerry to look for her. Away went Jerry. He saw a toy train and said, "This is my train. Alice was here. But she is not here now." Just then he saw Jack. Jack was willing to help Jerry look. And the boys walked on. (Play "One, Two, Three! How Many for Me?" to have word cards reread and removed from card holder.)

Introducing new vocabulary. (Have these sentences on board.)

Jip ran and jumped on May.
He wanted to say, "Come and play."
"Get down, Jip, get down.
Go, Jip, go!"

One morning—(sentence 1). Jip barked and said—(wait for suggestion *bow-wow*). When Jip barked, he really wanted to talk. This is what he wanted to do. (Sentence 2.) You know how this word begins. (Indicate *say*.) You know that this part says—(underline *ay*). So the word is *s—ā*. (Add word card *say* to card holder.) Read the whole sentence. What was Jip trying to say?

Guidance in methods of word attack

I guess May didn't understand dog talk because she said—(sentences 3 and 4; have sentences and word reread).

Reading page numbers

If you can read this number (write *66*) and can turn quickly to that page, we can learn if the boys find Alice.

SILENT READING

Page 66. Where have the boys come now? Would a toy store be a good place to find a little girl? Why? Jerry is sure he is going to find Alice. Read four sentences and find the reason. He asks the man a question. What is the question? How does the man answer? Finish the page and see.

Page 67. And here comes Jip. Could he be of any help? (Discuss a dog's ability to scent.) Now read four lines. What did Jip do, and what did Jerry say to him?

Oral language

I wonder if Jip is trying to—(indicate word card *say*) something when he barks this time. Finish the page and find out.

ORAL READING

Rereading by page units. The one who can tell me two words we use when we talk about a girl or a woman may read page 66 (*she, her*). The one who knows this word (indicate *say*) may read page 67.

VOCABULARY ENRICHMENT AND EXTENSION

Word concepts. Today we have airplanes. *Now* we ride in airplanes. A long time ago people used horses. *Then* they rode in wagons and buggies. *Now* people live in houses and apartments. *Then* they lived in log cabins. What did you find out about these words? (Write *Now— Then*.)

Opposites

WORD RECOGNITION TECHNIQUES

Phonics

Auditory-visual perception. *Initial sounds.* If you will show me how *find* begins, I will finish the word for you. (Continue with *for, get, man, rain.*)

Here are four new words. (Write *farm, Mr., rooster, girl.*) Are your eyes sharp enough to see which word says *Mr.?* (Continue in same way.)

SUPPLEMENTARY ACTIVITIES

1. *Vocabulary Primer Workbook,* pages 42, 43.
2. *Workbook for Day In and Day Out,* page 41.

Unit 34: Can You Find Alice? (*cont.*)

Pp. 68-69

PREPARATION

Have the following materials ready for use:

Pocket Card Holder
Word Cards

122 with	132 Do	493 again	496 surprise
126 at	150 going	494 was	

INITIAL PROCEDURE

Vocabulary review. (Have these sentences on board.)

What a surprise for Alice!
Do not say that.
That dog is just a puppy.
He is not going with me.
That puppy was at the store again.

One morning Alice ran to the store. She thought she was alone; but when she opened the door of the store, Jip ran in, too. (Sentence 1.) Jip started to bark and bark. Alice said, "Keep still! (Sentence 2.)" The storekeeper smiled and said—(sentence 3). The next day Alice had to go to the store again. She shut Jip up in the kitchen and said—(sentence 4). But when she got to the store—(sentence 5). How do you suppose that happened? I am going to draw a line under certain words. Be ready to tell me what each word says. (Underline each word listed under word cards.) Now can you read these cards? (Add word cards to card holder, one at a time.)

Building sight vocabulary

Maybe Jip won't get into mischief today. Maybe he will find Alice. Turn to this page (write *68*) so that we can find out.

SILENT READING

Page 68. Jip *has* found Alice, hasn't he? And where is she? That is a joke on Jack and Jerry.

When Jerry sees Jip running home, he is disgusted. Read four lines. What does he say? Jack has a better opinion of Jip. Finish the page and find out what Jack says.

Page 69. I wonder how Jerry felt when he saw Alice. I wonder if he remembered to tell her that Mother wanted her. Read three sentences and see. Alice asks two questions. What are they? How does Jerry answer? Read until you find out. How does Jack answer Jerry? I hope you notice that the last two sentences are two-line sentences. Get ready to read them as if they were each on one line.

Two-line sentences

ORAL READING

Organization. (Write: _____*Mother wants Jerry to look for Alice.* _____*Jerry finds Jack.* _____*Jerry finds a box and a train.*) One of these sentences tells what happens on page 63 in our story. Which sentence is that? Who will come to the board and mark that sentence *1?* Who will find the sentence which tells what happens on page 64? Mark that sentence *2.* (Continue by having remaining sentence numbered *3.* Then proceed in similar fashion for pages 66, 67, 68, 69. Have some child read sentence 1 and the corresponding story page, etc.)

Following events in sequence

WORD RECOGNITION TECHNIQUES

Phonics

Auditory-visual perception. *Phonetic parts.* (Write *new*.) *New* begins like *not*, and this part in *new* says *ū*. (Underline *ew*.) Remember that the part says—(*ū*). That will help you remember that the word is—. (Review *ay* in *say, stay, play, away, day, may*.)

Initial sounds. Do you remember how *the* begins? It takes two letters to begin *the*. (Write *the;* then *th;* then erase word and letters.) Listen as I say *then, the*. What do your ears tell you about these two words? If you can show me how *then* begins, I will finish the word. (Continue with *that, this; say, surprise; toys, to; find, father; kitten, kite*.)

One day I went for a ride on a b— (*bus*). (Proceed as in previous units.) I did not have to pay any m— (*money*) because I had a t— (*ticket*). The bus stopped at every c— (*corner*). Some of the people on the bus were m— (*men*). Some were w— (*women*). Some were b— (*boys*). Some were g— (*girls*). The bus driver wore a blue s— (*suit*).

SUPPLEMENTARY ACTIVITIES

Guiding Workbook activities

1. *Vocabulary Primer Workbook,* pages 44, 45.
2. *Workbook for Day In and Day Out,* page 42. This page should be done under teacher guidance.

Unit 35: (Supplementary)

1. Textfilm for *Day In and Day Out,* Frames 19-20. See Textfilm manual for directions.
2. Additional reading. In the following preprimers the pages noted ᵇe used as supplementary reading under teacher guidance:

ᴾete, and Ginger, pages 11-16.

ᴳreen Story Book, pages 29-34. (Give help with the ᵖage 29.)

Time to Play, pages 26-33.
We Work and Play (Scott, Foresman and Co.), pages 3-10. (Give
help with the words *work,* page 3; and *Baby,* page 6.)

Pp. 70-73 Unit 36: A Walk with Mother

NEW VOCABULARY: mew

PREPARATION

Have the following materials ready for use:

Pocket Card Holder
Word Cards

159 This	468 But	486 wanted	503 now
162 Yes	471 please	494 was	504 say
459 So	474 laughed	496 surprise	505 mew
461 Away	484 walk	502 her	

INITIAL PROCEDURE

Building sight
vocabulary

Vocabulary review. (Have all word cards listed above, except
mew, in card holder.) Who can bring and read for me three cards?
four? five? the last two? How many cards can you read and return
to card holder?

Today some people you know are going to take a—(indicate word
card *walk*). If you can read this number (write *70*), we can turn to
that page and find out who they are.

SILENT READING

Page 70. Here they are! But where do you think they are going?
I wonder whose guess will be the right one.

Mother asks a question. Read the title and enough of the story to find out what her question is. Now read until you find out how Alice and Jerry answer. Does Mother tell the surprise? What does happen? The next three sentences tell. Alice seems to be lagging behind. I wonder why. Finish the page and see.

Page 71. Is Jerry also getting tired? Read until you find out. Mother doesn't tell what the surprise is. But she tells something about it. Finish the page and find out what she says. What do you suppose that surprise is?

Page 72. Is this kitten the surprise? Is it little and brown? Can you ride on it? Then I guess it isn't the surprise. You remember that, in the word *new* (write *new*), this part (underline *ew*) says *ū*. Here is a word which rhymes with *new*. (Write *mew*.) Do you see the part which says *ū*? (Underline *ew* in *mew*.) The kitten says m——. And this word card says—(add *mew* to card holder).

Now read four sentences. Find out what the kitten wanted to say when it said, "*Mew, mew!*" Was Alice as smart as you are? Did she know that the kitten could not be the surprise? Finish the page and find out.

Page 73. And who is this? Are you sure it is Mac? Read three sentences and see. Can this dog be the surprise? Is he little? Then he can't be the surprise. I wonder what Jerry thinks about it. Finish the page and find out.

Guidance in methods of word attack

ORAL READING

Rereading by page units. My favorite book is the book I like best. I have a favorite page in this story, also. It is page 70. I will read it for you. Is page 71 anyone's favorite page? Who wants to read that? (Continue in same manner with pages 72 and 73.)

Setting pattern for expressive reading

WORD RECOGNITION TECHNIQUES

Auditory-visual perception. *Phonetic parts.* What does this word say? (Write *new*.) Who can draw a line under the part you see in *new* and tell me what the part says? (Repeat with *mew;* then with *play, say, stay,* etc.)

Phonics

Initial sounds. It takes two letters to begin the word *Then.* If someone can show me how *then* begins, I will finish the word. (Continue
with *that, now, not, boy, by, come, can.*)

Here are four new words. (Write *There, nest, baby, candle.*) How
sharp are your eyes? Which word says *candle?* Light the *candle.*
(Continue in usual way.)

SUPPLEMENTARY ACTIVITIES

Guiding
Workbook
activities

1. *Vocabulary Primer Workbook,* page 46.
2. *Workbook for Day In and Day Out,* pages 43, 44. The first two
sections on page 44 should be done under teacher supervision.

Pp. 74-76 # Unit 37: A Walk with Mother (*cont.*)

PREPARATION

Have the following materials ready for use:

Pocket Card Holder
Word Cards

159 this	460 happy	465 out	482 By	497 get
459 So	464 came	467 for	492 will	503 Now

INITIAL PROCEDURE

Vocabulary review. (Have these sentences on the board.)

> By and by she came out.
> So this is Alice.
> I like something like this.
> Now I will get something for you.
> Alice looked so happy.

One day Mother asked Alice to take some fresh biscuits to Mrs. Smith. Alice rang Mrs. Smith's bell again and again. Then—(sentence 1). Mrs. Smith had never seen Alice before. So she said—(sentence 2). When she saw the biscuits, she said—(sentences 3, 4). I don't know what she got for Alice, but it must have been something very nice because—(sentence 5). How quickly can you read the words I underline? (Underline each word listed above under word cards.) How quickly can you read the cards I put into the card holder? (All cards listed.)

We still haven't found out what Mother's surprise is. Read this number and turn quickly to this page. (Write *74*.)

Drill on carrier words

SILENT READING

Page 74. One of the pictures gives away the surprise, doesn't it? Would you be as frightened as Alice and Jerry look if you were on that pony? How can you tell that they are frightened? Which one is the more frightened?

When I read the first two sentences on page 74, I know where the walk ended. When I read the next two, I know what Mother said and what happened when she got to the red house.

Maybe the man hasn't seen Alice and Jerry before, but I think he has heard about them. Read all he says and find out why I think so. I don't believe Alice and Jerry have seen that pony yet. Finish the page and find out why.

Page 75. Who was the first to discover the pony? The first two sentences tell. What do the children say the minute they see him? Read the sentences that tell. I believe the man helped them up. Read three lines and see if you can find out why I think so. Finish the page and start Alice and Jerry on their ride.

Page 76. Would you feel like Jerry? Read the first sentence and see. Jerry remembers something. Read six sentences and see what he remembers. If Jerry wants to ride on forever, I don't believe he will ride alone. Why not? Finish the page and see.

Predicting outcomes

Well, I suppose Alice and Jerry come to live with the man in the red house and ride the pony day and night. Is that the way you think things turn out? Why not?

Page 77. What do you call all these things you see in the picture? That must be why the new part of our book is called *Animals*. Who will read the title? Who will tell us the name of each animal? The first animal we will read about is Little—(write g_____ and wait for suggestion *goat*).

Independent word attack— goat

ORAL READING

Organization. (Write on board: _____*Alice sees a kitten.* _____*Alice and Jerry do not want to walk.* _____*Alice, Jerry, and Mother go for a walk.* Have pupils decide which sentence should be numbered *1* because it tells what happened first in the story. Have someone read the part of page 70 which corresponds with that sentence. Continue in similar way, adding the following sentences for the remaining pages: _____*Alice and Jerry jump on the pony.* _____*Alice and Jerry have a good ride.* _____*Jerry sees a big dog.* _____*Mother, Alice, and Jerry come to a red house.*)

Following events in sequence

WORD RECOGNITION TECHNIQUES

Auditory-visual perception. *Phonetic parts.* When Mother made a —(write *garden*), Alice wanted a garden, also. I will tell you something about the word *garden*. This part (underline *ar*) says—(give sound). Say the word *garden* and see if you can hear the *ar* sound. *Farm, cow!* In which word did you hear the part *ar*? (Give sound.) (Continue in similar manner with the words *car, bus; bowl, jar; some, part;* etc.)

Can you read this word? Can you draw a line under the part and tell me what the part says? (Use *day, stay, new, mew.*)

Initial sounds. Show me how *that* begins, and I will finish the word. (Continue with *dog, find, get.*)

(Conduct in usual way.) One morning Jerry jumped out of b—— (*bed*). He put on his s—— (*socks*) and then his sh—— (*shoes*). He took off his p—— (*pajamas*) and put on his sh—— (*shirt*) and his p—— (*pants*). He washed his f—— (*face*) and h—— (*hands*) and combed his h—— (*hair*). Then he ran downstairs to eat his br—— (*breakfast*).

Phonics

SUPPLEMENTARY ACTIVITIES

1. *Vocabulary Primer Workbook,* pages 47, 48.

2. *Workbook for Day In and Day Out,* pages 45, 46.

3. Tests. Give the informal tests on pages 47 and 48 of the *Workbook for Day In and Day Out.* A score of 1 is given for each item correctly marked. Pupils should make a score of at least 16 on the vocabulary test; a score of at least 3 on the sentence-meaning test. If scores are lower than this, CHECK YOUR TEACHING WITH THE UNIT PLANS. At this time, each child should be tested with the word cards for the new Primer vocabulary. (See page 159 of the Primer.) READING DEVELOPMENT CANNOT TAKE PLACE WITHOUT AN ADEQUATE SIGHT VOCABULARY.

Individual check on sight vocabulary

Unit 38: (Supplementary)

1. Textfilm for *Day In and Day Out,* Frames 21-22. See Textfilm manual for directions.

2. Additional reading. In the following preprimers the pages noted may be used as supplementary reading under teacher guidance:

Molly, Pete, and Ginger, pages 17-24. (Give help on page 22 with the sound word *Wuff* and the word *no.*)

Time to Play, pages 34-41.

We Work and Play, pages 15-18. (Give help with the word *funny* on page 18.)

My Little Red Story Book, pages 27-34. (Give help with the word *apple* on page 31.)

Pp. 77-81 # Unit 39: Little Goat

NEW VOCABULARY: animals   ate   Goat   old   stopped

PREPARATION

Have the following materials ready for use:

Pocket Card Holder
Word Cards
507 Goat   508 stopped   509 ate   **510 old**

INITIAL PROCEDURE

Introducing new vocabulary. (Have these sentences on board.)

> By and by he stopped.
> He saw a house, a little old house.
> I will find something to eat.
> "Here is something to eat,"
> he said.
> And then Jerry ate and ate.

Guidance in
methods of
word attack

One day Jerry ran as fast as he could down the road. Then—(indicate sentence 1). This word (indicate *stopped*) begins like *store*. By and by he st——. (Wait for suggestion *stopped*.) Then this word card says—(add *stopped* to card holder).

When Jerry stopped—(underline *He saw a house* and have that much of sentence read). This tells what kind of house it was. (Underline *a little old house*.) Remember that the name of the first letter in the new word is $\bar{o}$ (indicate $\bar{o}$ in *old*); and the word means just the opposite of *new*, a little o—— house. (Wait for suggestion *old;* then add word card *old* to card holder.) Now let me read the sentence for you.

Purpose of
comma

This little mark (indicate comma) tells me to read the first part of the sentence, then to pause a second, and then to read the second part.

Listen to see if I pause at the comma. (Have several children read sentence after you have set pattern.)

A friend of Jerry's lived in that house. It was Fisherman Jack. The minute he saw Jerry he said, "You must stay to dinner and—(sentence 3)." Before long, some fish that he had caught were frying in the pan, and Fisherman Jack looked at Jerry. (Sentence 4.) Of course, you know what happened then. (Indicate sentence 5.) If you remember that the first letter in the new word (indicate *ate*) says *ā*, you can get the word. And then Jerry a——. (Wait for suggestion *ate* and add word card *ate* to card holder. Have sentences and words reread.)

Guidance in methods of word attack

Introducing the contents pages. Now suppose we look at some very important pages in our book. This page (open to title page) is called the title page because it has the title of the book on it. Who will read the title as I run my hand under it? Now turn to pages 2 and 3.

These pages are called the contents pages, and this word (run your hand under *Contents*) says Contents. The contents of your pockets are all the things you have in them, and the contents of a book are the stories which are in it. Our book is divided into parts, and these words in big letters (indicate unit titles) are the names of the parts. Who will read the name of the first part? of the second? If you remember (turn to page 77) what we call these things in the picture and what this word says (write *Animals* on board), someone can read the title of the next part. By the time you are through the book, you will be able to read the names of the other parts, also.

Learning to use the table of contents

Now look again at Part 1. How many stories are in that part? What is the name of the first story? Do you remember the joke Little Rabbit played on Alice and Jerry? Let your eyes follow the dotted line. What do you find at the end of the line? The number 6 tells what page the story starts on. Turn to page 6. Did the contents pages give us the right information? (Repeat with one other story.)

Now look at the part called—(indicate *Animals* on board). Of course, you know the name of the animal we will read about first (write *goat*) because you see the little word—(underline *go* in *goat*). (Wait for suggestion *goat;* then add capitalized form of word to card holder.) Now who will read the title of the first story in the part called "Animals"? Let your eye follow the dotted line. On what page will the story begin?

SILENT READING

Page 78. (Allow time for enjoyment of pictures. Have pupils discover that the goat has a coat of curly hair and hoofs like a cow's. Have them infer that Little Goat has run away from his home in the valley. Discuss the penchant goats have for eating everything, and have pupils predict that he may eat the cap.)

Oral language

You thought Little Goat may have run away. Read the title and three sentences to see if you are right. We said that goats are always hungry. Is Little Goat that way? Finish the page and see.

Page 79. The first sentence is a question. The second is the answer. Read so that you can ask the question and answer it. Now listen as I read the second sentence. Can you hear the pause at the comma?

Purpose of a comma

You thought Little Goat would eat that cap. Finish the page and see if he does. What do you think may happen on the next page?

Pages 80-81. (Conduct in usual way.) What do you think Little Goat may find to eat tomorrow?

Predicting outcomes

ORAL READING

Fluency and expression. (The rhythm of sentences in this story is very apparent. Suggest that you like the story so well that you would like to have a chance to read the four pages. Set the pattern; then have several children read their favorite pages. Compliment evidences of expressive reading.)

Setting oral reading standards

WORD RECOGNITION TECHNIQUES

Accurate word recognition. Sometimes knowing names of certain letters helps us remember words. The name of this letter is *ē,* and the word is—(write *eat*). The name of this letter is *ā,* and the word is—(write *ate*). The name of this letter is *ō,* and the word is—(write *old*). (Play "Watch Me Go" with *eat, ate, old.*)

Auditory-visual perception. *Initial sounds. What* is the question word. (Write *What.*) It takes two letters to begin *what.* (Trace *Wh;* then erase word.) If anyone can show me how *What* begins, I will finish the word. *White* begins like *what.* Show me how *white* begins,

Phonics

and I will finish the word. (Continue with *then, this, that, kitten, pony, toy*.)

Here are four new words. (Write *whistle, them, kitchen, porch.* Proceed as in previous units.)

SUPPLEMENTARY ACTIVITIES

Guiding
Workbook
activities

1. *Vocabulary Primer Workbook*, pages 49, 50, 51.
2. *Workbook for Day In and Day Out*, pages 49, 50. Do first section on page 50 with pupils.

Unit 40: Little Goat (*cont.*)   Pp. 82-83

NEW VOCABULARY: am   are   started

PREPARATION

Have the following materials ready for use:

Pocket Card Holder
Word Cards

483 eat	507 goat	509 ate	511 started	513 are
506 Animal	508 stopped	510 old	512 am	

INITIAL PROCEDURE

Vocabulary review. Another name for a cow or a horse is—(add word card *Animal* to card holder; continue to add other suggested word cards). The animal we are reading about is a—(*goat*). The name of the first letter in this word is $\bar{e}$, and the word is—(*eat*). The name of this first letter is $\bar{a}$, and the word is—(*ate*). The name of this first letter is $\bar{o}$, and the word is—(*old*). Jerry ran down the road, but at last he—(*stopped*). How fast can someone read up and down the word ladder?

Introducing new vocabulary. (Have these sentences on board.)

I am the rabbit.
You are the man in the garden.
So Alice stopped.
Then the play started.

Alice, Jerry, and some other children were having a play. It was the play of Peter Rabbit. Alice was going to be Peter. So when she was dressed up in the rabbit suit, she said, "I am not Alice, now." (Indicate sentence 1.) Hop over the new word (indicate *am*) and let the sentence help you. (Wait for suggestion *am;* then add word card *am* to card holder.) Alice pointed to Jack, dressed in his father's old clothes, and she said—(indicate sentence 2). Remember that this part (underline *ar* in *are*) says—(give sound). Who is ready with the sentence? Then this word (add *are* to card holder) says—.

Alice went on talking until Jerry said, "Oh, please stop, Alice." (Sentence 3.) And—(indicate sentence 4). This word (indicate *started*) begins like *store*. Do you see the part in it which says—(give sound of *ar*)? Then the play star——. Then this word card says—(add *started* to card holder). What kind of words are *started* and *stopped*? Why do we call them opposites? (Have sentences and all cards in card holder reread.)

Do you think Little Goat will continue to eat everything in sight today? This page number is—(write *82*). It is more than halfway through our book. So make one big turn to find it.

SILENT READING

Page 82. Do you know what Little Goat is looking at on page 82? Do you think he knows? Read three sentences and see if he is as wise as you are. I think he is going to get into trouble. Finish the page and find out why. Why do you think that last sentence says that Little Goat *started* to eat, instead of saying, "He ate and ate and ate"?

Page 83. (Allow time for enjoyment of picture.) The minute Little Goat started to eat, what happened? Read four lines to find out. A big goat will not be afraid of a little kitten, will he? What will he do? Finish the page and see. Was he afraid? How do you know?

Margin notes:

Guidance in methods of word attack

Opposites

Locating page numbers quickly

Oral language

ORAL READING

Fluency and expression. Maybe we can choose someone to be Little Goat, someone to be the kitten, someone to be the ball (etc.) and play this story just as Alice and the children played Peter Rabbit.

Dramatization

Of course we will have to have a little goat who talks in an interesting way. Suppose you each choose your favorite page in this story and read it for us. The rest of us will listen to see which one in the group will make the best goat.

VOCABULARY ENRICHMENT AND EXTENSION

Word concepts. See if you can read these words as quickly as I write them on the board. (Write *new, started, old, stopped, came, went, in, ran, out, walked.*) Now who can come to the board and

Opposites

erase two words which have opposite meanings? Then use each word in a sentence.

WORD RECOGNITION TECHNIQUES

√**Auditory-visual perception.** *Phonetic parts.* This word says—(write *day*), and this part says—(underline *ay;* repeat with *say, stay, away*).

Phonics

This word says—(write *new*), and this part says—(underline *ew* and repeat with *mew*). This word says—(write *garden*), and this part says —(underline *ar;* then repeat with *started, are*).

SUPPLEMENTARY ACTIVITIES

1. *Vocabulary Primer Workbook,* pages 52, 53, 54.
2. *Workbook for Day In and Day Out,* pages 51, 52. On page 52, give whatever guidance is necessary.

Unit 41: (Supplementary)

1. Textfilm for *Day In and Day Out,* Frames 23-24. See Textfilm manual for directions.

2. Additional reading. In the following preprimers the pages noted may be used as supplementary reading under teacher guidance:

Molly, Pete, and Ginger, pages 25-28. (Give help with the words *cakes,* page 25; and *has,* page 28.)

My Little Blue Story Book (Ginn and Co.), pages 3-12. (Give help with the words *we* and *fast* on page 7.)

My Little Red Story Book, pages 35-48.

Time to Play, pages 42-51.

We Work and Play, pages 23-26.

Pp. 84-87 # Unit 42: The Little Duck

NEW VOCABULARY:	cluck	could	hen	talk
	cock-a-doodle-doo		rooster	tweet

PREPARATION

Have the following materials ready for use:

Pocket Card Holder

Word Cards:	96 kitten	515 could	519 rooster
	463 bird	516 hen	520 cock-a-
	505 mew	517 cluck	doodle-doo
	514 talk	518 tweet	

INITIAL PROCEDURE

Introducing new vocabulary. (Have these sentences on board.)

> Alice went for a walk.
> Alice stopped to talk to her.
> "What pretty talk that is!"
> said Alice.
> "I wish I could talk like that."
> But she could not do it.

Guidance in methods of word attack

Not long ago a little girl moved in near Alice's house. She could speak only French because she had just come from France, a country across the ocean. One morning—(sentence 1). She saw the little French girl by the gate, and—(indicate sentence 2). If you think how this word begins (indicate *talk*) and make it rhyme with *walk* (indicate *walk* in sentence 1), you can get the word. Alice stopped to t—— to her. (Wait for suggestion *talk;* then add word card *talk* to card holder.)

Alice couldn't understand a word the little girl said. But she liked the way the words sounded. And this is what Alice said to herself. (Sentence 3. Have the sentence read several times.) Then she said—(indicate sentence 4). Think how this word (indicate *could*) begins. Jump over it to let the sense of the sentence help you. I wish I c—— talk like that. (Wait for suggestion *could;* then add word card *could* to card holder. Have sentence read several times.) Alice tried and tried to say one French word. (Sentence 5.) Who will read all the sentences and the two new words?

Working for fluency

Contents pages. Turn to your contents page. Find the part of the book called Animals. The first one to find and read the title of the second story in that part and the page number on which the story starts may write the page number on the board. How quickly can you find page 84?

Using the table of contents

SILENT READING

Page 84. Can you guess who wants to talk? Read the title and two sentences. What did the little duck do one day? Read two more sentences. What happened when the kitten said, "Mew"? The little duck is like Alice. Finish the page and find out why.

Page 85. Whom does the little duck see now? You know how *hen* begins. How many times can you find it on this page? What does a hen say? Can you find *cluck?* How many times? Then what do these words say? (Add *hen* and *cluck* to card holder.) Now read the whole page. What happens? What do you think may happen on the next page?

Independent word attack— hen, cluck

Page 86. Of course, you know whom Little Duck sees now. If I tell you that birds say *tweet,* can you find that word? How many times? Then what does this say? (Add *tweet* to card holder.) Now read the whole page. What happens when Little Duck meets the bird?

Independent word attack— cock-a-doodle- doo, rooster

Page 87. Who is this crowing away? You know how *rooster* begins. How many times can you find the word? What does a rooster say? *Cock-a-doodle-doo* is a long word. Can you find it in two places? Then these cards say—(add *rooster* and *cock-a-doodle-doo* to card holder; have page read in usual way). By tomorrow Little Duck may have learned to say something. I hope so, don't you?

ORAL READING

Rereading by page units. (Add word cards *mew* and *bird* to card holder.) The one who can read this card and can find the card in the card holder which tells what this animal says (hold up *kitten*) may read page 84. (Hold up *hen* for page 85, *bird* for page 86, *rooster* for page 87.)

WORD RECOGNITION TECHNIQUES

Auditory-visual perception. *Phonetic parts.* (Write each of the following words on board. Have each word read. Then have the part to be seen and heard in each word underlined, and the part read: *new, mew, are, started, say, away.*)

Phonics

This word (write *now*) says—. This part (underline *ow*) makes the sound you make when you are hurt. (Give sound.) Can you see that part in this word? Draw a line under it and tell what the word says. (Use *down;* then *brown.*)

Rhyming words. I want to *look* at my new *book.* Which two words sound alike? Which two words rhyme? Every *day* I go to see *May.* Did you hear two more rhyming words? (Continue with *duck, truck; goat, coat; hop, top; hole, coal; ate, skate; that, hat.*)

SUPPLEMENTARY ACTIVITIES

1. *Vocabulary Primer Workbook,* pages 55, 56.
2. *Workbook for Day In and Day Out,* pages 53, 54. Give whatever guidance is necessary on page 54.

Unit 43: The Little Duck (*cont.*) `Pp. 88-89`

NEW VOCABULARY: quack

PREPARATION

Have the following materials ready for use:

Pocket Card Holder

Word Cards:	96 kitten	516 hen	520 cock-a-
	463 bird	517 cluck	doodle-doo
	466 duck	518 tweet	521 Quack
	505 mew	519 rooster	

INITIAL PROCEDURE

Following events in sequence

Vocabulary review. (Have all cards listed above, except *duck* and *quack,* in card holder.) Who will tell about the first animal Little Duck met and what happened? As you talk, take from the card holder the name of the animal and the sound it makes. (Continue in similar way.) We hope by the time we have finished reading today that this animal (add word card *duck*) can say something, also.

Our story begins on page 88. Can anyone write *88?* Remember to make one big turn as you look for the page.

SILENT READING

Oral language

Page 88. (Allow time for careful interpretation of pictures. Call attention to the web feet, the bill and breathing holes, and the yellow down which changes to white feathers.)

Little Duck is certainly going along in a hurry. I wonder what he is saying to himself. Read five sentences and find out. How did he happen to see Mother Duck? Finish the page and see.

Page 89. If you know anything about ducks, you can read that first sentence without stopping on the new words. Who is ready?

Independent word attack

Then what does this card say? (Hold up *Quack.*) I wonder if Little Duck will be able to say that. Finish the page and see. Then I guess I can put the word card *Quack* under—(indicate *duck* in card holder).

Predicting outcomes. If you should see Little Duck a few weeks from now, what do you think will have happened to him?

ORAL READING

Organization. (Have these sentences on board.)

_____Little Duck saw a rooster.
_____Little Duck saw a kitten.
_____Little Duck saw Mother Duck.

Following events in sequence

_____Little Duck saw a bird.
_____Little Duck said, "Quack, quack!"
_____Little Duck saw Mother Hen.

Which animal did Little Duck see first? Then which sentence should be numbered *1?* Who will number the sentence and then read the page which goes with the sentence? (Continue in similar way.)

WORD RECOGNITION TECHNIQUES

Auditory-visual perception. *Phonetic parts.* (Write the following words one at a time: *say, are, mew, now.* Have some pupil read each

Phonics

word, underline the part, and then tell what the part says.)

Phonics

Initial sounds. (Write *she.*) It takes two letters to begin *she.* (Trace *sh;* then erase word.) Listen as I say *cow, sheep, turkey.* Which word begins like *she?* Show me how *sheep* begins, and I will finish the word. What do you notice about *show, sheep,* and *she?* Then show me how *show* begins so that I may finish that word.

Here are four new words. (Write *wheel, there, ship, soap.* Proceed as in previous units.)

Once there was a little duck who had had nothing to eat for a long time. (Proceed as in previous units.) He was very h—— (*hungry*). First he saw a fly. He caught it in his b—— (*bill*) and ate it. Then he saw a big fat w—— (*worm*) and ate that. Then he thought he would like a swim. He did not go to the r—— (*river*). He went to the p—— (*pond*). Down he went into the w—— (*water*). He knew how to sw—— (*swim*), and he knew how to d—— (*dive*).

SUPPLEMENTARY ACTIVITIES

1. *Vocabulary Primer Workbook,* pages 57, 58.
2. *Workbook for Day In and Day Out,* pages 55, 56. Be sure directions are understood.

Unit 44: (Supplementary)

1. Textfilm for *Day In and Day Out,* Frames 25-26. See Textfilm manual for directions.

2. Additional reading. In the following preprimers the pages noted may be used as supplementary reading under teacher guidance:

Molly, Pete, and Ginger, pages 29-34. (Give help with the words *make,* page 31; and *bigger,* page 33.)

My Little Blue Story Book, pages 13-16. (Give help with the words *pie,* page 13; *funny* and *apple,* page 16.)

Ned and Nancy, pages 41-45. (Give help with *school,* page 41.)

Time to Play, pages 52-63.

We Work and Play, pages 35-38.

Unit 45: Little Jack Rabbit

NEW VOCABULARY: lived   nest   run

PREPARATION

Have the following materials ready for use:

Pocket Card Holder

Word Cards:	131 did	464 came	494 was	523 nest
	161 went	468 But	513 are	524 run
	460 happy	472 Then	522 lived	

INITIAL PROCEDURE

Vocabulary review. (Have all word cards listed above, except *lived, nest,* and *run,* in card holder.) How sharp are your eyes and ears? Who *are* you? Bring me the word from the card holder which

Drill on carrier words

I used in my sentence. (Continue with: Jack *came* to my house. He *did* not stay long. He looked *happy*. *But* he had to hurry. He *was* going to a show. So he *went* home. *Then* he started for the show.) How many of my cards can you read and return to the card holder? How high up the word ladder can you climb? How far down?

Introducing new vocabulary. (Have these sentences on board.)

> A little boy lived in that house.
> I will not stay in this house.
> I can run away,
> and I will run away.
> I am a big boy now.

Guidance in methods of word attack

Not far from Jerry's house was a pretty yellow house, and—(indicate sentence 1). Think how this word (indicate *lived*) begins. Then jump over it and let the sentence help you. A little boy l—— in that house. (Wait for suggestion *lived;* then add word card *lived* to card holder.)

This little boy was only two years old, but he wanted to be outdoors all the time. One day he said—(sentence 2). When he got out onto the sidewalk, he thought it would be fun to run away. So first he said—(indicate line 3). Think how this word (indicate *run*) begins. I can r—— away. (Wait for suggestion *run;* then add word card *run* to card holder.) Next he said—(line 4). Now read the two-line sentence as if it were all on one line. The last sentence tells why he thought it was all right for him to run away. I am sure his mother caught up with him before he had gone very far. (Have sentences and new words reread.)

Contents pages. I hope you remember the name of Jerry's friend. (Write *Jack.*) In the title of the new story, we are going to hear about another Jack, but it will not be a boy. Who will be the first to find the title on the contents pages? Who will be the first to find the number of the page on which the story begins? Who can write *90* on the board? How many of you can find page 90 with one big turn?

Two-line sentence

Using the table of contents

SILENT READING

Page 90. Do you think these are tame rabbits or wild rabbits? Why? In what do tame rabbits live? (*hutch*) What do you think Mother Wild Rabbit has made down here in the grass? (Explain the habit of lining the nest with fur.) *Nest* begins like *not.* How many times can you find the new word *nest?* Then this word card says— (add *nest* to card holder). How many rabbits are in the nest? Can you find the word *Three?* Read the first two sentences. Do they tell you what the picture tells you?

Read two more sentences. Find out something important about one little rabbit. Finish the page. What did Jack Rabbit want to do? What did Mother Rabbit say about it?

Page 91. What happened one day? Read the first sentence and see. The minute Mother Rabbit was gone, what did Jack Rabbit say? The next three sentences tell you. Watch out! Two of them are two-line sentences. Finish the page. What did Jack Rabbit do? To what place did he come?

Independent word attack

Two-line sentences

When I see the sky in the picture, I fear something may happen. What do you think may happen? Maybe Jack will wish he had not run away. We will find out when we read again.

ORAL READING

Rereading by page units. The one who can read these two cards (hold up *lived* and *nest*) may read page 90. The one who knows— (hold up *run*) may read page 91. Maybe someone knows all three words and can read both pages.

WORD RECOGNITION TECHNIQUES

Drill on carrier words

Accurate word recognition. Jack Rabbit wanted to—(write *run* and have word read). So he—(write *ran* and have word read). I always remember which word says *run* because I remember this letter. (Trace *u*.) Suppose we play "Magic." (Use *ran, run* several times; then *lived, little; not, now*.)

Phonics

Auditory-visual perception. *Initial sounds.* You remember that it takes two letters to begin—(write *she;* then *sh;* then erase word and *sh*). *She, shine!* What do your ears tell you about these words? If someone will show me how *shine* begins, I will finish the word. (Continue with *shell, sheep; this, that, then; what, white, whistle; kitten, kite, king*.)

Here are four new words. (Write *shed, them, whisper, kick*.) Which word says *whisper?* How do you know? (Continue in similar way with the other words; then use *shelf, there, wheel, key*.)

SUPPLEMENTARY ACTIVITIES

1. *Vocabulary Primer Workbook,* page 59.
2. *Workbook for Day In and Day Out,* page 57.

Unit 46: Little Jack Rabbit (*cont.*)

NEW VOCABULARY: all   played   white

___

PREPARATION

Have the following materials ready for use:

Pocket Card Holder

Word Cards:

51 And	488 day	522 lived	526 white
468 But	490 stay	523 nest	527 played
470 coat	512 am	525 all	

INITIAL PROCEDURE

Building sight vocabulary

Vocabulary review. (Have all cards listed above, except *all, played,* and *white,* in card holder.) Who can take one card from the card holder, read it, and use it in a sentence? (When all cards have been removed, have them given to pupils who did not take cards. Have these pupils read the cards given them and return them to card holder. Then have several pupils read up and down the word ladder.)

Introducing new vocabulary. (Have these sentences on board.)

> You are all here.
> I like to hop.
> I like to play.
> I am too big to stay
> in the house all day.

Guidance in methods of word attack

Everyone is here this morning. I might say that in another way. I might say, "You are (write *all*) all here." Can you find the word *all* in the first sentence? Who can read the sentence? Then this word says—(add *all* to card holder).

Working for
fluency

You remember the little boy who ran away from home. When his mother caught up with him that morning, this is what he said. (Sentences 2, 3.) What else did he say? I hope you notice (indicate sentence 4) that this is a two-line sentence. (Have sentences 2, 3, 4 reread until pupils sense the rhythm.)

If you can read this number (write *92*) and can make one big turn and find that page, we can learn what happened to Jack Rabbit in the garden.

SILENT READING

Page 92. What kind of rabbits live in that garden? How can you tell that they are tame? What do we call the house they live in? Do you suppose Jack Rabbit will nibble at one of these carrots? Watch the sky. Does it still look like a storm? Jack is too busy having a good time to notice that sky. That will be too bad for him.

How does Jack Rabbit feel about himself? Read the first sentence and see. Now he reminds me of that little boy who ran away from home. Read four sentences and find out why.

Independent
word attack—
white

What color are the rabbits? *White* begins like *what*. Can you find the word *white?* Now finish the page. Are there any more rabbits inside the house? How many rabbits really live there?

Page 93. Look at that sky. I wish Jack Rabbit would look at it. What did he look at? Read the first sentence and see. I don't believe he had ever seen a rabbit with a white coat before. Read the next four sentences. What did he say to the two rabbits? What color were their coats? (Add *white* to card holder.)

Word
structure

You know this word. (Write *look.*) Now what does it say? (Write *looked.*) This word says—(write *play*). And now it says—(write *played*). How many times can you find *played* in your books? Finish the page. How long did the rabbits play? What may happen when we read tomorrow?

ORAL READING

Rereading by page units. The one who can read these two words (hold up *all* and *white*) may read page 92. The one who knows this word (hold up *played*) may read page 93. The one who can read all the words in the card holder may read both pages.

WORD RECOGNITION TECHNIQUES

Phonics

Auditory-visual perception. *Rhyming words.* I ran out the *door* to go to the *store.* Which two words sound very much alike? Which two words rhyme? The hen said, "Cluck, *cluck!* Here comes a little *duck.*" Did you hear two more rhyming words? (Continue in the same way with *hen–pen, ran–can, now–cow, wish–fish, all–ball, quack–track, white–kite, nest–vest.*)

Verbs ending
in ed

Word structure. We found that this word said–(write *play*). If I add these letters (add *ed*), the word says–. This word says–(write *jump*). Who can come to the board and make it say *jumped?* (Continue with *walk, stay, wish, talk.*)

SUPPLEMENTARY ACTIVITIES

1. *Vocabulary Primer Workbook,* pages 60, 61.
2. *Workbook for Day In and Day Out,* page 58.

Unit 47: Little Jack Rabbit (*cont.*)

Pp. 94-95

NEW VOCABULARY: gate   his   open

PREPARATION

Have the following materials ready for use:

Pocket Card Holder
Word Cards

459 So	468 But	486 wanted	522 lived	528 gate
457 Just	483 eat	492 will	523 nest	529 open
461 Away	485 That	503 now	524 Run	530 his

INITIAL PROCEDURE

Building sight vocabulary

Vocabulary review. Can you read these words as quickly as I add them to the card holder? (Put the following word cards in the card holder, one at a time: *Away, But, eat, Just, lived, nest, now, Run, So, That, wanted, will.*) Who can climb five steps up the word ladder? the rest of the way? five steps down? the rest of the way? Who can read and remove five cards? the rest of the cards?

Introducing new vocabulary. (Have the following sentences on the board.)

> The garden gate was open.
> He ran in at the open gate.
> He could not find his ball.
> By and by he stopped.

Guidance in methods of word attack

Behind Jerry's house was a lovely—(indicate the word *garden* in sentence 1). Around the garden was a white fence, and in the fence was a—(indicate the word *gate,* sentence 1). Think how the word begins. Notice that inside the word is the little word *ate.* (Underline *ate* in *gate.*) The whole word says—. Since it was a gate that opened into a garden, it was called—(underline the phrase *The garden gate* and have it read several times).

One morning Jerry was playing ball just outside the fence, and—(indicate sentence 1). Remember that the name of this letter (indicate *o* in *open*) is—. Now read the sentence and get the word. What do these two cards say? (Add *gate* and *open* to card holder.)

Jerry's new ball went over the fence. So—(sentence 2). But look where he would—(sentence 3). You can get this word. (Indicate *his.*) You know how it begins, and inside you see the little word—(underline *is*). Who is ready to read the sentence and tell me what this word says? (Add *his* to card holder.) Since he could not find that ball—(sentence 4). And there, right under a bush, Jerry found his ball. (Have sentences and words reread.)

Locating page numbers quickly

Has Jack Rabbit grown more sensible since we read about him yesterday? Did he get home before the rain? If you can read this number (write *94*) and can find that page with one big turn, we can soon find out.

SILENT READING

Page 94. Poor Jack Rabbit! Here is something much worse than the rain! Where will the tame rabbits go the minute they see the dog? Will Jack run into the hutch? Why not? Let's read and see if we have been good thinkers.

I don't believe Jack Rabbit knew what a dog was. I don't believe he had ever seen one before. Read two sentences and see why I feel that way.

What happened the minute that dog saw the rabbits? The next two sentences tell. I think the white rabbits knew what a dog was. They also knew what to do to protect themselves. Finish the page. What did they say? What did they do? Will they be safe in the hutch? Why?

Page 95. Read four sentences. Were we right when we said that Jack Rabbit would not run into the hutch? Were we right about the reason? Were we right when we thought those clouds meant a storm?

No rabbit can run forever, even with a dog behind him. What will Jack have to do? Why? Finish the page. Check to see if you are good thinkers.

Predicting
outcomes

What do you think your mother might do if she came home on a stormy day and found you gone? What do you think Mother Rabbit may do? I hope she finds Jack when we read our story tomorrow, don't you?

ORAL READING

Rereading by page units. The one who can read these two cards (indicate *gate* and *open*) may read page 94. The one who can read this word (indicate *his*) may read page 95.

WORD RECOGNITION TECHNIQUES

Little words
in big words

Word structure. Many times if we see a little word inside a big word, the little word helps us get the big word. Inside the word— (write *gate*) we see a little word. Who can underline the little word and tell us what it says? You see the word *ate* inside this word also. (Write *late*.) Think how the new word begins. Let the word *ate* help you. The new word is—. (Continue with *date, hate;* repeat procedures with *and* in *band, hand, land;* then with *is* in *his.*)

Capitalization. Sometimes words begin with capital, or big, letters. Sometimes they begin with small letters. Watch as I write—(write *Run—run*). What does each word say? Which *run* begins with a capital letter? (Write *Away, So, But, Then, Down, Come* in one row on board. In a parallel row reverse the order and write the same words in lower-case form. Have pupils draw a line from the capitalized to the lower-case form of a word and read the word.)

Capital letter
for sentence
beginning

Suppose we look carefully at the sentences on the board. What do you notice about the first letter in every sentence? Let's look at page 6 in our book. Check to see if each sentence begins with a capital letter. Check page 7. Remember that a sentence always begins with a capital letter.

SUPPLEMENTARY ACTIVITY

Vocabulary Primer Workbook, page 62.

Pp. 96-97 # Unit 48: Little Jack Rabbit (*cont.*)

NEW VOCABULARY: night

PREPARATION

Have the following materials ready for use:

Pocket Card Holder
Word Cards

54	come	141	ran	486	wanted	513	are
94	It	145	she	496	surprise	524	run
120	want	148	What	502	her	530	his
134	he	464	came	512	am	531	Night

INITIAL PROCEDURE

Vocabulary review. The words I use when I talk about a girl are—(add *she* and *her* to card holder); about a boy—(add *he* and *his*). Do you know these words which are almost alike, but not quite? (Add *came—come, ran—run, want—wanted.*) The riddle word is—(add *It*). The question word is—(add *What*). Something we do not expect is a—(add *surprise*). You hear this word in the sentence *I am too big to stay in a nest.* (Add *am.*) You hear this one when I say *You are too little to run away.* (Add *are.*) Who can read and remove ten words? five?

(Have the following sentences on board.)

> Now he started for home.
> "I can run home.
> And I will run home.
> I will stay in the house,"
> said the runaway boy.

Guidance in methods of word attack

You remember the boy who wanted to be outdoors all the time. When his mother caught up with him that morning, she soon turned him around in the other direction. So—(sentence 1). If you have forgotten this word (indicate *started*), remember that it begins like *store* and this part (underline *ar*) says—. Who is ready to tell what the runaway boy did? On the way home, this is what he said. (Sentences 2, 3, 4.) Don't let this word bother you. It is just two words put together, a compound word. (Indicate *runaway*.) The first word (underline *run*) says—. The other word (underline *away*) says—. The whole word says—. Who is ready to read all that the runaway boy said?

Compound words

I wonder if Mother Rabbit is looking for a runaway little rabbit. If you can read this number (write *96*) and can find the page with one quick turn, we can find out.

SILENT READING

Independent word attack— night

Page 96. The pictures tell me that we are good thinkers. Why? Do you think the storm is over? How can you tell? What time do you think it is when Mother Rabbit finds her baby? Can you find the word

Night in the first sentence? Can you find it again? Then this card (add *Night* to card holder) says—.

What happened when night came? Read three sentences to see. Poor Jack Rabbit is cold and miserable in that top picture, isn't he? How does he look in the bottom picture? How did he know that the rabbit he saw was Mother Rabbit? Finish the page and see.

Page 97. What was the first thing Mother Rabbit did? The first sentence tells. Would your mother have done that? What did she say to Jack Rabbit? Read four sentences and see. Even though Mother Rabbit is cross, how does Jack feel? The next two sentences will tell you. Jack reminds me of the runaway boy. Finish the page and find out why.

Predicting outcomes

Suppose Mother Rabbit had to go away looking for food the next morning. Suppose you found that rabbit nest. How many rabbits would be in it?

ORAL READING

Establishing standards. (Assign one page from the entire story to each of eight pupils. Have them prepare to read their pages to the entire group. Have other members of group be ready to tell what they enjoyed about the reading.)

Audience reading

WORD RECOGNITION TECHNIQUES

Capitalization. What does each of these words say? (Write *this—This.*) Which one begins with a capital letter? What kind of letter did we find out we must use to begin a sentence? Then which of these words would we use? (Continue with *Just—just, Her—her, that—That, Night—night.*)

Capital letter for sentence beginning

(Write the lower-case forms of the following words in one row, the capitalized forms in different order in a second row. Have pupils draw a line from the lower-case form of a word to the capitalized form and read word: *this, she, away, fly, all, what.*)

Auditory-visual perception. *Phonetic parts.* This word says—(write *new*), and this part says—(write *ew*). (Repeat with s*tay*, n*ow*, s*tarted*.) Since you know how the word begins and what the part says, can you get this new word? (Write *car*. Continue with *far, cow, few, pay.*)

Word attack— using phonetic parts

SUPPLEMENTARY ACTIVITIES

1. *Vocabulary Primer Workbook,* page 63.
2. *Workbook for Day In and Day Out,* pages 59, 60. Be sure directions are understood.

Unit 49: (Supplementary)

1. Textfilm for *Day In and Day Out,* Frames 27-28. See Textfilm manual for directions.
2. Additional reading. In the following preprimers the pages noted may be used as supplementary reading under teacher guidance:
    All in a Day (American Book Co.), pages 3-11.
    Molly, Pete, and Ginger, pages 61-66. (Give help with the word *we* on page 64.)
    My Little Blue Story Book, pages 17-32. (Give help with the words *Bunny,* page 18; *cakes* and *dinner,* page 20.)
    We Come and Go, pages 17-22.
    We Work and Play, pages 39-42. (Give help with the words *makes,* page 39; and *yellow,* page 41.)

Unit 50: A Good Breakfast   Pp. 98-101

NEW VOCABULARY: breakfast   cow   moo   pig   wee

PREPARATION

Have the following materials ready for use:

332   IMMATURE GROUP

Pocket Card Holder
Word Cards

161 went	479 into	532 breakfast	535 cow
464 came	508 stopped	533 pig	536 moo
465 out	511 started	534 Wee	

INITIAL PROCEDURE

Drill on
carrier words

Vocabulary review. These two words have opposite meanings. How quickly can you read them? (Add *started–stopped* to card holder. Continue with *came–went, into–out.*)

Introducing new vocabulary. (Have these sentences on the board.)

I had something good to eat.
I had a good breakfast.

Guidance in
methods of
word attack

This morning I was up early. As soon as I was dressed–(sentence 1). Now read the second sentence. The new word (indicate *breakfast*) begins like *brown.* Think how it begins; then let the sense of the sentence help you. I had a good br––. (Wait for suggestion *breakfast;* then add word card to card holder.)

Using table
of contents

Contents pages. If you can read this phrase (underline *a good breakfast* in sentence 2), you can read the title of the new story. How quickly can you find it on the contents pages? On what page will the story begin? Who can write *98* on the board? Turn quickly to page 98 so that we can find out who will have a good breakfast.

SILENT READING

Independent
word attack—
pig, wee

Page 98. The picture gives the secret away, doesn't it? You know how the word *pig* begins. How many times can you find it on page 98? on page 99? (Add *pig* to card holder.) What do you think little pig will have for breakfast?

How did little pig happen to find this garden? Read two sentences and see. Someone has been careless. Read the next sentence and look at the picture. Why do I say that? If I were the little pig, I would do just what he does. Read the next sentence. Now finish the page. What did he say, and what did he do next?

Page 99. Who came by next, and what did she do? Read two sentences and find out.

If you think how this word begins (hold up word card *Wee*) and if you remember that the name of these letters is—(indicate *ee*), you will know that a little pig says—(wait for suggestion *Wee* and add card to card holder).

Will the pig let the white hen come in? Look at the picture and see what you think. Now read three more sentences. Were you right? Finish the page. What did the white hen do then?

Predicting outcomes

There won't be much garden left at this rate. What do you hope may happen on the next page? Turn and see if it does.

Page 100. (Have pupils note and read page number. Explain that farmers call reddish brown cows *red* cows.) You know how *cow* begins. How many times can you find it? How many times on page 101? What does a cow say? You know how *moo* begins. How many times can you find *moo* on page 100? on page 101? (Add *cow* and *moo* to card holder.)

Independent word attack— cow, moo

Read four sentences. What did red cow do when she came to the gate? What did she say? Finish the page. Will the other animals invite her in? What happens?

Page 101. Readers as good as you, can read the whole page and find out what happens.

Predicting outcomes

Can this go on forever? What do you think may happen tomorrow when we read?

ORAL READING

Organization. (Write the following sentences on board.)

_____The pony comes to the garden.
_____The hen comes to the garden.
_____The pig comes to the garden.
_____The cow comes to the garden.

Following events in sequence

The one who can find the sentence which tells what animal came to the garden first and can number that sentence *1* may read the page of the story which goes with that sentence. (Continue in similar way with the other sentences.)

WORD RECOGNITION TECHNIQUES

Auditory-visual perception. *Initial sounds.* Show me how *came* begins so that I may finish the word. (Continue with *boy, day, find, gate, his, just, kitten, lived, moo.*)

Phonics

(Conduct as in previous units.) I have a garden, and in my garden I will plant some c—— (*carrots*) and some l—— (*lettuce*). I will want some p—— (*peas* or *potatoes*) and some b—— (*beans* or *beets*). I will take care of my garden. I will pull the w—— (*weeds*), and I will use my father's h—— (*hoe*). If it does not rain, I will w—— (*water*) my garden. It will be a v—— (*vegetable*) garden.

Phonetic parts. The red cow said—(write *moo*). This part in *moo* (underline *oo*) says—(give long double *o* sound). What does this word say? (Write *too*.) Can you draw a line under the part you see and hear in *too* and tell me what the part says? (Repeat with *rooster.* Then review n*ew*, g*arden*, n*ow*, s*ay*.)

SUPPLEMENTARY ACTIVITIES

1. *Vocabulary Primer Workbook,* pages 64, 65, 66.
2. *Workbook for Day In and Day Out,* page 61.

Pp. 102-4 # Unit 51: A Good Breakfast (*cont.*)

NEW VOCABULARY: barnyard

PREPARATION

Have the following materials ready for use:

Pocket Card Holder
Word Cards

120 want	161 went	493 again	511 started	537 barnyard
141 ran	492 will	494 was	524 run	

INITIAL PROCEDURE

Drill on carrier words

Vocabulary review. (Have all words listed above, except *barnyard,* in card holder.) Can anyone play "One, Two, Three! How Many for Me?" and remove all the cards from the card holder? (Reverse order of cards and repeat game several times.)

Introducing new vocabulary. (Have these sentences on the board.)

> All the animals in the barnyard
> will have breakfast in his garden.
> Get out! Get out!
> Go home to the barnyard.
> And stay in that barnyard, too.

Little words in big words

When you are in the country, you sometimes see the farmer's animals in the barn. (Write *barn.*) But many times you see them in the yard around the barn. You see them in the—(add *yard* to *barn* and wait for suggestion *barnyard*). Then this word says—(add *barnyard* to card holder).

If that careless farmer doesn't get home in a hurry, I am afraid—(indicate sentence 1). I hope you know how the sentence begins. (Indicate *All* and wait for suggestion *All.*) I hope you know what you call cows and pigs when they are all together. (Indicate *animals.*) I hope you know what the animals want. (Indicate *breakfast.*) I hope you know whose garden it is. (Indicate *his.*) Who is ready with the long two-line sentence?

Two-line sentence

That farmer needs to say what Alice said when she saw Jip in her garden. He needs to say—(sentences 2, 3, 4). If you can find this page (write *102* and have number read), we can soon find out what he does.

SILENT READING

Page 102. (Allow time for enjoyment of picture.) Read five sentences. Do they tell exactly what the picture tells? Finish the page. What is the man saying?

Page 103. I don't believe these animals ran all the way home. Read the page and see if you can find out why I think so. If they do not go home, what may they do? What is the first thing the farmer will do now? Turn to see if our thinking is right.

Page 104. Were we right? Read until you find out what the pig says as he looks through the gate. Find out what the pony says; what the hen says; what the cow says. Was the farmer ever careless again? Finish the page and see.

Page 105. Of course, you know what the next story will be about. Whose new doll is this? If you tell me what is on her cap, I will tell you her name. Do you like the name Betsy Lee? Will you read the title?

ORAL READING

Organization. (Have the following sentences on board.)

Following
events in
sequence

____The animals ran out of the garden.
____The man came home.
____The pig came to the garden.
____The cow came.
____The pony came.
____The white hen came.
____The animals came to the garden again.

The one who can find the sentence which tells about the first page in the story may number that sentence *1* and read the page which goes with it. (Continue in similar way.)

WORD RECOGNITION TECHNIQUES

Auditory-visual perception. *Initial sounds.* If I want to write *chair,* it will take two letters to begin my word. (Write *ch;* pause; then complete word and erase.) If I wanted to write *child,* how would I begin my word? Show me, and I will finish the word. (Repeat with *chair, cherry, church.*) If you will show me how *now* begins, I will finish the word. (Continue with *pig, run, surprise, talk, wee, that, she, what, chimney.*)

Phonics

Here are four new words. (Write *picture, race, supper, table.*) Think how each word begins. Which word says *table?* (Continue in same way with the other words; then repeat procedure with *woods, there, ship, whistle, chalk.*)

Rhyming words. I will say three words. You tell which two rhyme. (Use *boat, coat, train; this, tree, three; game, ran, name; May, stay, saw; down, do, clown; will, wall, ball; my, tie, shirt; come, pan, man; plate, gate, cap.*)

SUPPLEMENTARY ACTIVITIES

1. *Vocabulary Primer Workbook,* page 67.

2. *Workbook for Day In and Day Out,* pages 62, 63, 64.

3. Tests. Give the two informal tests on pages 65 and 66 of the *Workbook for Day In and Day Out.* Pupils are given a score of 1 for each item marked correctly. They should make a score of at least 16 on the vocabulary test; a score of at least 3 on the sentence-meaning test. If scores fall lower than this, TEST YOUR TEACHING WITH THE UNIT PLANS. At this point, test each child individually with the word cards for the Primer vocabulary developed so far. (See pages 159-60 of the Primer.)

Individual check on sight vocabulary

Unit 52: (Supplementary)

1. Textfilm for *Day In and Day Out,* Frames 29-30. See Textfilm manual for directions.

2. Additional reading. In the following preprimers the pages noted may be used as supplementary reading under teacher guidance:

All in a Day, pages 12-19. (Give help with *stop,* page 15.)

Molly, Pete, and Ginger, pages 35-40. (Give help with the words *there,* page 39; and *car,* page 40.)

My Little Blue Story Book, pages 33-40. (Give help with the words *chair,* page 34; and *work,* page 35.)

Under the Tree (Silver Burdett Co.), pages 9-13. (Give help with the word *stop* on page 12.)

We Work and Play, pages 47-50.

Pp. 105-7 # Unit 53: The New Doll

NEW VOCABULARY: Betsy   Lee   very

PREPARATION

Have the following materials ready for use:

Pocket Card Holder
Word Cards: 508 stopped   532 breakfast   540 very

INITIAL PROCEDURE

Vocabulary review. (Have the following phrases and words on board: *He had, I am, I will, It had, It was, One morning, So, Then, This is.*)

Drill on sentence beginnings

If we are to enjoy the story of Betsy Lee, it is very important that our sentences get started on the right track. Who can draw a line under one of the sentence beginnings on the board, read it, and then use it to begin a sentence?

I hope you have not forgotten what the animals wanted in the garden (add *breakfast* to card holder); or this word (add *stopped*).

Introducing new vocabulary. Sometimes things are—(write *pretty*).

Guidance in methods of word attack

Sometimes they are more than pretty. They are—(write *very* to the left of *pretty*). This new word begins like *valentine* and *vacation*. Sometimes things are v—— pretty. (Put lips, teeth, and tongue in position to form *v* but give no sound. Wait for suggestion *very;* then add *very* to card holder.) When you read about that doll, I am sure you will find that—(write *It was very, very pretty*).

Contents pages. The title of the new part of our book is the name of the doll. Can you find that title and read it? The title of the first story tells me something else about Betsy Lee. Who is ready with the title? On what page will the story "The New Doll" begin?

SILENT READING

Oral language   **Page 106.** (Allow time for thorough discussion of picture.)

What happened that morning when Alice hopped out of bed? Read two sentences and see. When Alice got to the gate, what happened? The next two sentences tell. Now read the next sentence. What did the man say? Who in the world is Alice White? Has the mailman stopped at the wrong house? Finish the page and see.

Page 107. When Alice got that box, what did she do? The first sentence tells. Read four more lines. What did she say to Mother? Now finish the page. Are you as good a reader as I am? Can you find out five things about that doll?

Predicting outcomes

Do you think that doll has a name? What may Alice do when we read the next time?

ORAL READING

The one who can tell me Jerry's whole name may read page 106. The one who knows this word (indicate *very*) may read page 107.

VOCABULARY ENRICHMENT AND EXTENSION

Word associations. You found out today that Alice's full name is —(write *Alice White*). Then Jerry's name is—(write *Jerry White*). Father's name is—(write *Mr. White;* continue with Mother's name). When we have them all together, we call them a f— (*family*); the White family.

WORD RECOGNITION TECHNIQUES

Auditory-visual perception. *Final sounds.* Listen as I say *boat— want.* (Say the *t* sound very clearly.) My ears heard the same sound on the end of *boat* that they heard on the end of *want.* Listen again and see if the words end alike. (Repeat *boat—want.*) Let's see if our ears told us the truth. Do *boat* and *want* really end with the same letter and the same sound? (Write *boat—want* and direct attention to final *t* in each.) Now listen as I say *rabbit—pig.* Which word ends like

Phonics

boat and *want?* Let's see if you are right. (Write *rabbit* under *boat* and *want,* and check final *t*. (Continue with *went—walk, just—then, had—put.*)

Phonetic parts. You remember that this word (write *moo*) says—. And this part (underline *oo*) says—. This word (write *now*) says—, and this part (underline *ow*) says—. (Continue with d*ay,* *are,* n*ew.*)

SUPPLEMENTARY ACTIVITIES

1. *Vocabulary Primer Workbook,* page 68.

2. *Workbook for Day In and Day Out,* pages 67, 68. Have all pictures on page 67 identified before pupils begin to work.

Pp. 108-9 # Unit 54: The New Doll (*cont.*)

NEW VOCABULARY: word

PREPARATION

Have the following materials ready for use:

Pocket Card Holder
Word Cards

| 158 name | 485 That | 498 wish | 513 are | 541 word |
| 469 new | 492 will | 502 her | 540 very | |

INITIAL PROCEDURE

Building sight
vocabulary

Vocabulary review. Something more than pretty is—(add *very* to card holder) pretty. One of the words I use when I talk about a girl is—. (Add *her.* Continue in similar way with all words listed above, except *word.* Have pupils play "One, Two, Three! How Many for Me?" to remove cards from card holder.)

Introducing new vocabulary. (Have these sentences on board.)

She could not talk.

She could not say a word.

One day Father called Mother to the front door. There in the street was a new car with Father at the wheel. Mother was so surprised that—(sentence 1). In fact, she was so surprised that—(sentence 2). Think how the word begins. (Indicate *word.*) Then let the sense of the sentence help you. The new word is—(add *word* to card holder).

We decided that Alice might name her doll today. This page number is—(write *108*). How quickly can you find that page?

Guidance in methods of word attack

SILENT READING

Page 108. (Take time for enjoyment of pictures.) Read four sentences. Read carefully. What does Alice decide to name her doll? Read four more sentences. Why doesn't Alice call her doll just Betsy? Does Mother like the name Betsy Lee? Finish the page and see.

Page 109. I am sure by the way Alice looks at Betsy Lee that she likes her very much. But Alice is not quite satisfied. What does she want Betsy Lee to do? Read four sentences to find out. Do dolls ever talk? What do they say? Maybe Betsy Lee is a talking doll after all. Finish the page and see.

ORAL READING

Rereading by page units. The one who can tell me the name of the toy standing up against Alice's bookcase (*tennis racket*) may read page 108. The one who knows this word (indicate *word*) may read page 109.

VOCABULARY ENRICHMENT AND EXTENSION

Synonymous meanings

If I want to say *after a while,* I may say—(write *by and by*). If I do something every day, I do it—(write *day in and day out*). When I do something once in a while, I do it—(write *now and then*). When something happens just when I am looking, it happens—(write *Just then*).

WORD RECOGNITION TECHNIQUES

Auditory-visual perception. *Final sounds.* Listen as I say *boat, want, rabbit.* What did our ears tell us about these words? Let's see

Phonics

if we are right. (Write the words and direct attention to final *t*.) If I want to write another word which ends like *boat,* shall I write *new* or *but?* Let's prove that you are right. (Write *but* and have pupils point out the final *t*. Continue with *coat—please, eat—green, got— man, wanted—that.* DO NOT OMIT THESE ACTIVITIES.)

SUPPLEMENTARY ACTIVITIES

1. *Vocabulary Primer Workbook,* page 69.
2. *Workbook for Day In and Day Out,* pages 69, 70.

Unit 55: (Supplementary)

Additional reading. In the following preprimers the pages noted may be used as supplementary reading under teacher guidance:

All in a Day, pages 20-29. (Give help with *we,* page 26.)

Molly, Pete, and Ginger, pages 41-46. (Give help with the words *honk,* page 44; and *our,* page 46.)

Under the Tree, pages 20-25. (Give help with the word *Baby* on page 20.)

We Come and Go, pages 23-28. (Give help with the word *work* on page 25.)

Unit 56: In the Garden

NEW VOCABULARY: gave

PREPARATION

Have the following materials ready for use:

Pocket Card Holder
Word Card: 542 gave

INITIAL PROCEDURE

Vocabulary review. (Have these phrases on the board: *Away went, By and by, Do you see, He lived, Her coat, I will not stay, You can talk, You have.*) Who can draw a line under one of the phrases on the board, read it, and use it to begin a sentence?

Drill on sentence beginnings

(Have the following sentences on board.)

Come, Betsy Lee.
Come, walk with me.
I will say it again.

Alice was talking to Betsy Lee and made up a little rhyme. If you can read these two sentences (indicate sentences 1, 2), you will know what her rhyme was. (Have rhyme reread until pupils sense the rhythm. Have them decide which words rhyme.) Alice liked to say that rhyme. As soon as she was through saying it once, she said— (sentence 3).

Working for fluency

Introducing new vocabulary. (Have these sentences on board.)

I gave you a book.
Then she gave a big hop.
She gave one big hop and ran away.

Guidance in
methods of
word attack

(Hand a book to some child.) This sentence tells exactly what **I** did. (Indicate sentence 1.) Think about this word. (Indicate *gave*.) It begins like *go*. The name of this letter (indicate *a*) is—. I ga—— you a b——. Who is ready? Then this word (add *gave* to card holder) says—.

Do you remember the day Alice and Jerry discovered the little rabbit? For a moment the rabbit sat up, stiff and straight. But—(sentence 2). And then—(sentence 3). (Have sentences and new word reread.)

Using the table
of contents

Contents pages. If you will find the title of the story, you will find out where Alice takes Betsy Lee today. On what page will the story begin?

SILENT READING

Page 110. Is this a wild rabbit or a tame rabbit? How do you know?

If I had a garden like this, I would say just what Alice says in the first two sentences. What does she say? Now Alice makes up that rhyme. Read until she has said it a second time. Now finish the page and get her into the garden.

Page 111. Is this rabbit just visiting in the garden? Read the first sentence and see what you think.

Now read four sentences. How is Betsy Lee different from the rabbit? Read three more sentences. What did Mother Rabbit do when she was through looking? Mother Rabbit doesn't feel the way Alice does. How does Mother Rabbit feel? How does Alice feel? Finish the page and see.

Page 112. Did Brown Bird just happen to fly into this garden? Read two sentences and see what you think. What did Alice say to Brown Bird? Read four sentences and you will know. Did Brown Bird do what all birds do when you come close to them? The next sentence tells.

Alice is disappointed in Betsy Lee. Finish the page and find out why.

Predicting
outcomes

Page 113. That rooster makes me know where Alice and Betsy Lee go next. Who can read the title and tell us? What might they meet in the barnyard? What may happen?

ORAL READING

Rereading by page units. The one who can say Alice's rhyme without looking at the book may read page 110. The one who knows this word (indicate *gave*) may read page 111. The one who can tell me what you call a gate which opens into a garden may read page 112.

WORD RECOGNITION TECHNIQUES

Phonics

Auditory-visual perception. *Final sounds.* You remember how the word *boat* ends. (Write *boat;* direct attention to final *t;* then erase word.) If I write *boat,* all but the last letter, will you put on the last letter? (Write *boa*____ and have some child add *t.* Continue with *goat, tweet, nest.*)

Capital letter
for sentence
beginning

Capitalization. We found out that every sentence begins with what kind of letter? Here is a sentence with a word left out. (Write____ *me go.*) Which of these words do I need to complete the sentence? (Write *See—see* below sentence. Have pupils choose capitalized form and give reasons for choice; then write in word and complete the sentence. Change sentence to read *I can*____ *you go* and repeat procedure. For other suggestions see page 72 in the *Workbook for Day In and Day Out.*)

SUPPLEMENTARY ACTIVITIES

1. *Vocabulary Primer Workbook,* page 70.
2. *Workbook for Day In and Day Out,* pages 71, 72, 73, 74.

Unit 57: (Supplementary)

1. Textfilm for *Day In and Day Out,* Frames 31-32. See Textfilm manual for directions.

2. Additional reading. In the following preprimers the pages noted may be used for supplementary reading under teacher supervision: *All in a Day,* pages 30-41. (Give help with *fun,* page 30.)

Molly, Pete, and Ginger, pages 67-69. (Give help with the word
school on page 67.)
Under the Tree, pages 26-31.
We Come and Go, pages 29-32.

Pp. 113-15   # Unit 58: In the Barnyard

PREPARATION

Have the following materials ready for use:

Pocket Card Holder
Word Cards

| 483 eat | 493 again | 509 ate | 510 old | 540 very |

INITIAL PROCEDURE

Drill on
sentence
beginnings

Drill on
carrier words

Vocabulary review. (Have these phrases on board: *Alice went, All
the white hens, Here is, He started to talk, I wish you could, Red
Rooster lived, You are.* Then proceed as in previous units.)

When you do things over, you do them—(add *again* to card holder).
The name of the first letter in this word is—(add *eat* to card holder),
and the word is—. The name of the first letter in this word is—(add
old), and the word is—. The name of the first letter is—(add *ate*),
and the word is—. When something is more than pretty, it is—(add
very) pretty. How many of you can read all five words? (Reverse
order continually.)

Contents pages. If you can read the title of the new story, you will
recall where Alice and Betsy Lee are going today. Who is ready with
the title? What page will the story begin on?

SILENT READING

Page 113. It looks as if Alice is saying that rhyme again. Read the
title and the first two sentences and see if she is. Does this rooster

belong in the barnyard? What does he do when he sees Alice? The next three sentences tell. I believe Alice is teasing Betsy Lee to do something. Finish the page and see if she is.

Page 114. Read three sentences and find out two things about this red cow. Read four more and find out what Alice says to her. I am afraid Alice is more disappointed than ever. Finish the page and find out why.

Page 115. Maybe these white hens will wake up Betsy Lee. What did they do when they saw Alice, and why? The first two sentences tell.

Predicting
outcomes

What did the hens say and what did they do? Read two sentences to find out. Does Betsy Lee surprise Alice by talking? Finish the page and see. I hope she talks tomorrow. Do you think she will?

ORAL READING

Organization. (Write the following sentences on board.)

Following
events in
sequence

_____Alice talks to the hens.
_____Alice talks to the cow.
_____Alice talks to the rooster.

The one who can find the sentence which tells what happened first in the story today and can number that sentence *1* may read the page which goes with that sentence. (Continue in similar way.)

WORD RECOGNITION TECHNIQUES

Auditory-visual perception. *Final sounds.* Here are two new words.

Phonics

(Write *best—bed.*) One says *best.* You are getting to be the *best* readers. One says *bed.* Go to *bed* early. Which word says *best?* How do you know? (Repeat with *hat—hand, face—fat.*)

Word structure. (Write *I like to_____ ball.* Under the sentence write *play* and *plays.*) Which of these words (indicate *play* and *plays*) do I need to complete my sentence? Who will write in the right word?

Using verb
forms correctly

(Change sentence to read *Jerry_____ ball* and repeat procedure. For other suggestions, see page 77 of the *Workbook for Day In and Day Out.*)

SUPPLEMENTARY ACTIVITIES

1. *Vocabulary Primer Workbook,* pages 71, 72.
2. *Workbook for Day In and Day Out,* pages 75, 76.

Pp. 116-19 # Unit 59: In the Barnyard (*cont.*)

PREPARATION

Have the following materials ready for use:

Pocket Card Holder
Word Cards: 474 laughed   511 started

INITIAL PROCEDURE

Drill on
sentence
beginnings

Vocabulary review. (Have the following phrases on board: *All he can do, Away went, He may want, I am going, She could not, She lived, She was, The barnyard gate was.* Proceed as in previous units.)

I hope you have not forgotten this word (add *laughed* to card holder) or this word (add *started*).

If you can read this number (write *116*) and turn quickly to that page, we can find out if Betsy Lee is any smarter than she was yesterday. Maybe she can talk by this time.

SILENT READING

Page 116. (Allow time for enjoyment of picture.) How many of the ducks talked to Alice? Read six sentences and find out. Is Betsy Lee any smarter than she was yesterday? Finish reading the page and find out.

Page 117. Read until you find out what Alice did when the pigs started to talk to her. What did she say to the pigs? Read until you find out. Finish the page. Is Betsy Lee any smarter?

Oral language

Page 118. (Allow time for picture discussion.) The first three sentences tell what started the trouble. Read and see. I don't believe the red cow has seen that goat yet, do you? Will she run, too? Finish the page and see.

Page 119. What does Alice tell Betsy Lee she is going to do? Read two sentences and find out. Why is Alice so frightened? The next four sentences tell. Did Alice and Betsy Lee get home safely? Read the last sentence and see what you think. We finish the story tomorrow. Do you think Betsy Lee will talk?

Predicting outcomes

ORAL READING

Organization. (Have the following sentences on board. Proceed as in previous units.)

Following events in sequence

_____Alice runs home.
_____The ducks talk to Alice.
_____The goat runs into the barnyard.
_____The pigs talk to Alice.

VOCABULARY ENRICHMENT AND EXTENSION

Word concepts. Alice has a friend named—(write *May*). So May is sometimes the name of a person. When Alice wants to go to see her friend, she says, "May I go, Mother?" What does Alice mean by that *may*? (*allow*) Today Alice said, "That goat may eat Betsy Lee." What did she mean that time? (*might*) My birthday is in May. What do we mean by that *May*? Think what *May* means when you read.

WORD RECOGNITION TECHNIQUES

Auditory-visual perception. *Final sounds.* Listen as I say *goat, duck, cat.* Which two words end with the same sound? If I write *goat,* all but the last sound, will you finish the word? (Repeat with *tent, farm, nut; street, road, suit.*)

Here are two new words. (Write *bag—bat.*) One says *bat;* bat the ball. One says *bag;* I have a bag of popcorn. Which word says *bat*? How do you know? (Repeat with *wet—well.*)

Phonics

Using verb
forms
correctly

Word structure. (Use procedures similar to those in preceding unit. See page 77 of the *Workbook for Day In and Day Out* for suggestions.)

SUPPLEMENTARY ACTIVITIES

1. *Vocabulary Primer Workbook,* pages 73, 74, 75.
2. *Workbook for Day In and Day Out,* pages 77, 78.

Unit 60: (Supplementary)

Additional reading. In the following preprimers, the pages noted may be used as supplementary reading under teacher guidance:

All in a Day, pages 42-51.

Under the Tree, pages 44-47. (Give help with the word *Daddy* on page 44.)

We Come and Go, pages 47-52. (Give help with the words *cars,* on page 47; and *yellow,* page 48.)

Pp. 120-22 # Unit 61: Betsy Lee Talks

NEW VOCABULARY: hug   Ma-ma

PREPARATION

Have the following materials ready for use:

Pocket Card Holder
Word Cards

493 again	515 could	541 word	543 hug
498 wish	531 night	542 gave	544 Ma-ma

INITIAL PROCEDURE

Drill on
sentence
beginnings

Vocabulary review. (Have the following phrases on board. Follow procedure suggested in previous units. *All the animals, That night, Then she gave, You are.*)

Building sight
vocabulary

Can you read these cards as quickly as I put them into the card holder? (Add *could, gave, again, night, wish, word.* Have several pupils climb up and down the word ladder.)

Contents pages. I am afraid the title of our story today gives away a secret. Who will be the first to find and read the title? On what page will the story begin?

SILENT READING

Page 120. Good readers like you can read a whole page. Find out what Alice is saying to Betsy Lee.

Page 121. You can read this whole page. Find out what Alice is thinking. Betsy Lee hasn't talked. If she does talk, what will she say? *Ma-ma* looks like this. (Hold up word card.) Turn quickly and see if you can find it on the next page.

Page 122. How many times can you find *Ma-ma?* Betsy Lee certainly talks when she once starts. What time is it in the picture? Can you find *night* in the first sentence? Now read the two-line sentence. What happened that night?

What is Alice giving Betsy Lee? You know how *hug* begins. Can you find it in the next sentence? (Add *hug* to card holder.) Now read two sentences and find out what happens. Why hasn't Betsy Lee been talking all the time? Read the next two lines. What does Alice say

Independent
word attack—
hug, Carl

when she hears that *Ma-ma?* I am afraid Alice may break Betsy Lee's talking machine. Read the rest of the page and find out why.

Page 123. Of course, you know the boy in the picture. His name is—. If I tell you that this word (write *Mr.*) says *mister,* I am sure you can get this name for yourselves. (Write *Carl.*) You know how the name begins. You know that this part (underline *ar*) says—. Who is smart enough to know the man's name? Do you think you might like Mr. Carl? Do you think Jack does? Who is ready with the title of the next part of our book?

ORAL READING

Audience reading. (Assign one or two pages of the Betsy Lee stories to each pupil. Have each pupil prepare to read part assigned. Then organize group into a reading party where assigned pages are read for enjoyment of group.)

WORD RECOGNITION TECHNIQUES

Auditory-visual perception. *Final sounds.* Listen as I say *went, want, was.* Which two words end with the same sound? (Continue as in previous units.)

Phonics

Here are two new words. (Write *rest—read.*) Which word says *rest?* You may have the *rest* of the cake. How do you know? (Repeat with *right—road.*)

Using verb forms correctly

Word structure. (See page 81 in *Workbook for Day In and Day Out* for suggestions. Write sentences on board similar to the ones there. Have pupils draw lines from blanks to correct verb forms.)

SUPPLEMENTARY ACTIVITIES

1. *Vocabulary Primer Workbook,* page 76.
2. *Workbook for Day In and Day Out,* pages 79, 80, 81, 82.
3. Tests. Before beginning the next unit give the two informal tests on pages 83 and 84 in the *Workbook for Day In and Day Out.* A score of 1 is given for each item marked correctly. Pupils should make a score of at least 18 on the vocabulary test; 4 on the sentence-meaning test. As in previous units, test each pupil individually with the word cards for the Primer vocabulary developed so far. (See pages 159-60 of the Primer.)

Individual check on sight vocabulary

Unit 62: (Supplementary)

1. Textfilm for *Day In and Day Out,* Frames 33-34. See Textfilm manual for directions.

2. Additional reading. In the following preprimers the pages noted may be used for supplementary reading under teaching guidance:

All in a Day, pages 52-61. (Give help with *make*, page 58.)
Under the Tree, pages 32-37. (Give help with *we* on page 36.)
We Come and Go, pages 33-42. (Give help with the words *help*, page 33; *we*, page 37.)

Unit 63: My Little Girl

Pp. 124-27

New Vocabulary: **Carl**   girl   hello   liked   **Mr.**

PREPARATION

Have the following materials ready for use:

Pocket Card Holder
Word Cards

162 Yes	525 All	540 very	546 Carl	548 liked
502 her	530 his	545 Mr.	547 girl	549 Hello

INITIAL PROCEDURE

Vocabulary review. (Have the following phrases on board: *Again*

Drill on
sentence
beginnings

and again, Alice ate, Alice lived, Do you like, Here comes, Mr. Carl was, One morning, So she stopped, Then she went.) I hope you remember that the man we will read about in the next part of our book is—(add *Mr. Carl* to card holder). Now will you draw a line under a phrase you know on the board, read it, and then use it to begin a sentence?

When you mean "everyone," you say—(add *All* to card holder). The opposite of *no* is—(add *Yes*). Something more than pretty is—

Drill on
carrier words

(add *very*) pretty. A word which goes with a boy is—(add *his*); with a girl,—(add *her*). Who can read all five words?

Introducing new vocabulary. (Have these sentences on board.)

> Alice is a girl.
> She liked Betsy Lee.
> Do you say, "Hello!"

Guidance in methods of word attack

Think how this word begins. (Indicate *girl* in sentence **1.**) I am sure you will need no further help with this sentence. Who is ready? Then this word (add *girl* to card holder) says—.

This word (write *look*) says—. Now it says—(write *looked*). This word says—(write *like*). Now it will say—(write *liked*). Who is ready to read sentence 2? Then this word (add *liked* to card holder) says—.

When you walk down the street and meet a friend of Mother's, what do you say? (Indicate sentence 3.) Think how this word begins. (Indicate *Hello.*) Think what you would say. (If someone suggests *Hi,* remind him that he might say that to a child but not to a friend of Mother's.) Then this new word says—. (Add *Hello* to card holder; then reverse to show lower-case form. Have sentences and new words reread.)

Contents pages. How quickly can you find the new part of our book and read the title? What is the name of the first story? Do you suppose Mr. Carl has a little girl? To what page shall we turn to find out?

SILENT READING

Gathering information from pictures

Page 124. Suppose we see how many things we can find out about Mr. Carl from the pictures. Is he old or young? What kind of house does he live in? What does he like? Would you like him? Why? Do you suppose he is in a bird store on page 125? Suppose we read and check to see if we are good thinkers.

Read page 124. In what way is Mr. Carl like Alice?

Page 125. Read three sentences. Find out two more things about Mr. Carl. Now read the next sentence. Does Mr. Carl really have a little girl?

What else does Mr. Carl like? Read the next two sentences and see. Were we right in our thinking about the bird store? Read the three short sentences. What kind of birds does Mr. Carl have in his house? Finish the page. What did Alice like to do?

Page 126. (Allow time for enjoyment of picture.) Read the first two sentences. Find out what happened one morning. How did Alice happen to stop at the garden? The next two sentences tell. What does she ask Betsy Lee? Finish the page and see.

Page 127. Alice must have given Betsy Lee a hug. Read the first sentence and find out why I think so. What does Mr. Carl say? You will have to read four sentences to find out. Did Alice go on walking, or did she go with Mr. Carl? Finish reading the page and find out what she did.

Predicting
outcomes

What do you think may happen when Alice and Betsy Lee go into the house?

ORAL READING

Rereading by page units. The one who knows this word (indicate *girl*) may read page 124. (Use *liked* for 125, *hello* for 126.) The one who knows all three words may read page 127.

WORD RECOGNITION TECHNIQUES

Auditory-visual perception. *Final sounds.* Listen as I say *can, down.* (Say *n* sound very clearly.) My ears tell me that *can* and *down* end with the same sound. I wonder if my ears told the truth. (Write words and direct attention to final *n*.) If I wanted to write another word which ends like *can* and *down*, should I write *red* or *brown?* Let's prove that you are right. (Write *brown*, direct attention to final *n*, and then repeat procedure with *puppy, kitten; is, in.*)

If I write *breakfast,* all but the last letter, will someone finish it for me? (Continue with *night, nest, tweet.*)

Phonics

Initial sounds. When something is more than pretty, it is—(write *very*) pretty. Watch how *very* begins. (Trace *v;* then erase word.) Listen as I say *valentine, postman.* Which word begins like *very?* If someone will show me how *very* begins, I will finish the word for you. (Repeat with *valentine;* then with *vacation, violin, visit.*)

Here are four new words. (Write *vegetable, corn, beets, peas.*) Which word says *vegetable?* How do you know? (Continue with the other words; repeat procedure with *rose, pansy, violet, tulip.*)

Vocabulary Primer Workbook, pages 77, 78, 79, 80, 81.

Pp. 128-29

Unit 64: My Little Girl (*cont.*)

PREPARATION

Have the following materials ready for use:

Pocket Card Holder
Word Cards

| 94 it | 483 eat | 518 tweet | 525 All | 542 gave |

INITIAL PROCEDURE

Drill on
carrier words

Vocabulary review. If you can read these cards as quickly as I add them to the card holder, we can soon find out what happened when Mr. Carl, Alice, and Betsy Lee went into the house. (Add all listed cards.)

Can anyone write *128?* Now how quickly can you find that page?

SILENT READING

Oral language

Page 128. (Allow time for enjoyment of pictures and for identification of perches, feeding cups, water cups.)

Now read six sentences. What did the birds do the minute they saw Alice and Betsy Lee? Why do you think they gave two "tweets" for Alice and just one for Betsy Lee?

Now Alice makes a discovery. Finish the page. What does she find out? What will she feed the birds?

Page 129. Before long the birds will like Alice as well as they like Mr. Carl if she takes care of them as well as this. What does she do? Read three sentences and find out. How do the birds say "thank you"? Finish the page and see.

ORAL READING

Organization. (Have the following phrases on board.)

Following
events in
sequence

_____What Alice did
_____Mr. Carl's house
_____What Mr. Carl liked
_____Alice's morning walk
_____What Mr. Carl said
_____What the birds said

Turn back to page 124. The one who can find the phrase on the board which tells what this page is about may number that phrase *1* and then read the phrase and the page. (Continue in similar way.)

WORD RECOGNITION TECHNIQUES

Auditory-visual perception. *Final sounds.* Listen carefully as I say *man, boy, green.* My ears told me that two of those words ended with the same sound. Which words were they? Let's prove that you are right. (Write *man, green* and direct attention to final *n.* Continue as in previous units.)

Phonics

Phonetic parts. This word (write *Carl*) says—, and this part (underline *ar*) says—. (Continue with *ay* in *say, oo* in *moo, ew* in *new, ow* in *now.*)

SUPPLEMENTARY ACTIVITIES

Workbook for Day In and Day Out, pages 85, 86, 87, 88. Supervise marking of first section on page 87.

Unit 65: (Supplementary)

Additional reading. In the following preprimers the pages noted may be used as supplementary reading under teacher guidance:

All in a Day, pages 62-71.
Under the Tree, pages 48-51. (Give help with the words *make* and *thank* on page 50.)
We Come and Go, pages 43-46. (Give help with the words *cookies,* page 44; and *where,* page 45.)
We Work and Play, pages 27-30.

Pp. 130-31   # Unit 66: The Big Green Bird

NEW VOCABULARY: help

PREPARATION

Have the following materials ready for use:

Pocket Card Holder

Word Cards:			
51 And	471 Please	503 now	542 gave
139 Not	474 laughed	510 old	550 help
162 yes	485 that	513 are	
460 happy	493 again	515 could	
469 new	501 find	525 all	

INITIAL PROCEDURE

Drill on
carrier words

Vocabulary review. If I do something over, I do it—(add *again* to holder). If you ask me if everyone is here today, I will say—. (Add *Not all.* Continue in similar fashion with other listed words, except *help.* Have pupils play "One, Two, Three! How Many for Me?" to remove cards from card holder.)

Contents pages. Turn quickly to the contents pages. Who will be the first one ready with the title of the new story? Have we heard anything about a green bird before? Maybe Mr. Carl bought a new bird. To what page must we turn to find out?

SILENT READING

Oral language   **Page 130.** (Take plenty of time for picture discussion. Have all items identified. Have pupils decide what Mr. Carl has been doing and what the bird sticks are for.) What does Alice seem to be doing? Why do you suppose she is pulling Mr. Carl?

Read the title and the first two sentences on page 130. Alice is very sure of something. What is she sure of, and why? Mr. Carl has a big surprise for Alice. Read three more sentences. What is the surprise? Do you think Alice can find the bird? What does she think? Read the next two sentences and see. Finish the page. What does Mr. Carl tell her to do?

Independent
word attack—
help
Page 131. When you just can't do something, you sometimes have to say—(write *Please help me*). Think how the new word begins (indicate *help*); then let the sentence help you. Who is ready? Then the new word (add *help* to card holder) says—. How many times can you find *help* on page 131? Now read the page. Why is Alice pulling Mr. Carl?

ORAL READING

Expressing
mood of
characters
Rereading by two-page units. One or two people who are sure they do not need any—(hold up word card *help*) might try to read both these pages. I hope our readers talk like Alice and Mr. Carl.

WORD RECOGNITION TECHNIQUES

Auditory-visual perception. *Phonetic parts.* Of course, you know that Alice is a—(write *girl*). But you didn't know that this part in the word says—(underline *ir* and give sound). Listen as I say *bird—duck.* In which word did you hear the part *ir*? (Give sound.) Let's see if you are right. (Write *bird;* then have some pupil underline *ir* and give sound.)

Can someone read this word? (Write *Carl*.) Can you draw a line under the part you see and hear in the word and tell me what the part says? (Continue with *stay, down, mew, too.*)

Phonics   *Final sounds.* You remember how the word *rabbit* ends. (Write *rabbit* and direct attention to final *t*.) You also know how *down* ends. (Write *down* and direct attention to final *n*. Erase both words.) If I wanted to write *basket,* would I end it like this (write *n*) or like this (write *t*)? I will write *basket,* all but the last letter. The one who can show me how the word should end may put on the last letter. (Repeat with *brown, just, went, man, green,* etc. DO NOT OMIT THESE ACTIVITIES.)

SUPPLEMENTARY ACTIVITIES

1. *Vocabulary Primer Workbook,* page 82.
2. *Workbook for Day In and Day Out,* pages 89, 90.

Pp. 132-33   Unit 67: The Big Green Bird (*cont.*)

PREPARATION

Have the following materials ready for use:

Pocket Card Holder
Word Cards

158 name	494 was	513 are	543 hug	549 hello
485 that	504 say	514 talk	547 girl	

INITIAL PROCEDURE

Drill on
sentence
beginnings

Vocabulary review. (Have the following phrases on board: *Alice gave, Alice laughed, It said, Just then, Mr. Carl got up and, Then Alice went.* Have a pupil underline a phrase he knows, read it, and then use it to begin a sentence.)

When Alice gives Betsy Lee a—(add *hug* to card holder), Betsy Lee can—(add *say*) her—(add *name*). (Use similar procedure for other listed words.) How quickly can someone read all the words?

Will Alice find the green bird today? If you can turn to this page (write *132*), we can soon find out.

SILENT READING

Page 132. Have you found the green bird? What kind of bird is it? What can parrots do? What do they say? I wonder if this parrot will say, "Polly wants a cracker"? Let's read and see.

When Alice was pulling Mr. Carl, Mr. Carl was sitting down. What does he do now, and what does he say? Read two sentences and see. Then what happens? Read until you come to the two questions, and see if you can answer them. Finish the page. How do you suppose the parrot ever learned to say, "Hello, Alice"? (Suggest that Mr. Carl has owned the parrot for some time and has taught him to say *Alice*.)

Page 133. What did Alice say as soon as she could stop laughing? The first four sentences tell. She must have given Betsy Lee a squeeze. Read two more sentences. See what happens.

Will Alice be as good to the green bird as she was to the others? The next sentence tells. How does the green bird say, "Thank you"? Finish the page and see.

ORAL READING

Audience reading. (Assign the entire story by pages to different members of the group. Have them prepare to read the page assigned for the enjoyment of the whole group. Read several pages yourself to stress expression and rhythmic phrasing.)

Working for fluency and expression

WORD RECOGNITION TECHNIQUES

Phonics

Auditory-visual perception. *Final sounds. Rabbit!* (Say the final *t* clearly.) If I write the word, all but the last sound, will someone finish it for me? (Continue with *went, just, rain, again*.)

Here are two new words. One says *pan;* there is a *pan* of water on the stove. One says *pet;* Jip is Alice's *pet*. Which word says *pet?* How do you know? (Repeat with *fan—feet*.)

Using verb forms correctly

Word structure. (Write *help, helps, helped* on board and have the words read.) I am going to write a sentence and leave out one word. Be ready to show me which of these words I should put into my sentence. (Write *Jerry _____ Father*. Have some child choose the correct verb form; then write it for him in the sentence and have him read sentence. Repeat procedure with the other two verb forms. For other suggestions, see page 91 in the *Workbook for Day In and Day Out*.)

SUPPLEMENTARY ACTIVITIES

1. *Vocabulary Primer Workbook,* page 83. This page should be done under teacher guidance.

2. *Workbook for Day In and Day Out,* pages 91, 92.

Unit 68: (Supplementary)

1. Textfilm for *Day In and Day Out,* Frames **35-36.** See Textfilm manual for directions.

2. Additional reading. In the following preprimers the pages noted may be used as supplementary reading under teacher guidance:

My Little Blue Story Book, pages 41-48. (Give help with the word *make,* page 43.)

My Little Green Story Book, pages 35-42.

Under the Tree, pages 2-7.

We Work and Play, pages 31-34.

Pp. 134-37 # Unit 69: The Best Store

NEW VOCABULARY: best

PREPARATION

Have the following materials ready for use:

Pocket Card Holder
Word Cards

455 toy	485 that	506 animal	549 hello
483 eat	493 again	524 run	551 best

INITIAL PROCEDURE

Drill on
sentence
beginnings

Vocabulary review. (Have the following phrases on board: *In the morning, Then he liked, One day, You are, I wish I could have, That dog was, Jack came, He wanted to say.* Have a pupil underline a phrase he knows, read it, and then use it to begin a sentence.)

Betsy Lee is a doll, but she is also a—(add *toy* to card holder). Alice gave the birds something to—(add *eat;* use similar procedure with other words listed above, except *best*). Who can climb both up and down the word ladder?

Guidance in
methods of
word attack

Introducing new vocabulary. Mr. Carl liked all the children who lived on his street. The reason he called Alice "my little girl" is because—(write *He liked Alice best*). Think how the new word begins. (Indicate *best*.) He liked all the boys and girls, but he liked Alice b——. (Wait for suggestion *best;* then add word card to card holder.)

Contents pages. The next story will not be about the best girl. But it will be about the best—. Who is ready to read the title?

SILENT READING

Page 134. If you are very smart, you can tell me the name of the store (*pet, animal*). Maybe Jack thinks this is the—(indicate *best*) store. Would you agree with Jack? Which pet do you like best? How many kittens do you see, and what are they doing?

Read the title and the first two sentences. Find out what stores Jack likes. Are toy stores the only kind he likes? Read the next sentence and see. What is another name for a store that has something good to eat?

Now read the next sentence. Does Jack like still another kind of store? What are other names for stores where coats and caps are sold?

Does Jack agree with you? Does he think the animal store is best? Finish the page and see.

Page 135. I wonder how often Jack went to the animal store. Read two sentences and see. Now read the question. Can you answer it?

Read the next two sentences. Do they tell about one thing you saw in the window? Read two more sentences. Does Jack see the kittens doing just what you see them doing? Now finish the page. Which pet is Jack watching especially?

Page 136. Does the puppy like Jack? How can you tell? How many puppies can you see?

Now read two sentences. What did Jack say to the dog, and what did the dog do when he heard Jack? Read three more sentences. What is Jack saying? If the dog barks, what will his bark mean? Finish the page and see.

Page 137. Are there any pets in the window we have not seen before? Would you rather have a monkey than a dog? I wonder if Jack would. What do you think he is counting? It would take many, many pennies to buy a puppy like this. Who do you think this man is? If you look quickly over the page, you might be able to find his name. Why is Mr. Green looking at Jack?

Now read the first sentence. How many days did that puppy stay in the window? Read the next sentence. Did Jack do just what you might
Predicting
outcomes
expect him to do? Read the last sentence and tell us the name of the man once again. What may happen tomorrow?

ORAL READING

Rereading by page units. The one who knows this word (indicate *best*) may read page 134. The one who can tell how many rabbits are in the window may read page 135. The one who can tell the name of the pets on the shelf may read page 136. The one who can tell how many kittens are in the window now may read page 137.

WORD RECOGNITION TECHNIQUES

Auditory-visual perception. *Final sounds.* If I wanted to write the
Phonics
word *best* (give final sound clearly), would I end it like this (write *t*) or like this (write *n*)? I will write *best,* all but the last letter. Who can show me how to put on the last letter? (Repeat with *open, night, run.*)

Here are two new words. (Write *soon, suit.*) One says *suit;* I have a new *suit.* One says *soon;* come home *soon.* Which word says *soon?*

SUPPLEMENTARY ACTIVITIES

1. *Vocabulary Primer Workbook,* page 84.
2. *Workbook for Day In and Day Out,* page 93.

Unit 70: The Best Store (*cont.*)   Pp. 138-39

NEW VOCABULARY: Snap

───────────────────────────────

PREPARATION

Have the following materials ready for use:

Pocket Card Holder
Word Cards

159 this	485 that	525 all	530 his
474 laughed	492 will	529 open	543 hug

INITIAL PROCEDURE

Drill on sentence beginnings

Vocabulary review. (Have the following phrases on board: *For three days, So by and by, Out jumped, Jack gave, He started.* Have some child underline a phrase he knows and use it to begin a sentence.)

Another word for *everyone* is—. (Add *all* to card holder. Use similar procedure to add all cards listed to card holder. Have some pupil play "One, Two, Three! How Many for Me?" to read and remove cards from card holder. Reverse order of cards and repeat game several times.)

Has Jack found enough pennies to buy that dog? If you can read this number (write *138*), we can turn quickly to that page and see.

SILENT READING

Page 138. Do you remember how many days the dog was in the window? I wonder if Jack came back every day. Read the first sentence and find out. Mr. Green asks Jack a question. Read until you find the question and see if you can answer it. Jack answers Mr. Green. Then he asks a question. Read until you find what Jack's question is. Can you answer it?

Sometimes when a puppy sees someone he does not like, he does not bite; but he does—(write *Snap*). This new word begins like *snow*. It rhymes with *cap*. The puppy will sn——. (Wait for suggestion *snap*.) Show me how he might snap.

Guidance in methods of word attack

Now read the next two sentences. Find out what Mr. Green thinks about the dog. Now read three more sentences. Where did the puppy get his name? Does Jack still like that dog? Finish the page and see.

Page 139. Maybe that dog will snap, after all. Look at the picture and see what you think. What is Mr. Green doing?

Now read three sentences. What happened the minute Mr. Green opened the window? Read three more sentences. Did the dog snap at Jack? Finish the page. What did Mr. Green say, and what did Jack and the puppy do?

Predicting outcomes

What do you think may happen tomorrow, the next day, and many days after this?

ORAL READING

Organization. (Have the following sentences on board.)

_____Jack finds out the dog's name.
_____Jack looks at the store he likes best.
_____Jack plays with the dog.
_____Jack talks to the dog.
_____Mr. Green sees Jack at the window.
_____Jack sees something in the window.

Following events in sequence

Turn back to page 134 and look over the page quickly. What is this whole page telling us about? Yes, about the stores Jack likes. Finally it tells us about the one he likes—. I see a sentence on the board which tells us what this page is about. The one who can find that sentence and number it *1* may read the page. (Continue in similar manner with other sentences.)

WORD RECOGNITION TECHNIQUES

Phonics

Auditory-visual perception. *Final sounds.* If I write the word *rabbit,* all but the last sound, will someone finish the word? (Continue with *brown, kitten, not.*)

Here are two new words. (Write *moon, meat.*) If you think how the words begin and end, you can tell me which word says *moon.* How did you know? (Repeat with *meat;* then with *burn* and *beet.* DO NOT OMIT THESE ACTIVITIES.)

SUPPLEMENTARY ACTIVITIES

1. *Vocabulary Primer Workbook,* page 85.

Guiding Workbook activities

2. *Workbook for Day In and Day Out,* pages 94, 95, 96. On page 95 discuss story of picture sequence and have the first three pictures and corresponding sentences marked under teacher guidance. On page 96 the first two questions should be marked under teacher guidance.

Unit 71: The Best Store (*cont.*)   Pp. 140-43

PREPARATION

Have the following materials ready for use:

Pocket Card Holder

Word Cards:	89 Good	493 again	551 best
	139 Not	540 very	552 Snap

INITIAL PROCEDURE

Vocabulary review. (Have the following sentences on the board.)

He saw Alice
on the walk by his house.
I want a girl to help me.
Are you the girl to help me?
Yes, I am.
I will stay and help you now.
That is all for now.
You are a good help.

One morning Mr. Carl walked out into his garden and—(sentence 1). Then he said—(sentences 2, 3). Of course Alice said—(sentences 4, 5). Have you any ideas what she might have done to help Mr. Carl?

After a while the work was done. Mr. Carl said—(sentences 6, 7). What did he mean when he said, "That is all for now"? Then he gave Alice a big red apple, and she ran home.

If you are the—(add *best* to card holder) reader I have, you can read the rest of these words as quickly as I put them into the card holder. (Add all other words listed above and have words read several times.)

Will Jack go to the store every morning? Will Mr. Green open the cage door and let the puppy out? If you can read this page number (write *140*) and can turn quickly to that page, we can soon find out.

SILENT READING

Oral language

Page 140. (Allow time for discussion of picture on page 141.) I don't believe that that puppy, Snap, minds well. Read two sentences and find out why I think he doesn't. Do you suppose Jack can make him mind? Read the next three sentences. Why did Snap mind Jack and not Mr. Green?

Mr. Green has a fine plan. If you are big enough readers to read five sentences, you can find out about the plan.

Does Jack like the plan? Finish the page and see.

Page 141. Now we know why Jack is so busy. Will he treat Snap just a little bit better then he does the other dogs? Finish the page and find out.

Page 142. What does Jack seem to be doing in the picture? Evidently he has not worked long enough to earn a dog yet. Dogs cost a great deal of money.

Mr. Green reminds me of Mr. Carl. He tells Jack just what Mr. Carl told Alice. Read three sentences and see how he liked the work Jack did.

On the way home something happens. Finish the page and find out what happened.

Page 143. What seems to be happening here? What can Alice and Jack be quarreling about? I wonder if Jerry is in the quarrel? If you read three sentences, you will know. What does Alice think about the matter? Read until you find out. Does Jack admit that Jip is the best dog? Read until you find out.

Read the last sentence to see how the quarrel comes out.

ORAL READING

Organization. (Have these sentences on board. Follow techniques suggested in previous unit.)

Following events in sequence

_____Jack talks to Alice and Jerry.

_____Mr. Green wants Jack to help in the store.

_____Jack is going home.

_____Jack helps Mr. Green.

VOCABULARY ENRICHMENT AND EXTENSION

Descriptive phrases. Suppose we put some pets in Mr. Green's window this morning. Suppose we start this way. "I walked by Mr. Green's store, and in the window I saw a brown and white kitten with pointed ears." (Have next pupil repeat what has been said and add another pet. Continue to repeat and add.)

WORD RECOGNITION TECHNIQUES

Phonics

Auditory-visual perception. *Initial sounds.* If someone will show me how *best* begins, I will finish the word. (Continue with *Carl, day, find, gave, help, Jack, kitten, like, morning, night.*)

SUPPLEMENTARY ACTIVITIES

Vocabulary Primer Workbook, pages 86, 87, 88, 89, 90, 91.

Unit 72: (Supplementary)

Additional reading. In the following preprimers the pages noted may be used as supplementary reading under teacher guidance:

My Little Blue Story Book, pages 49-52. (Give help with the word *stop* on page 52.)

My Little Green Story Book, pages 43-54.

Under the Tree, pages 58-63.

We Come and Go, pages 53-60. (Give help with the word *make* on page 54.)

We Work and Play, pages 11-14.

Pp. 144-46

Unit 73: A Dog for Jack

INITIAL PROCEDURE

Vocabulary review. (Have the following on the board.)

Day in and day out
Now and then
Can you help me out?

When you do something day after day, you do it—(phrase 1). When you do something only once in a while, you do it—(phrase 2). Who will read both phrases? Sometimes when Mother has too much work to do, she will say to Alice—(line 3). Today Mr. Green wants to be helped out of some trouble. Turn to the contents pages so that we may locate the new story and find out what the trouble is.

Contents pages. The title of the next story gives away a secret. Who can read the title and tell us what you think the secret is?

SILENT READING

Page 144. If you are good enough readers to read the title and three sentences, you can find out two things Jack does—(indicate *Day in and day out*) and one thing he does—(indicate *Now and then*). Show me that you are really good readers.

Three-line
sentence

Now Mr. Green tells you about the trouble he is in. The next sentence is a three-line sentence. Read it and find out what the trouble is. Now finish the page. Mr. Green asks Jack two questions. Find out what the questions are. How would you answer?

Page 145. Jack just can't believe that Mr. Green said what he did say. Read the first two sentences and find out how he answers Mr. Green. Did Mr. Green really mean what he said? The next two sentences tell.

Jack reminds me of Betsy Lee. Read three sentences and find out why. Do you suppose he said "thank you" with his eyes?

How long did it take Mr. Green to open the window? Finish the page and see.

Page 146. Jack can't go home without stopping to hug his dog, can he? How is the puppy showing that he likes Jack?

Read three sentences and find out what happened when the window opened. Read the next sentence. What did Jack do?

Don't call that dog Snap from this time on. If you can finish the page, you will find out why. Could you help Jack? Could you suggest a good name for his dog?

Page 147. One look at this picture and I know what time it is. Do you? What do you suppose these mischief-makers are saying as they lean over the bannister? Then can you read the title of the last part of our book?

ORAL READING

Working for
fluency and
expression

Audience reading. (Divide group into two smaller groups. Assign *The Best Store* to one group, *A Dog for Jack* to the other. Proceed as in previous units.)

VOCABULARY ENRICHMENT AND EXTENSION

Descriptive phrases. Suppose we make believe we have a toy store and begin this way: "I want a toy store, and in my toy store I will have a little red drum that says 'tum, tum.' " (Have each pupil repeat what has been said and add a toy.)

WORD RECOGNITION TECHNIQUES

Phonics

Auditory-visual perception. *Final sounds.* If I write *nest,* all but the last letter, will someone finish it? (Continue with *man, just, green, then, rain, eat, got, that, again.*)

Here are two new words. (Write *win, wet.*) One says *win;* I want to *win* the race. One says *wet;* the rain is *wet.* Which says *wet?* How do you know? (Repeat the procedure with *win;* then with *pin, pet; fun, fat.*)

SUPPLEMENTARY ACTIVITIES

1. *Workbook for Day In and Day Out,* pages 97, 98, 99, 100.
2. Tests. Before beginning the next unit, give the two informal tests on pages 101 and 102 of the *Workbook for Day In and Day Out.* A score of 1 is given for each item marked correctly. Pupils in immature groups should make a score of at least 18 on the vocabulary test, a score of at least 4 on the sentence-comprehension test. At this point check each child individually with the word cards for the Primer vocabulary.

Individual check on sight vocabulary

Unit 74: (Supplementary)

1. Textfilm for *Day In and Day Out,* Frames 37-38. See Textfilm manual for directions.

2. Additional reading. In the following preprimers the pages noted may be used as supplementary reading under teacher guidance:

Molly, Pete, and Ginger, pages 47-52. (Give help with the words *cat,* page 51; and *kitty,* page 52.)

My Little Green Story Book, pages 55-63. (Give help with the word *cake* on page 59.)

Under the Tree, pages 14-19.

We Work and Play, pages 19-22.

Unit 75: A Happy Day

Pp. 147-49

PREPARATION

Have the following materials ready for use:

Pocket Card Holder

Word Cards:

152 got	497 get	549 hello
483 eat	509 ate	550 help
493 again	525 all	551 best

INITIAL PROCEDURE

Vocabulary review. I hope you know these two partner words (add *get–got* to card holder); and these two (add *eat–ate*); and these two (add *hello–help*). I am glad you are–(add *all*) here. I hope you will be the–(add *best*) readers. If you do not know a word the first time you see it, try–(add *again*). Can someone read four words? five? How many words are in the card holder? Then five and four must be–.

Drill on carrier words

(Have the following sentence on board.)

> I am going to help Jack get
> a new name for his dog Snap.

Boys and girls who are about to finish a book are able to read long, long sentences. When Jack got home that day, a boy Jack knew said to his mother—(underline *I am going to help Jack* and have that much of the sentence read). You know this word. (Underline *get* and have word read.) You can read this phrase. (Underline *a new name*.) Now you can finish the sentence. (Underline *for his dog Snap* and have phrase read.) Who can read the whole sentence? (Swing your hand under each phrase as sentence is read. Have it read several times.)

Working for fluency

I wonder who the boy was. Let's find out.

Contents pages. The last time we saw Alice and Jerry, they were looking over the bannister and saying good night. Can you find the part in your book entitled "Good Night"? Read the title of the first story in that part.

SILENT READING

Page 148. Read the title and the first two sentences. What was the first thing Jerry did that morning? Then what did he tell Mother? The next two sentences will tell you. Did the boys name the dog? Finish the page and see. Would you have had such a good time playing that you would have forgotten to name your dog?

Page 149. What happened to Alice the first thing in the morning? Read two sentences and you will know. Where did Alice spend the morning? The next three sentences will tell you. What happened when the children came home again? Finish the page and see. Did they have a happy day? Would you have enjoyed a day like that? No wonder this story is called "A Happy Day."

ORAL READING

Rereading by page units. The one who can tell me how many two-line sentences there are on page 148 may read the page for us. Remember that periods tell where sentences end.

The one who can find out how many two-line sentences there are on page 149 may read that page. (Do not try to explain exclamation point at this time.)

VOCABULARY ENRICHMENT AND EXTENSION

Descriptive words. Suppose we imagine that we have a fruit store. Suppose we begin like this. I want a fruit store. In my fruit store I will have some big juicy grapes. Who will repeat what I said and put something more into our store?

WORD RECOGNITION TECHNIQUES

Auditory-visual perception. *Initial sounds.* If someone will show me how *puppy* begins, I will finish the word. (Continue with *rabbit,*

Phonics

say, talk, very, window, she, what, that, chair.)

Phonetic parts. (Write these words on board: *garden, brown, day, bird, mew, rooster.*) I see a word in which I hear and see the part— (give sound of long $\overline{oo}$). Who can find and read the word? Can you draw a line under the part and tell me what it says? (Continue in same way with other words.)

SUPPLEMENTARY ACTIVITIES

Workbook for Day In and Day Out, pages 103, 104, 105, 106.

Unit 76: (Supplementary)

Additional reading. In the following preprimers the pages noted may be used as supplementary reading under teacher guidance:

Molly, Pete, and Ginger, pages 53-56. (Give help with the sound word *Meow* on page 53.)

Under the Tree, pages 38-43. (Give help with the word *cake* on page 38.)

We Come and Go, pages 61-64.

We Work and Play, pages 43-46. (Give help with the word *cars* on page 43.)

p. 150-55 # Unit 77: Good Night

INITIAL PROCEDURE

Drill on
sentence
beginnings

Vocabulary review. (Have the following phrases on board: *Now it was, Mother came, She gave, That is what, In my barnyard*. Have some pupil draw a line under a phrase he knows and use it to begin a sentence.)

(Have the following on board: *The girls liked to splash in the rain puddles. I have had something to eat. Animals in the barnyard*.)

Working for
fluency

One rainy day Alice went to see May. For a time the girls played outdoors because—(sentence 1). Then May's mother called them and gave them lunch. When Alice went home, there was Jerry at the table with a glass of milk and a cooky. Alice said—(sentence 2). (Have this sentence repeated until phrase *I have had* is read without hesitation.) Mother wanted the children to stay in the house, out of the rain. So they decided to play a game called—(indicate *Animals in the barnyard*). Do you know how to play that game? Maybe our story will tell us.

Contents pages. Can you find the title of the very last story in the book? I think you know who is going to bed. To what page shall we turn to find out if you are right?

SILENT READING

Page 150. Is this the bed you saw Alice in on page 122? Look back and see. Whose bed do you think it is? What kind of bed do you call it? Where would you like to sleep? Do you suppose Mother will let Jip stay where he is all night?

Now read the title and the first four sentences. Find out exactly what Mother did when bedtime came. I hope you remember this phrase. (Indicate *I have had*.) Now finish the page. What did Alice and Jerry say to Mother?

Page 151. It looks as if mischief is starting. Do you suppose Mother expected this to happen? Who starts the mischief? Read four lines and see.

I believe Jerry is as bad as Alice. Read two more lines and see if you think so, and why.

Now Jerry starts the game. Finish the page to see how the game goes.

Page 152. I wonder if Alice will put something more into that barnyard just as we have been putting something more into our store windows. If you read five lines, you will know.

Will Jerry add something to the barnyard? Finish the page and see.

Pages 153, 154, 155. (Use techniques similar to those for page 152.)

Will this game never end? What might happen if Alice and Jerry get too noisy?

ORAL READING

Expressing
mood of
characters

Dramatization. Will someone read page 150 for us and put Alice and Jerry safely to bed? Will someone read enough of page 151 to get the game started? (From this point on, choose one pupil to be Alice, one to be Jerry and have them play the game by reading what each character says.)

VOCABULARY ENRICHMENT AND EXTENSION

Descriptive phrases. What is another way of saying "after a while" (*by and by*)? "suddenly" (*All at once*)? "every day" (*day in and day out*)? "once in a while" (*now and then*)?

WORD RECOGNITION TECHNIQUES

Phonics

Auditory-visual perception. *Final sounds.* If I had a barnyard, I would want a *colt.* If I write *colt,* all but the last letter, will someone finish the word? (Continue with *barn, hen, nest, night.*)

Here are two new words. (Write *noon, nut.*) One says *noon;* twelve o'clock is *noon.* The other word says *nut;* crack this *nut.*

Which says *nut?* How do you know? (Repeat with *noon;* then with *seen* and *seat.*)

SUPPLEMENTARY ACTIVITIES

Vocabulary Primer Workbook, pages 92, 93, 94, 95, 96.

Pp. 156-57 # Unit 78: Good Night (*cont.*)

PREPARATION

Have the following materials ready for use:

Pocket Card Holder
Word Cards

457 Just	474 laughed	503 now	537 barnyard	543 hug
464 came	485 that	504 say	541 word	547 girl
472 then	489 boy	531 night	542 gave	

INITIAL PROCEDURE

Vocabulary review. (Have all the words listed above in two columns in card holder.) Boys and girls about to finish a book should be able to read up and down these word ladders without any trouble. Who wants to be the first to try?

Reading numbers

Will Alice and Jerry go on playing that game all night? Will someone put a stop to their fun? If you can read this page number, we can find out. (Write *156.*)

SILENT READING

Page 156. Anyway, we know the fun has stopped. How do we know? Is Jip where he ought to be? (Suggest that the *F.V.* on the banner suggests the name of the village where the children live, Friendly Village.)

Three-line sentences

Read the first three sentences. Who puts a stop to the fun and what does she say? What does Mother want? Read the next sentence and see. The next sentence is a three-line sentence. Can you read it with your eyes and then read it aloud for me as if it were all on one line? The next sentence tells exactly what Mother wants done. What is that? Now who can go back to the top of the page and read everything that Mother did and said?

Alice makes a promise. Read four sentences and find out what she promises. Does Jerry promise? Finish the page and see.

Page 157. Read the whole page and see if Alice kept her promise. Did Jerry? Do you suppose Alice, Jerry, and Jip may wake up in another book with some more good stories?

ORAL READING

Working for fluency and expression

Audience reading. (Divide the group into two smaller groups. Assign *A Happy Day* to one group, *Good Night* to the other. Proceed as in previous units.)

WORD RECOGNITION TECHNIQUES

Auditory-visual perception. *Final sounds.* If I write *night,* all but the last letter, who will put that on for me? (Continue with *garden, rain, man, boat, not, want, what.*)

Here are two new words. (Write *wagon, west.* Proceed as in previous units.)

Phonics

Phonetic parts. I will write a word. Read the word, tell me the part you hear and see in the word, and then draw a line under the part. (Use *down, new, girl, play, started, too.*)

SUPPLEMENTARY ACTIVITIES

1. *Workbook for Day In and Day Out,* pages 107, 108, 109, 110. Read text on page 109 with pupils before they begin work.

2. Tests. Give the informal tests on pages 111 and 112 of the *Workbook for Day In and Day Out.* A score of 1 is given for each

item marked correctly. Pupils in immature groups should make a score of at least 18 on the vocabulary test, a score of at least 4 on the sentence-meaning test. At this point, test all pupils with the vocabulary word cards for the Primer vocabulary. Keep a record of the words which each child does not recognize automatically. Stress these again when the reading of the First Reader is begun.

Individual check on sight vocabulary

3. *My Own Book,* Nos. 5, 6, 7, 8. If possible, have copies of each of these books to give to pupils to take home to read to their fathers and mothers. See page 100 for explanation.

Unit 79: (Supplementary)

1. Textfilm for *Day In and Day Out,* Frames 39-40. See Textfilm manual for directions.

2. Additional reading. In the following preprimers, the pages noted may be used as supplementary reading under teacher guidance:

Molly, Pete, and Ginger, pages 57-60.

My Little Blue Story Book, pages 53-63.

Under the Tree, pages 52-57. (Give help with the words *bed,* page 52; and *sleep,* page 57.)

We Come and Go, pages 65-70.

We Work and Play, pages 51-62.

STANDARDIZED ACHIEVEMENT TEST

A Reading Achievement Test for use at the end of the Primer can be bought from Harper & Row, Publishers. This test should be given before beginning the Basic First Reader, *Round About.*

PARALLEL PRIMER

The Parallel Primer, *Wishing Well,* can be read with a minimum of vocabulary difficulty upon the completion of *Day In and Day Out.*

Diagnosis of Pupil Growth

(Upon completion of *Day In and Day Out*)

1. Are pupils having a thoroughly enjoyable time learning to read? Can they enter into the spirit of a story so that characters and occurrences seem real to them as they read?

2. Have pupils mastered the 180 words of the basic vocabulary so well that they can apply these words with ease and confidence to the reading of new context?

3. Can they read silently with little or no evidence of head or lip movement? Has the habit of reading silently before reading orally been well established?

4. Is oral reading fluent, rhythmic, and expressive?

5. Have pupils' ability in auditory and visual perception developed to the degree that pupils can:

   a) hear as well as see that certain words begin with the same sound?

   b) combine picture clues with initial consonant clues to unlock new words?

   c) combine context clues with initial consonant clues to unlock new words?

6. Are they using their reading ability in the activities of the school day: reading signs, bulletin boards, etc?

7. Are you, the teacher, diagnosing the needs of individuals in this group and adapting the unit plans to meet these needs instead of rushing on to new text material?

8. Have you, the teacher, a sense of satisfactory accomplishment? Do you feel that a firm foundation has been laid upon which further reading development can take place?

UNIT REFERENCES TO WORD RECOGNITION TECHNIQUES

Initial consonant sounds	Superior Group		Average Group		Immature Group	
	Intro.	Review	Intro.	Review	Intro.	Review
b		3, 8, 18, 24	**5**	6, 7, 8, 9, 10, 12, 14, 15, 16, 17, 20, 21, 25, 31	4	5, 7, 9, 13, 16, 19, 36, 50, 71
c		2, 24	7	8, 9, 10, 12, 14, 15, 16, 17, 20, 22, 25, 31	11	13, 16, 19, 36, **50, 71**
ch		22, 26, 27	30	33, 36	51	75
d		1, 2, 3, 8	1	12, 14, 15, 16, 17, 20, 21, 25	19	22, 23, 25, 37, 50, 71
f	11		4	5, 6, 7, 8, 9, 10, 12, 14, 15, 16, 17, 20, 25	26	28, 29, 30, 33, 34, 37, 50, 71
g	8, 11		12	14, 15, 16, 17, 20, 21, 22, 26, 31	25	26, 28, 29, 33, 37, 50, 71
h	2, 3		2	3, 4, 5, 6, 7, 8, 9, 10, 12, 14, 15, 16, 17, 20, 21, 26, 31	2	4, 5, 7, 9, 13, 16, 19, 50, 71
j	3, 11		14	15, 16, 17, 20, 26	7	8, 9, 13, 16, 19, 50, 71
k	6		20	21, 26	30	34, 39, 45, 50, 71
l	6, 18		15	16, 17, 20, 22, 26, 31	13	16, 19, 22, 50, 71
m	8		6	7, 8, 9, 10, 12, 14, 15, 16, 17, 20, 27	22	23, 25, 26, 30, 33, 50, 71
n	16, 24		9	10, 12, 14, 15, 16, 17, 20, 22, 27	23	25, 26, 28, 29, 36, 51, 71
p	6, 11		8	9, 10, 12, 14, 15, 16, 17, 20, 27	28	29, 30, 39, 51, 75

	Intro.	Review	Intro.	Review	Intro.	Review
Initial consonant sounds (cont.)						
r	......	2, 3, 6	2	3, 4, 5, 6, 7, 8, 9, 10, 12, 14, 15, 16, 17, 20, 21, 22, 27	16	19, 22, 33, 34, 51, 75
s	......	2, 3	3	4, 5, 6, 7, 8, 9, 10, 12, 14, 15, 16, 17, 20, 27	1	2, 4, 5, 7, 9, 13, 16, 19, 34, 51, 75
sh	......	16, 21, 22, 26, 27	19	20, 22, 28, 30, 33, 36	43	45, 51, 75
t	......	3	16	17, 20, 22, 28	29	30, 34, 39, 51, 75
th	......	15, 16, 22, 26, 27	17	19, 20, 22, 28, 30, 33, 36	34	36, 37, 39, 45, 51, 75
v	......	18	25	26, 28, 31	63	75
w	......	2, 3, 8, 11, 18	10	12, 14, 15, 16, 17, 20, 28	20	22, 23, 25, 28, 51, 75
wh	......	15, 16, 21, 22, 26, 27	22	28, 30, 33, 36	39	45, 51, 75
Phonetic parts						
ar	13	15, 17, 20, 22, 25, 26	20	23, 27, 29, 35	37	40, 42, 43, 48, 50, 53, 64, 66, 75, 78
ay	8	9, 10, 11, 12, 13, 20, 22, 25, 26, 28	11	12, 13, 14, 17, 18, 19, 20, 23, 27, 29, 35	22	23, 32, 34, 36, 37, 40, 42, 43, 48, 50, 53, 64, 66, 75, 78
er	11	12, 13, 14, 18, 20, 23	17	18, 19, 20, 23, 24, 27, 29, 32, 35	......	......
ew	12	13, 15, 18, 20, 22, 25, 28	19	20, 23, 27, 29, 35	34	36, 37, 40, 42, 43, 48, 50, 53, 64, 66, 75, 78
ir	22	23	29	32, 35	66	75, 78
oo	20	21, 22, 25, 28	24	27, 29, 35	50	53, 64, 66, 75, 78
ou	1	8, 9, 10, 11, 12, 13, 20, 22, 23, 25	1	12, 13, 14, 17, 18, 19, 20, 23, 27, 29, 32, 35	......	......
ow	9	10, 11, 12, 13, 17, 20, 22, 23, 25	18	19, 20, 23, 24, 27, 29, 32, 35	42	43, 48, 50, 53, 64, 66, 75, 78
oy	10	11, 12, 13, 15, 20, 22, 25, 26, 28	13	14, 17, 18, 19, 20, 23, 27, 29, 35	......	......

(Continued on next page)

UNIT REFERENCES TO WORD RECOGNITION TECHNIQUES (cont.)

	Superior Group		Average Group		Immature Group	
	Intro.	Review	Intro.	Review	Intro.	Review
Final sounds						
d	14	16, 17, 18, 19, 20, 21, 23, 24, 25, 26	21	22, 23, 25, 26, 27, 30, 32, 34, 35, 36	. . . .	. . . .
g	17	18, 19, 20, 21, 23, 24, 25, 26	28	29, 30, 32, 34, 35, 36	. . . .	. . . .
l	22	23, 24, 25, 26	. . . .	. . . .	. . . .	. . . .
n	5	6, 7, 8, 9, 10, 11, 16, 18, 19, 20, 21, 23, 24, 25, 26	18	19, 21, 22, 23, 25, 26, 27, 30, 32, 34, 35, 36	63	64, 66, 67, 69, 70, 73, 77, 78
p	9	10, 11, 16, 17, 18, 19, 20, 21, 23, 24, 25, 26	15	16, 17, 18, 21, 22, 23, 25, 26, 27, 30, 32, 34, 35, 36	. . . .	. . . .
t	2	3, 4, 5, 7, 8, 9, 10, 11, 16, 17, 18, 19, 20, 21, 23, 24, 25, 26	13	14, 15, 16, 17, 18, 20, 21, 22, 23, 25, 26, 27, 30, 32, 34, 35, 36	53	54, 56, 59, 61, 63, 66, 67, 69, 70, 73, 77, 78
y	27	28	25	26, 27, 30, 32, 34, 35, 36	. . . .	. . . .
Initial blends						
bl	5	8, 12, 25, 28	. . . .	. . . .	. . . .	. . . .
br	5	8, 12, 17, 19, 21, 25, 28	. . . .	. . . .	. . . .	. . . .
gr	5	8, 12, 25, 28	. . . .	. . . .	. . . .	. . . .
pl	5	8, 12, 17, 19, 21, 25, 28	. . . .	. . . .	. . . .	. . . .
sn	24	25, 28	. . . .	. . . .	. . . .	. . . .
st	8	12, 13, 17, 19, 21, 25, 28	. . . .	. . . .	. . . .	. . . .
tr	5	8, 25, 28	. . . .	. . . .	. . . .	. . . .
Long vowel sounds						
a	13	14, 16, 18, 23	. . . .	. . . .	. . . .	. . . .
e	13	14, 16, 18, 23	. . . .	. . . .	. . . .	. . . .
o	13	14, 16, 18, 23	. . . .	. . . .	. . . .	. . . .
Word structure	7, 21	15, 22, 24	7, 31	8, 22, 31, 34, 36	5, 16	20, 46, 58, 61, 67